THE SENSE OF BROWN

PERVERSE MODERNITIES
A series edited by Jack Halberstam and Lisa Lowe

José Esteban Muñoz

EDITED AND WITH AN INTRODUCTION BY
Joshua Chambers-Letson and Tavia Nyong'o

The Sense of Brown

DUKE UNIVERSITY PRESS *Durham and London* 2020

© 2020 Duke University Press
All rights reserved
Designed by Aimee C. Harrison
Typeset in Warnock Pro and Helvetica by Copperline Book Services

LIBRARY OF CONGRESS CATALOGING-IN-PUBLICATION DATA
Names: Muñoz, José Esteban, author. | Ochieng' Nyongó, Tavia Amolo, editor. | Chambers-Letson, Joshua Takano, editor.
Title: The sense of brown / José Esteban Muñoz ; edited and with an introduction by Joshua Chambers-Letson and Tavia Nyong'o. Other titles: Perverse modernities.
Description: Durham : Duke University Press, 2020. | Series: Perverse modernities | Includes bibliographical references and index. Identifiers: LCCN 2020006182 (print)
LCCN 2020006183 (ebook)
ISBN 9781478009979 (hardcover)
ISBN 9781478011033 (paperback)
ISBN 9781478012566 (ebook)
Subjects: LCSH: Hispanic Americans in the performing arts. | Hispanic Americans—Ethnic identity. | Performance art. | Queer theory. | Art and race.
Classification: LCC PN1590.H57 M866 2020 (print) |
LCC PN1590.H57 (ebook) | DDC 814/.6—dc23
LC record available at https://lccn.loc.gov/2020006182
LC ebook record available at https://lccn.loc.gov/2020006183

Cover art: Nao Bustamante performs *America, the Beautiful.* Photo by Lorie Novak.

Contents

ACKNOWLEDGMENTS   vii

EDITORS' INTRODUCTION The Aesthetic Resonance of Brown
Joshua Chambers-Letson and Tavia Nyong'o   ix

1 The Brown Commons   1
2 Feeling Brown: Ethnicity and Affect in Ricardo Bracho's *The Sweetest Hangover (and Other STDs)*   8
3 The Onus of Seeing Cuba: Nilo Cruz's *Cubanía*   24
4 Meandering South: Isaac Julien and *The Long Road to Mazatlán*   29
5 "Chico, What Does It Feel Like to Be a Problem?": The Transmission of Brownness   36
6 The Vulnerability Artist: Nao Bustamante and the Sad Beauty of Reparation   47
7 Queer Theater, Queer Theory: Luis Alfaro's *Cuerpo Politizado*   59
8 Performing the Bestiary: Carmelita Tropicana's *With What Ass Does the Cockroach Sit?/Con Qué Culo se Sienta la Cucaracha?*   78
9 Performing Greater Cuba: Tania Bruguera and the Burden of Guilt   86
10 Wise Latinas   100
11 Brown Worldings: José Rodríguez-Soltero, Tania Bruguera, and María Irene Fornés   118
12 The Sense of *Wildness*: The Brown Commons after Paris Burned   128
13 Vitalism's Afterburn: The Sense of Ana Mendieta   141

NOTES   151

BIBLIOGRAPHY   167

INDEX   175

Acknowledgments

The editors would like to thank the following for their help in bringing *The Sense of Brown* into the world. First, to the Muñoz family, especially Elena Pastora Muñoz, Antonio Muñoz, Alex Muñoz, and Albert Muñoz. We're also grateful to other kin to this project—those who contributed work, counsel, and support along the way: Luis Alfaro, John Andrews, Christine Balance, Georgia Boe, Barbara Browning, Tania Bruguera, Nao Bustamante, Kandice Chuh, Jorge Ignacio Cortiñas, Michal Daniel, Jennifer Doyle, Licia Fiol-Matta, Victor Gonzalez, Jack Halberstam, Christina Hanhardt, Joshua Javier Guzmán, Isaac Julien, Albert Laguna, Bill Letson, Shadi Letson, Lisa Lowe, Ricardo Montez, Fred Moten, Ren Ellis Neyra, Ann Pellegrini, Roy Pérez, Miriam Petty, José Quiroga, Joshua Rains, Iván Ramos, Sandra Ruiz, Matthew Leslie Santana, Karen Shimakawa, C. Riley Snorton, Rebecca Sumner-Burgos, Karen Tongson, Joshua Tranen, Alina Troyano, Ela Troyano, Wu Tsang, Guinevere Turner, Jeanne Vaccaro, Alexandra Vazquez, Victoria Miro Gallery, Antonio Viego, Shane Vogel, Hannah van den Wijngaard, Ken Wissoker, audiences at the University of Maryland, University of California, Riverside, New York University, Pérez Museum of Art, Wesleyan University, and the anonymous reviewers for Duke University Press. Ali Faraj provided invaluable support as a research assistant during the manuscript's final stages of preparation.

Editors' Introduction

THE AESTHETIC RESONANCE OF BROWN
Joshua Chambers-Letson and Tavia Nyong'o

It's late morning on November 3, 2013. He sits across from one of us on his couch, handing over a black binder with a manuscript in it. There were always manuscripts strewn across his apartment. All of them in different states of incompletion, not-yet, and becoming. There were the developing new works by his friends and the myriad projects he reviewed for publication; drafts of his students' unfinished dissertations alongside former students' nascent books; ideas waiting for a place in the world. This manuscript: a series of chapters gathered together. For many years this book traveled under the name *Feeling Brown*, but more recently he'd taken to calling it *The Sense of Brown*. The chapters were winnowed out of a decade and a half of writing that appeared in various forms as talks and essays. Sewn together into sequence in a binder, they approximated something like the first draft of a book. "There's still a lot of work to do," he said (or something like it). He was proud to have it at hand. And he knew, or thought, that he had time to finish it. This would be his final draft.

From *Feeling Brown* to *The Sense of Brown*

The task of offering an introduction to José Esteban Muñoz's *The Sense of Brown* is complicated by the book's incompletion as much as by the fact that it was a long time in the making. Muñoz was a prominent and well-regarded scholar of queer studies, Latinx studies, and performance studies. The author of a number of edited collections and monographs, including the influential books *Disidentifications* (1999) and *Cruising Utopia* (2009), Muñoz helped draft the horizons of contemporary queer of color critique, performance theory, and queer utopianism. *The Sense of Brown* is avowedly situated within (or in relationship to) performance studies, black studies, Asian American studies, and queer theory. In many ways it is an extension of concepts and questions that moved across his earlier books. But *The Sense of Brown* is also Muñoz's most direct address to the field of Latino/a studies and the queer intellectual formation that would come to be known, in the years since his death, as Latinx studies.

Theorizing brownness in relationship to "the people who are rendered brown by their personal and familial participation in South-to-North migration patterns," *The Sense of Brown* often looks toward (or back at) Cuba, where Muñoz was born in Havana in 1967. His family migrated to the U.S. mainland six years later, and he grew up in Hialeah, Florida, a predominantly Cuban suburb of Miami. He left his parents' home to attend Sarah Lawrence College before receiving a doctorate from Duke University in 1994 and moving to New York to begin an appointment in the Department of Performance Studies at New York University. He taught and lived in New York until his premature death on December 3, 2013, at the age of forty-six.

Muñoz compiled his draft manuscript for *The Sense of Brown* from pieces composed over a period of fifteen years (approximately 1998 to 2013). The project's extended drafting period meant that his ideas shifted and evolved in subtle, minor, and major ways. This was clearly signified by a revision to this project's long-standing title from *Feeling Brown* to *The Sense of Brown* around 2012. This shift was not so much away from feeling as toward sense, but, as the reader will discover, the manuscripts he left behind had varying degrees of alignment with the book's developing throughlines. In particular, the first half of the text tends to focus on affect, feeling, and brown feelings, which become interarticulated with a turn toward "the sense of brown" and the "brown commons" occupying the later chapters. And although the project's title marked a shift in emphasis from feeling to sense, his concerns with ethnicity and affect and his investments in theorizing black, brown, queer, and minor structures of feeling remained central to the project.

He began presenting material that he would include in the manuscript for *The Sense of Brown* in the late 1990s, shortly before the publication of *Disidentifications* in 1999. In November 1998 he delivered two papers ("Ethnic Feeling" and "This Bridge Called My Crack: Ricardo Bracho's *The Sweet-*

est Hangover") that culminated in the publication of his germinal 2000 essay "Feeling Brown: Ethnicity and Affect in Ricardo Bracho's *The Sweetest Hangover (and Other STDS)*." Around this time he contracted a book with Duke University Press under the title *Feeling Brown*. He researched and composed *Feeling Brown/The Sense of Brown* alongside 2009's *Cruising Utopia* (which has been released in an expanded tenth-anniversary edition). The latter text has been read as a key queer of color intervention in debates over the antirelational thesis in queer studies. But those debates, crucial as they were, did not represent Muñoz's full theoretical horizon at the time. One can see anticipatory glimmers of *The Sense of Brown* in both of his earlier books. Indeed, understanding *The Sense of Brown* as concurrently written with *Cruising Utopia* affords a renewed sense of the degree to which questions of race are central to both projects.

You can track the ideas at the center of *The Sense of Brown* throughout his body of work. In a chapter on Felix González-Torres in *Disidentifications*, for example, Muñoz argued that the artist deployed a "strategic obliquity" that eschewed a transparent address to identity, while nonetheless resonating within "a 'structure of feeling' that cuts through certain Latino and queer communities."[1] He drew the notion of a structure of feeling from Marxist critic Raymond Williams, and the concept would appear again in *Cruising Utopia* as Muñoz deployed it in his theorization of queerness. But this notion of queerness was always already relational to black and brown structures of feeling, as is palpably evident in *Cruising Utopia*'s chapters on the work of Samuel Delany, Amiri Baraka, Kevin Aviance, Kalup Linzy, and My Barbarian. In many ways, *The Sense of Brown* stands as a powerful rejoinder for those who would appropriate the pastier passages and ideas from *Cruising Utopia*, whitewashing it by excluding, subordinating, or simply ignoring the analytics of race and racialization that have always been central to Muñoz's work.

In *The Sense of Brown*'s second chapter ("Feeling Brown"), Muñoz insists on the brownness of the utopian impulse. He illustrates his claim via the work of Cherríe Moraga, Gloria Anzaldúa, and Ricardo Bracho, meditating on the relationship between queerness and what he would later call the sense of brown. In chapter 11 ("Brown Worldings") he explicitly addresses this overlapping, yet distinct, theorization of queerness and brownness:

> The ways in which my sense of brownness converges with what I have defined in *Cruising Utopia* as a queerness that is not ontologically fixed are many. But there is one crucial difference for me. I suggest queerness

is in the horizon, forward dawning and not-yet-here. Brownness diverges from my definition of queerness. Brownness is already here. Brownness is vast, present, and vital. It is the ontopoetic state not just of people who live in the United States under the sign of latinidad but of a majority of those who exist, strive, and flourish within the vast trajectory of multiple and intersecting regimes of colonial violence.

To attend to the *sense of brown* is thus to become attuned to the ways in which the world is *already brown*. It is also to sense the ways in which *brownness* was always already presupposed in Muñoz's theorization of queerness and utopia.

Though he describes brownness in various ways throughout *The Sense of Brown* (refusing to let it ossify into anything that might approximate a fixed identity marker), the actual phrase "sense of brown" first appears in chapter 10 ("Wise Latinas"). He began delivering "Wise Latinas" as a talk around 2010, and it evidences the increased influence of Jean-Luc Nancy on Muñoz's thought. In particular, in this essay Muñoz begins to employ the Nancean language of "sense." The turn to sense did not signify a break with his earlier emphasis on feeling and affect. Rather, it allowed him to elaborate on the notion that the affective particularity of brown feelings can serve as a conduit to other ways of knowing and being in the world. For Nancy, sense is, among other things, a conduit between a porous self and the world. Sense and the senses are how we experience, know, and relate interior to exterior worlds, the self to others. The language of sense thus gave Muñoz a way to further describe the politics of being with and being together-in-difference that animated his earlier works: "My aim, through the route of affect, is to chart a provisional de-universalizing of reason for the express purpose of imagining and describing multiple modes of being, feeling, and knowing in the world. This knowing the brownness of the world is, more nearly, participating in a shared sense of brown."[2]

Our preparation of Muñoz's incomplete manuscript for publication has involved the painful, gradual, and always incomplete process of accepting the fact that we will never know how he would have addressed some of the gaps and points of friction between the various manuscripts that make up its whole because he is not here to do that work himself. In some ways, the reader will find that the plurality of chapters that make up *The Sense of Brown* mirrors the structure and form of Muñoz's other monographs. The two earlier books have an accumulative feeling to them, in terms of both form and style of argumentation. Each contains ten to twelve concentrated case studies that collaboratively, and often elliptically, elaborate upon the book's central thematics. Yet each chapter can be (and in the classroom they often are) broken off from each other into individual monads since most have, each unto itself, the air of a self-contained manifesto. These formal elements are similar to another incomplete text of which Muñoz was fond, and briefly referenced in *Cruising Utopia*: Marx's *1844* manuscripts.[3] But in the case of *Disidentifications* and *Cruising Utopia*, Muñoz was able to revise across the different chapters to bring them into theoretical and conceptual alignment. In the case of *The Sense of Brown*, he did not have the time to do as much.

This introduction cannot make up for this fact. Instead, we present *The Sense of Brown* in relationship to the problem of its incompletion. What follows does not provide an authoritative account of *The Sense of Brown*. That labor must remain permanently unfinished. Though we worked with and alongside Muñoz for many years as colleague, student, and comrades, we have undertaken the task of editing this book in a spirit of intellectual friendship that is still marked by our own incommensurable differences from Muñoz. This includes our position on the outside of Latinx studies via the adjacent fields of black studies, Asian American studies, performance studies, and queer studies. In this respect, our editorial enterprise was animated by the "commons of the incommensurate" he wrote of in an essay on the black queer writer Gary Fisher and his mentor, Eve Kosofsky Sedgwick.[4] But there is a degree to which every work of theory, even when it is brought to completion by its author, is a performative utterance whose praxis can only be achieved and realized through its uptake. As such, we offer this elaboration on some of the major and minor themes in *The Sense of Brown* as a speculative engagement with the text, performing one practice (or set of practices) for taking up, working with, and working through the brown density of Muñoz's manuscripts. What follows is less an introduction than a portrait of our own attempt to gain a sense of Muñoz's sense of brown.

Snapshots of His Exilic Childhood

Let's begin (again) with the picture of a queer little Cuban boy in brown. Except what we're looking at is not a picture, but pictures. Not pictures, in fact, but puzzles. Two jigsaw puzzles displayed next to each other, side by side. One of the puzzles features the photo of the little boy: seated, soft, vulnerable. It has the air of a documentary photograph—for a passport or visa, perhaps. The other puzzle is a statue: some kind of (seemingly nationalist) monument:

erect, hard, domineering. Both puzzles are protected by and held in a plastic archivist's bag. Side by side, they are suspended against a white wall by two white pushpins. Printed above them, in red, are the words "Madrid 1971."

Felix González-Torres first materialized this piece, *"Untitled" (Madrid 1971)*, in 1988. Though the work does not explicitly state as much, the spectator may (correctly) assume that the boy in photograph is the artist himself. The statue's provenance is less clear, although the accompanying wall text might suggest Madrid. A sense of brown radiates from the puzzle/picture of the boy. The picture is itself brown as it is saturated by a pervasive, fading brown tone. But there is also the way that, as Muñoz described it in *Disidentifications*, "this image speaks to exile and ethnicity in a voice that is evocative and suggestive."[5] The "voice" is part of what Muñoz would come to describe as the sense of brown. It is a voice that speaks through its attunement to the sense of a brown world.

The brown tones of the little boy's photograph come into relief against the stark white of the wall on which the puzzle is suspended. In describing it this way, we mean to evoke a phrase by another of Florida's adopted children, Zora Neale Hurston, alongside a painting of the phrase by one of González-Torres's contemporaries, Glenn Ligon. In this painting Ligon appropriates and reproduces Hurston's phrase, "I feel most colored when I am thrown against a sharp white background." It is as if, against the whiteness of the wall, the boy in *"Untitled" (Madrid 1971)* is becoming brown such that the work comes to radiate a sense of immanence and brown becoming.

We'll come back to the boy but pause and linger here on Hurston and Ligon's articulation of a "colored" feeling. The 1928 essay that is the source of the sentence, "How It Feels to Be Colored Me," offers an account of Hurston's experience of becoming raced. From its title to the line that Ligon isolates and reproduces (eventually into blackening abstraction), Hurston underlines the complex affective contours of racial becoming as a deeply felt process.[6] For Hurston, "feeling colored" sometimes resonates with Fanon's description of the scene of racialization as one of shattering negation. Surely, Hurston describes what it is to "feel colored" as an experience of feeling like a problem.

One could imagine a dialogue between Hurston and W. E. B. Du Bois in which Du Bois asks his famous question, "How does it feel to be a problem?," before Hurston replies (though not necessarily to Du Bois), "I feel most colored when I am thrown against a sharp white background."[7] That she describes the feeling of being "most colored" as akin to being "thrown against a sharp white background" frames racialization as a violent and abject negotiation with a stark and seemingly unmoving wall of whiteness. But it is important to emphasize that Hurston's essay describes an attendant plurality of "colored" feelings that refuse to be reduced to mere and abject suffering. She insists on describing a complex archive of transitory feelings including even the absence of feeling racialized, as in, "I do not always feel colored." Throughout the essay, "color comes" and becomes in and on her body in a host of different ways.[8]

To sense a resonance between the mode of becoming brown in the image of a little boy suspended against a sharp white wall, or in the work of Hurston and Ligon, is to be attuned to the brown and black sense of the world that Muñoz describes throughout *The Sense of Brown*. Du Bois's question was one of the animating forces for Muñoz, and in chapter 5 ("'Chico, What Does It Feel Like to Be a Problem?'"), Muñoz opens with a revision and extension of Du Bois's question to frame his theory of brownness and/as brown feelings. As with Hurston, Ligon, González-Torres, and even Fanon, Muñoz's response to the Du Boisian question describes what it means to feel brown or to feel black as emerging in relationship to the clarifying, fragmenting violence of the white background against which one is thrown. But Muñoz also understood brown feelings as the grounds of shared consciousness and even insurgent action. For Muñoz, feeling brown is a conduit to knowing, sharing, and being with others (who have been blackened or browned by the world) in a collective attunement to the revolutionary potentials of what he called the "brown commons."

The little boy in *"Untitled" (Madrid 1971)* is isolated and alone, resonating with the first-person singular "I" that animates Hurston and Ligon's inquiry. In *The Sense of Brown*'s second chapter, "Feeling Brown," Muñoz notes that "feeling like a problem is about feeling apart, feeling separate." But he also insists that this isolating feeling is paradoxically the grounds on which other ways of being with and belonging-in-difference coalesce into a politics of collective relation: "feeling like a problem is also a mode of belonging, a belonging through recognition. Thus feeling like a problem is a mode of minoritarian recognition." Muñoz invites his reader to think "about the problem of feeling like a problem as not simply an impasse but, instead, an opening." If his reading of *"Untitled" (Madrid 1971)* suggests that González-Torres's work resonates with the deeply felt Cuban, brown, and queer of color structures of feelings that flow between the artist, his work, and his spectators, Muñoz also suggests that this is a "commonality [that] is not forged through shared images and fixed identifications but fashioned instead from connotative images that invoke communal structures of feeling. The structures of feeling that are invoked point to a world in which exile and ethnicity are not stigmatized aberrations, but instead everyday aspects of national culture."[9] In *The Sense of Brown* he sought to demonstrate how such structures of feeling are most often experienced and perceptible as a sense. As he did so, he routinely suggested that this sense often comes to us through the aesthetic experience and especially in the always already relational scene of a performance.

One might gain a sense of the brownness of *"Untitled" (Madrid 1971)* by reading it as a narrative of what Muñoz described as "participation in south to north migration patterns." González-Torres was sent to Madrid as an unaccompanied minor in 1971 as part of a broad diaspora of unaccompanied children from postrevolutionary Cuba.[10] For Muñoz, the juxtaposition of the picture of a little boy in brown and of the nationalist statue gives one a sense of the forces of colonialism, political economy, revolution, and nationalism that combined to create the precarious state in which a queer and brown boy was cast out, adrift, to sustain and survive an unknown and unknowing world. The photograph has the air of a documentary photograph (for a visa or passport), lending it a narrative of transport, movement, and becoming—even a process of becoming brown. Despite the lightness of the little boy's skin, and despite the contingent but favored status that has been offered to the Cuban American diaspora by the U.S. state—over and at times against other Latinx, black, Asian, and indigenous people in the U.S.—people like him are nonetheless made to be brown, especially when thrown against a sharp white background. But Muñoz insisted that an attunement to the sense of brown still provides an opening toward practices of collectivity and "shared flourishing": "Brownness as a grounded experience, for a brown commons, is often borne out of what, following John Dewey, we could call a shared sense of harm. But it is not just harm, it is also the shared flourishing that transpires and unfolds despite and in the face of systemic harm."[11]

It's worth noting that *"Untitled" (Madrid 1971)* involves an image of González-Torres's childhood. Muñoz was consistently interested in describing structures of feeling that resonate with and emerge from queer and brown experiences of childhood. One might think of the introduction to *Disidentifications*, which famously opens with an account of comedian Marga Gomez's childhood disidentification with lesbian women on sensationalistic television, or a sequence in *Cruising Utopia* where a young Muñoz comes to sense his queerness as he is teased for his effeminate gestures.[12] In *The Sense of Brown*, too, the reader will find that Muñoz repeatedly returns to the fraught and fractious structures of feeling that cluster around and emerge from queer and brown childhood. The figure of Elián González appears in several places, and chapter 7, in particular, offers a sustained meditation on a performance by the legendary Luis Alfaro. These meditations on Latinx childhood provided Muñoz with a means for illustrating the complex intersection of sexuality with race that he found lacking in most of the dominant practices of (white and antirelational) queer theories.

Queer of color subjects, and in Muñoz's case the queer Cuban child, don't necessarily have the privilege to choose between the brown structure of feeling performed and offered by the family and the forces of queer shame that are sometimes painfully manifest within the biological family's homophobic social sphere. As Muñoz describes it in chapter 7:

> Family has been much criticized in contemporary queer theory as an oppressive totality. But such a characterization, from the perspective of queers of color, is deeply reductive. On the one hand, it is true that not all families of color affirm their queer sons and daughters. On the other hand, the generalized gay community often feels like a sea of whiteness to queers of color, and thus the imagined ethnic family is often a refuge. It is a space where all those elements of the self that are fetishized, ignored, and rejected in the larger queer world are suddenly revalorized. Alfaro's memory performance attunes us to those enabling characteristics.

Queers of color thus come to feel themselves and each other in part because of the ways in which we, and our families, feel like a problem within "a sea of whiteness" against which the family (in either its real or imagined form) may function as refuge. At the same time, the family offers up a structure of feeling (brown feelings) through which "the problem of feeling like a problem becomes not simply an impasse but, instead, an opening" as the queer of color subject develops ways to incorporate and valorize "all those [brown] elements of the self that are fetishized, ignored, and rejected in the larger queer world."[13]

Cruising Cuba

These reflections on the place of queer childhood, exile, and ethnos in the early chapters' efforts to theorize brown feelings suggest that the sense of a brown world (or brown worldings) that Muñoz describes in *The Sense of Brown* was deeply influenced by the author's own entanglements with and theorizations of *cubanía*. In the manuscript draft of *The Sense of Brown*,

Muñoz indicated that the lead chapters were to be two essays that he published in 2000: "Feeling Brown: Ethnicity and Affect in Ricardo Bracho's *The Sweetest Hangover (and Other STDs)*" and "The Onus of Seeing Cuba: Nilo Cruz's *Cubanía*."[14] In "Feeling Brown," Muñoz famously describes feeling brown "as a way of being in the world, a path that does not conform to the conventions of a majoritarian public sphere and the national affect it sponsors." In a resonant fashion, his chapter on Cruz describes a particular structure of Cuban feeling to theorize "cubanía as a *manera de ser* (a way of being)" and as "a structure of feeling that supersedes national boundaries and pedagogies." As we undertook the work of assembling *The Sense of Brown* for publication, a key part of the puzzle was coming to grips with the Caribbean nation to which Muñoz had always assumed he would one day return, though his early death meant that he would never get to see Cuba as an adult.

In the spring of 2018, one of us traveled to Havana in search of further clues to the meaning of one of the city's lost and errant sons. The questions that brought us to Cuba were several. Among them were the kinds of idiosyncratic questions that come with missing a lost friend and a hope that his being in the world might have made it back to a place he had, in the later years of his life, spoken of going back to see. Was Muñoz read on the island? Were his work and influence known? More generally, how well known among the island's artists, intellectuals, and activists were the currents of queer theory and critical race theory in which he trafficked?

We also had questions about the scope and reach of the critical vocabulary developed within a U.S.-based Anglophone academic context. Words like "Latinx" and "blacktino" have been coined precisely to name the gendered and racialized experiences of migrants such as Muñoz, yet sit awkwardly on the Cuban tongue. Another English word puzzle particular to Muñoz's diction was "brownness." Finding a sense of brownness in Cuba would, in effect, evince the very dilemma the term names. "The study of brownness," writes Joshua Javier Guzmán, "is always an investigative process into the vital phenomena of mixture and immiscibility."[15] What would brownness mean on this brown island? Beyond the question of direct translation into Spanish, there was the larger and more consequential question of relevance. Would the sense of brown make sense in Cuba and to Cubans? What kind of sense would or could it make? And what, also, of the sense of queerness permeating all of Muñoz's work?

In contemporary Cuba, queerness remains a question mark, even if homosexuality is no longer officially a crime. Where gay men were once sent to reeducation camps by the regime, now those men meet for sex and sociality in an abandoned fort that lies within eyeshot of the skyline of Havana, the nation's capital. Contemporary Cuban artist Damian Sainz's film *Batería*—a work the artist relates was partially influenced by Muñoz's *Cruising Utopia*—tells a story about gay men cruising in Cuba. In it, shots of discarded condoms scattered inside stone walls hint at the combined and uneven development of urban gay male sexual ecologies. While they have apparent access to HIV prevention education and safer sex prophylactics, these men are on neither Grindr nor PrEP. And while the revolutionary disestablishment of organized religion and official support for gender equality might suggest that patriarchal norms are less in force for Cuban men seeking sex with other men, the anonymous subjects who speak in Sainz's film tell a different story. It is a story of enforced male gender conformity, little if any privacy for erotic pursuits in their homes, and the omnipresent threat of violence by homophobes lurking even here, in this queer sanctuary. Gay Cubans may now have an official patron in Mariella Castro, daughter of Raul Castro. But they do not have access to even ordinary rudiments of personal security as they pursue sexual contacts and intimate relationships that remain in shadow.

From the perspective of a North American mainlander, it would be all too easy to view Cuban queerness as backward, along the familiar lines of the underdevelopment thesis. But while *Batería* doesn't hesitate to militate for rights and freedoms comparable to those which U.S. American queers increasingly take for granted, it is not the case that Cuba simply lags behind. To assume this is the case would be to ignore the manner in which the histories of the U.S. and Cuba are thickly entangled with each other.

El Morro, the sixteenth-century fort that stands above the *batería*, is an iconic landmark of that entanglement, as well as an emblem of Havana harbor's strategic role in world politics over the centuries. In the postrevolutionary period it was a site of queer incarceration, as homosexuals and dissidents including the author Reinaldo Arenas were detained in the prison by the revolutionary state. Today, a cruising ground with obscene graffiti forms an undercommons beneath this popular tourist attraction. A short walk away, the Castillo de San Carlos de la Cabaña draws a crowd every evening for a historical reenactment ceremony, featuring young military conscripts dressed in period garb, in which the firing of a cannon announced the closing of the gates to the city. It is a purely sumptuary display of prowess; all the more incongruous in that it clothes young communist cadres in the costumes of the ancien régime. The contrast between these two uses of the former military complex is instructive: the one a tourist production designed to showcase historical continuity, the other a subterranean erotic zone that is overlooked at best, policed at worst. The young men who are conscripted into the spectacular military display could be the same young men, cruising for furtive contacts of another variety just meters away. The fort complex is thus what Michel Foucault would call a heterotopia. A social space that has been highly regimented and ordered for one set of purposes, it nonetheless opens itself up for appropriation by another regime of aims and desires. These discrepant uses of social space overlap each other uneasily. Havana's historic gateway to a seafaring world doubles as a home away from home for some of its queer residents, men who seek respite from policing, ironically, in catacombs that were once a military prison.

Moving from Sainz's oceanfront cruising ground to a more familiar setting of cosmopolitan queerness in Havana's gay district, the same trip that produced the encounter with Sainz's film involved spectatorship at a drag show staged for tourists and moneyed locals, yielding an encounter with a performer named Blankita. The ethnomusicologist Matthew Leslie Santana, who was conducting fieldwork on Havana drag at the time, introduced us to Blankita and her audience. Blankita was prominent in the gay scene, appearing on several different stages in a single weekend. She performs a version of drag that draws substantially upon *teatro bufo*, a theatrical tradition that the performance studies scholar Jill Lane has succinctly defined as "Cuban blackface."[16] Her act also resonates as a form of "queer assemblage" that Muñoz discusses in chapter 8 ("Performing the Bestiary"). Herself Afro-descended, Blankita cakes on even darker makeup and comically exaggerates her thick lips, bulging eyes, pronounced breasts, and thick ass. Most shockingly, rather than "tucking" as most drag queens do, she wears a grotesque simulacra of a vagina over her crotch, underscoring the degree to which the performance of femininity that she is staging is a specifically black one, depicted as at once uncontrollably sexual and disturbingly animalized. A piece of physical humor performed on at least two separate occasions seems from other reports to be a comic signature of her act. At a point each night, Blankita frantically scoots around the stage, legs extended, rubbing her ass as she goes, in imitation of a canine in heat. Many foreign visitors, us among them, are shocked by the crude racism and misogyny of this act. Blankita would appear to be a poster child for misogynoir, Moya Bailey's useful term for sexism directed specifically at black women. To some cuban queers, however, and particularly to some white Cuban queers, Blankita is simply Cuban culture.

Watching Blankita perform gave us a deepened sense of Muñoz's early writings on *chusma* and *chusmería*, a particular form of humor associated with Cuban blackness. Muñoz addresses chusma in *Disidentifications* in his discussions of the queer performances of his fellow Cuban exiles, filmmaker Ela Troyano and her performance artist sister, Alina (aka Carmelita Tropicana). "Chusmería" refers to people and behavior that "refuse standards of bourgeois comportment." Chusma, Muñoz notes, operates as "a barely veiled racial slur suggesting that one is too black."[17] Contemporary Anglophone cognates for chusma might thus include "ghetto," "cunty," or "ratchet." The relationship between this excessive and antibourgeois blackness and queerness is definite if complex. While working-class black culture is not necessarily known for its embrace of gays and lesbians—and in some countries, such as Jamaica, is notorious for its homophobia—there is a manner of being to this blackness that is always already queer.

In a similar sense, and as *The Sense of Brown*'s gravitation toward Du Bois's question makes clear, the questions of brownness and blackness were always already entangled in Muñoz's thought. His theory of brownness and brown feelings emerged, as he writes in chapter 5, in "the series of relays between the affective spike of what blackness meant and continues to mean within the historical field of U.S. culture and what brownness might mean today." This, as the trip to Havana made clear, was no less true for Cuban culture. Cuba is, after all, one of the crucial centers of Afro-diasporic religion, culture, and music in the New World. Writers like Lydia Cabrera—whose 1954 book *El Monte* has been declared by literary critic José Quiroga to be "one of the queerest books ever written by a Cuban author"—have made the study of Afrocubanismo central, and world music releases like *Buena Vista Social Club* (1996) have popularized the Afro-Cuban rhythms of son and rumba to a world music marketplace.[18] More recently, the anthropologist Jafari Allen released *Venceremos: The Erotics of Black Self-Making in Cuba* (2011), an ethnography of black queer world making in Cuba during the "special period" on the island that followed the fall of the Soviet Union. Blackness, in other words, remains a fraught matter on an island whose revolutionary ethos proclaims pride in Cuba's African heritage, but an island where black people remain disadvantaged and partly invisible, in part due to the lighter-skinned emigré community that dominates U.S. mainland perceptions of Cuba and *cubanidad*.[19] If the blackness of Cuba remains a perpetual surprise, a secret hidden in plain sight, then this blackness is not separate from, but deeply complicit with, the brownness that we had come to Cuba to begin to make sense of.

Mundos Alternos

We encountered this resonant convergence of a black, brown, and queer sense of the world when we traveled together to Riverside, California, to take in a performance by the Troyano sisters. "Hybrid Alternos" was performed in 2018 at the University of California, Riverside's Culver Center of the Arts on the occasion of the groundbreaking exhibition *Mundos Alternos*. "Hybrid Alternos" began with a particularly vivid instance of queer chusma. Entering the performance space in a rickety, cardboard "spaceship" lined with newspaper held together with tape marked "caution do not enter," Tropicana as the hyena/human hybrid Hye wandered into the audience to ask individual members if they, like her, came from a "shithole country." The joke referenced the obscene term that the sitting U.S. president had recently used to characterize the national origin of refugees and asylum seekers coming to America from Africa, Latin America, and the Middle East. Tropicana's witty disidentification with this abusive epithet served as an early clue to the convergence of blackness and brownness in "Hybrid Alternos." Her chusma turned presidential scorn into an unlikely occasion for Third World solidarity against the arrogance of imperialist white machismo. While impersonating an otherworldly alien creature, Tropicana's chusma performs analogously to Quiroga's appraisal of Cabrera's writings on Santería: "Queerness marks the status of the book as a hybrid that in turn comments on the very queer position of Cuba within Western discourse and Western modernity."[20]

While it would be simple enough to read the science fictional narrative of "Hybrid Alternos" as an allegory of Cuban migrants seeking refuge on North American shores, the Troyano sisters would trouble any such triumphalist reading. The plot concerns Hye's voyage to Nebula, the only planet accepting hybrid, interplanetary refugees. At the performance we saw, a discussion afterward broached the question of whether Nebula, as a stand-in for the United States, was in some sense a queer utopia. The Troyano sisters rebutted this interpretation, pointing out that Nebula, like the U.S., is far from a utopia. Indeed, the opening moments of the performance, with their call to a subaltern "shithole" solidarity, should have provided as much of a reminder as is needed. The dilemma of visibility for the class-race-gender-nonconforming chusma, Muñoz noted, was that "live performance for an audience of elites is the only imaginable mode of survival for minoritarian subjects within the hegemonic order that the chusma live within and in opposition to."[21] It was as a search for the lineaments of a heterotopia not characterized by the surveillance and paranoia of visibility in Trump's U.S. that the brownness of "Hybrid Alternos" operated.

Yet, if Nebula was not the stuff of utopia, Muñoz would be the first to insist that the Troyano sisters' mobilization of performance was itself rich with utopian potential that cannot be extricated from the ways in which, as he writes in *The Sense of Brown*, "performance attunes us to the world" and the world's latent utopian potential. The phrase "performance attunes" appears twice in the book (chapters 7 and 11), and in both cases it gestures to performance's ability to attune us twofold to the utopian potentiality of queer worlds that are not-yet-here and the brownness of a world that is already here. As performance does this, it does so in ways that can aid us in the struggle to overcome, as he writes in chapter 1, "the various blockages that keep us from knowing or being attuned to [the world's] brownness."

Our (re)turn to the work of the Troyano sisters is meant to underscore Muñoz's engagement with the artists about whom he wrote not merely as objects of analysis, but as theorists of brownness and queerness in their own right. Muñoz's interest in the work of the Troyanos, and in the performances of Carmelita Tropicana, spanned his career. Some of his very first writings, as well as one of his very last unpublished essays ("Performing the Bestiary") concerned Tropicana's work. Included here as chapter 8, "Performing the Bestiary" offers insight into the sense of brown that he always located in her work, even if he had not always known that this is what he would call it. Similarly, Nao Bustamante, the subject of chapters 6 and 10 and the artist who appears on the cover of this book, was a recurrent muse and interlocutor. Indeed, Muñoz published one additional essay on her work that was not included in his final manuscript for *Sense of Brown* (and thus is not included here) but that is well worth reading in dialogue with chapter 6.[22]

The manuscript for *The Sense of Brown* includes writings from his entire working career as a critic. They all were tending toward a concept of the sense of brown that he was developing in dialogue with more familiar concepts like latinidad and cubanía. Muñoz issued an outright rejection of the term "Hispanic," but he remained interested in the political utility of the term "Latino." This was in part because of the way the term could be mobilized to describe a concept that was central to Muñoz's work: "identity-in-difference."[23] As he explains in both *Disidentifications* and *The Sense of Brown*, he drew the concept from the work of Norma Alarcón, as much as it owed a debt to woman of color feminists and black feminists including Gloria Anzaldúa, Cherríe Moraga (especially their groundbreaking anthology *This Bridge Called My Back*), Chela Sandoval, and Audre Lorde. Muñoz commonly deployed "identities-in-difference" to describe a mode of being-together-in-difference that he understood to be relational to, and in some cases exchangeable with, "queers of color" and the Deleuze/Guattari–inflected "minoritarian subjects."[24] Yet, in *The Sense of Brown*, Muñoz suggests that the framework of "Feeling Brown is [his] attempt to frame the particularity of group identification that temporarily displaces terms like 'Hispanic' or even 'Latina/o.'"[25] Throughout the text he proposes a "capacious sense of brown" that indexes, but is not fixed within, the racial and national contours of latinidad.

If Tropicana's "shithole" solidarity hints at one manner in which brownness might perform a transection of race and nation, that insight is corroborated by Guzmán as he writes:

> To brown America is to bring it down, [to] depress what is notably and nobly understood as White America, thereby staining it and dragging it to its limits. Even the philosopher of colors, Goethe, associated brown, a color he did not necessarily enjoy, with seriousness and melancholy. The sobering intensity of the disenfranchisement of minoritarian people in the United States is nothing less than browning the way we understand the misapplication and abuses of those suspended realities known as justice, democracy, and freedom. Here is the drama within the color brown: it is itself a mixture of yellow, red, and black—the iridescent reminder that we are in brownness and of brownness, here and now.[26]

For Guzmán, brownness holds a political potential insofar as it cannot be reduced to a given identity within neoliberal multiculturalism, but is to the contrary a difference that "stains" the fantasy of a white America.

Questions of ontological consistency and political solidarity form the context in which *The Sense of Brown* will reverberate. The aesthetic sense of brown Muñoz makes the case for militates against conservative national discourses of hybridity. There is a sense of brown, that is to say, that emerges out of the centuries-long process of so-called miscegenation, or the mixing of the races: a violent and coercive process that resulted, in many locations in the Americas and across the colonized world, in distinct castes of brown people wedged between, very often, a black majority population and a ruling white elite. Or, in the case of the U.S., occupying the vanishing middle ground between a white supremacist majoritarian settler society and the oppressed and exploited black minority. While this usage of "brown" often intersects with discourses of racial mixing and hybridity, it is also compatible, from a structural point of view, with a much more bounded racial hierarchy. In East Africa, for instance, a brown middling class of South Asian descent rose up in the belly of the British Empire in the early twentieth century, even though this class was emphatically not the result of mixing between British colonizers and African subjects. In the West Indies, to give another example, Chinese and South Asian "coolie" labor was brought into British colonies such as Trinidad in the aftermath of the overthrow of colonial slavery. The examples proliferate. Generalizing from such cases, it is again very easy to walk away with a picture of brown minorities, competing with, mediating, and in some cases ruling an oppressed black population, with the long-term interests of white supremacy on a global scale being conveniently perpetuated regardless of the scenario.

Such discourses of mestizaje and miscegenation have of course been rigorously scrutinized, for instance in Jared Sexton's *Amalgamation Schemes: Antiblackness and the Critique of Multiracialism*. This critique bears heavily upon, as he puts it, the "restaging of sexual politics in the name of progressive change."[27] Sexton's critique serves as an exposé of the familiar icon of a future multiracial American whose brownness will encompass all the shades of color, in the orthodox sequence of a nationalist rhetoric whose motto is "Out of many, one." But the temporality of brownness encountered in *The Sense of Brown*, as we have seen, is not quite reducible to the reproductive futurity embedded in discourses of mestizaje and racial mixture. Instead, brownness seems to point to a different phenomenon, more attuned to the negative and the abject within sexuality, highlighting bodies, acts, and desires that have been rejected by the nation and shunted from myths of cosmic destiny. Returning briefly to Damian Sainz's film about cruising in Cuba may help underscore this point.

Batería

In his essay "Ephemera as Evidence" and again in *Cruising Utopia*, Muñoz wrote eloquently about "the ghosts of public sex," detailing how mainstream LGBT culture increasingly scrubbed and sanitized the cultures of public cruising that had sustained gay male sex worlds in New York City during the era of the closet, worlds that were increasingly clamped down upon in the U.S. during the 1980s' moral panic over the spread of HIV/AIDS. As he described a photo by the conceptual artist Tony Just:

Tony Just visited a run-down public men's room, a tea room where public sex flourishes. He scrubbed and sanitized the space, laboring to make it look pristinely, shimmeringly clean. The result is a photograph that indexes not only the haunted space and spectral bodies of those anonymous sex acts, and Just's performance after them, but also his act of documentation. This extended performance is, in multiple ways, an exemplary "queer act." It accesses a hidden queer history of public sex outside the dominant public sphere's visible historical narratives. It taps into the lifeworld of tea room sex, a space that is usually only shadowed in semipublicness, and makes this space legible outside of its insular sphere. *But it does this through negation, through a process of erasure that redoubles and marks the systematic erasure of minoritarian histories.*[28]

Muñoz's lifelong interest in the paradoxical power of such acts of negation, that is, in seeming erasures of queer existence that would somehow index and indeed protest the structural exclusion of queerness from the majoritarian frame, is powerfully on view here. As familiar as this move may now be in some circles, however, it is less often brought to bear in the context of the sexual politics of mestizaje, which tend to rest on more heteronormative assumptions regarding reproductive futurity.

What if we can understand brownness, however, not simply as the ideal future outcome of race mixing—the mythic racial democracy ostensibly achieved in official state ideology in Brazil, for instance—but instead by reflecting on the brownness of the stains that Just has carefully scrubbed away in order to produce his haunting image of idealized, abstract whiteness? What if we think of brownness not as the color of the cosmic race, but instead in a more Ellisonian sense of the drop of black that is required to make the most optic white? This sense of brown has less to do with mestizaje and the reproductive futurity that undergirds it, and more to do with the hauntology Muñoz describes here as a "queer act." At one level, then, *Batería* would seem to be a representation of such a hauntology. But to draw a direct equivalence between, say, Muñoz's analysis of a Tony Just photo of a scrubbed, pristine toilet and Sainz's shots of used condoms, dirty walls, and obscene graffiti would be to miss the degree to which the cruising cultures Sainz records are not in the past, but all too present, in the here and now.

We might attenuate our invocation of the brownness of the (missing) stain in Just's photograph with the elaboration on brownness taken up by another of Muñoz's students. In her work on the artist Ryan Rivera, Sandra Ruiz issues a description of "a queer Brown subject that is thrown into the world to endure the bodily residue of historical violence."²⁹ Here, brownness surfaces as the stain of enduring historical violence: a stain deeply felt at the level of the body that is subject to the ongoing histories of colonialism and empire, as well as the inherent violence of migration, displacement, refusal, and removal. Akin to Muñoz, Ruiz insists that "brownness is accessed through a shared sense of endurance experienced within various scenographies of waiting" as much as it "transpires within the senses."³⁰ The encounter with *Batería* similarly suggests that the sensory valences of the aesthetic can be a powerful conduit to the sense of brown. Sainz's lush colors, dramatic swoops of the camera, and interspersed testimony from cruising men all endow the space he investigates with a sensorial thickness and texture somewhat absent from the Tony Just photo. And yet this is, of course, a queer act, albeit one that registers its negation of a majoritarian public sphere through a different set of aesthetic strategies. This difference is key to the manner in which brownness is deployed precisely to disperse the state fantasies of a putatively brown nation.

Batería, in other words, is a signal instance of the kind of contemporary queer Cuban cultural production that calls for a transectional analysis, one that moves across the ideological haze that frames U.S.-Cuban relations. Muñoz understood the myriad Cuban and Cuban diasporic artists encountered within *The Sense of Brown* (including the Troyano sisters, Nilo Cruz, Jorge Ignacio Cortiñas, Coco Fusco, Marga Gomez, Felix González-Torres, and Tania Bruguera) to be mobilizing the aesthetic to, as he writes in chapter 3, "negotiate the onus of seeing Cuba, which is again the almost impossible project of looking beyond this vision-obscuring haze to a rich lifeworld of affective particularity." Similarly, *Batería* must be read in terms of the specific place and time that it documents, and the ongoingness of antiblackness in and beyond contemporary Cuba.

Yet it still makes sense to hold *Batería* in dialogue with work like Muñoz's writings about the ghosts of public sex, which were largely concerned with the lifeworld of urban gay men in New York City, rather than Havana (or even Miami). This is another negation, another erasure, that paradoxically redoubles and marks that which it erases. Muñoz wrote in English and at present his work circulates in Cuba only in limited ways (often in digitized files traded on thumb drives like samizdat). Nonetheless, Sainz told us that he had been able to read Muñoz's 2009 book, *Cruising Utopia*, and that Muñoz's analysis had influenced his making of the film. Charting the distance and proximity of Cuba and the U.S. has been the work of a new generation of scholars, including Alexandra Vazquez, Albert Laguna, and Aisha

Beliso-De Jesus.³¹ These scholars track flows of music, humor, culture, and commodities across officially interdicted spaces, charting a set of pragmatic negotiations and adaptations to a here and now that is always nonidentical to itself, one in which the distance between state ideology (in both the U.S. and Cuba) and lived reality has never been starker. Turn on the U.S.-based gay social networking app Grindr in Havana, and you are likely to connect with someone in Fort Lauderdale, Florida. Rather than lamenting spaces of queer contact that have been crowded out by gentrification in cities like San Francisco and New York, *Batería* testifies most anxiously to the arrival of a future Havana, asserting a queer right to the city that continues to be proscribed even in the current homonationalist era. As José Quiroga notes in *Tropics of Desire*, "In post–Cold War Cuba, the male homosexual is a cipher. His body stands for an excess of signification, or for *the* Excessive as a category. He is, first of all, a sexual body; as such, at times he promises sex for sale. He foreshadows the impending consumer economy, but also recalls the remnants of revolutionary history. He stands for the precarious sense of the present but also for the untangling of the past—an unfolding that can only be partial, simulated, directed, and mediated by his past victimization and his future despair."³² Nearly two decades after his writing, Quiroga's sketch of the Cuban male queer still resonates. We hear it, for instance, in the way in which Sainz's informants produce a distinctive polemic over the politics of cruising. This is especially acute in one anonymous cruiser's fantasy of police entering the cruising grounds, not to arrest the *maricónes* and faggots but instead to expose and interdict the men who come there to gay bash. This is of course quite a utopian image of the Cuban police (almost as utopian as Fredric Jameson's ersatz proposal for a universal army in the United States).³³ Like Jameson's soldier, this anonymous queer imagines a role for the policeman that is almost unrecognizable. To imagine the undercover police in the cruising ground, fucking and getting fucked, is quite an astonishing image given the police's actual role, which is to surveil and patrol Havana's urban gay nightlife, ostensibly to monitor and prevent sex work that remains illegal, but also to continue to proscribe and interdict modes of sociality that remain stigmatized. Like the fort itself, which stands proudly as an icon of the island's impenetrability to foreign invasion, even as a constant flow of licit and illicit commerce flows through its walls, the social logic of homosexuality remains indeterminate.³⁴

The queer utopia conjured up in *Batería* is not an apologia for policing or the police state, but performs a style of desiring production that at once occupies and transgresses the debased speaking position of the flaming queen, the one who cannot possibly hide the scandal of his homosexuality and gender nonconformity. It is here that the not-yet-hereness of queerness converges with a mode of persistent brownness that is always already here, as described here in chapter 1 ("The Brown Commons") when Muñoz writes, "Brownness is a kind of uncanny persistence in the face of distressed conditions of possibility."

Such queer, black, and brown excess is also on view in the performances of Blankita, who has a particularly cutting routine where she dances with a purse with magnets on the bottom. The trick is that the magnets pick up the coins of the dollarized currency—the so-called convertible peso—while leaving the national currency in the dust. During one performance an international audience threw money of various denominations at her, and her improvised reactions to the variety of bills she received was itself the stuff of high drama and low comedy. The black Cuban *travesti*, figure of all that has been left behind in both revolutionary society and its impending consumer-driven sequel, belies the imperialist nostalgia that often attaches itself to U.S. narratives of "vanishing" Cuba. Her blackness is her brownness insofar as both qualities overlie and intensify her abjection and exclusion, and, through that very same gesture, her vivid and undeniably spectacular presence.

The Brown Commons

In Juana María Rodríguez's *Sexual Futures, Queer Gestures, and Other Latina Longings*, a text that engages with Muñoz's work to offer a powerful elaboration upon the interarticulation of queer utopia and Latinx sexual world making, Rodríguez describes latinidad in a fashion that casts light on Blankita's queer transection of blackness and brownness: "Latin@ is therefore always already formed through embodiment and context. Yet our proximity to these other racialized forms of identifications inflects how we move in the world. These proximities create the conditions for social and sexual enactments that bring us closer to others touched by the African diaspora, to mixed-raced people everywhere, to the politics and passions of indigenous communities. . . . Through our friendships and sexual encounters, we become fluent in other political and erotic modalities, other gestures that mark ways of caring for each other."[35] Rodríguez here describes something akin to Muñoz's insistence that "brown people's very being is always a being-in-common. The commons is made of feelings, sounds, buildings, neighborhoods, environments, and the nonhuman organic life that might circulate in such an environment alongside humans, and the inorganic presences that life is very often so attached to."³⁶ But how to characterize the relationship between such a brown commons and the "brown people" to which Muñoz meant to refer "in a very immediate way"?³⁷

Since at least 1970, the year the Nixon administration decided to begin tracking demographic information regarding the Hispanic background of the U.S. population alongside, but distinct from, information about race, blackness and brownness in the American imaginary have been lived in entangled proximity. So far as the U.S. Census Bureau is considered, latinidad is an ethnicity while blackness is a race. A Hispanic or Latino, according to a 1997 notice from the Office of Management and Budget, includes "persons who trace their origin or descent to Mexico, Puerto Rico, Cuba, Central and South America, and other Spanish cultures." Being both black and Hispanic in this sense is as easy as ticking a box or two. But this bureaucratic intersectionality can hardly be said to correspond with the lived experience of U.S. minorities, and in particular it is belied in the very distinctive and difficult struggles faced by Afro-Latin peoples in the U.S., who are often considered betwixt and between. What the state readily admits for classificatory purposes, the fact that one can be both black and brown, is a fact that is only begrudgingly admitted in popular culture, electoral politics, or, indeed, in the academic interdisciplines, all sites in which blackness and brownness are held to possess distinct and discrete sociocultural itineraries. If one does a cursory survey of news reports regarding the immense demographic transition presently underway in the U.S.—with social scientists expecting the nation to be "majority minority" by the year 2043—you will discover that this historic shift is routinely described as "the browning of America" and almost never as "the blackening of America." This journalistic usage reflects the political elite's obsession with the consumer power, social attitudes, and voting behavior of an aggregate imagined to share something like Hispanic values.

Such an aggregate is of course one of the first myths deconstructed in any college-level course in Latinx studies, but its authority over the national imaginary is not diminished but rather probably enhanced by its status as a convenient fiction or shorthand. Certainly, much of Muñoz's work in the area of critical race studies was devoted to being both specific and capacious in his categories, and part of that involved insisting upon the ways in which Cuba and its diaspora was interpellated by both Latinx and African Americanist frames of analysis in the U.S. Although blackness and brownness are regularly cast as competitive with each other within a U.S. framework of ethnic segmentation and competition, and even held discrete and apart within the progressive dynamics of coalition politics, the case of queer Afro-Cuba underscores the insufficiency of this logic of either/or. It is a case that contests the established ways in which black and brown are held out as separate or separable in the mainland imaginary. It is to this intractable problem that Muñoz addresses his sense of a brown world.

The Sense of Brown's penultimate chapter ("The Sense of *Wildness*") offers an expansive vision of the brown commons populating and animating this world. In his analysis of Wu Tsang's film *Wildness*, Muñoz places Paul B. Preciado's *Testo Junkie* in conversation with Gilbert Simondon's concept of transindividuation to "give an account of a being-with that is intrinsic to both trans and brown, consisting of objects, human and otherwise, who are browned by the world, or taken up by the discourse of trans. . . . This is to imagine a brown commons, trans-relationality, and what Simondon would call the real collective." But Muñoz was careful to insist that this notion of a brown commons should not dissolve incommensurability and difference into equivalence. For example, when considering the relationship between Asianness and the sense of brown, Muñoz writes, "I hope I have made it clear that in my deployment of the term, Asian can potentially be [brown]. Not in a way that inhibits our thinking of a critical Asianness or even a yellowness; but a brownness that is a co-presence with other modes of difference, a choreography of singularities that touch and contact but do not meld. Brownness is coexistent, affiliates, and intermeshes with blackness, Asianness, indigenousness, and other terms that manifest descriptive force to render the particularities of various modes of striving in the world." This passage underscores Muñoz's lifelong theorization of minoritarian life as a practice of living in relation to other forms of difference that "touch and contact but do not meld."[38] The brown commons is a sphere of being with, between, across, and alongside each other in various positions of striving, flourishing, and becoming. Such a vision of the brown commons is not a utopian vision for the future, but instead a description of the actually existing reality of the here and now. Or, as Kandice Chuh (whose work Muñoz invokes in *The Sense of Brown*'s tenth chapter) describes it, while "Muñoz's sense of brown emerges in and through the historical specificities that precipitate *latinidad*, including migration, linguistic coding, and the geographies of colonial modernity and Indigenous dispossession, it cannot—like the color brown itself—be isolated or reduced to those specificities. Brownness *is*—full stop; it is not a something, a particular thing, an adjectival appendage or cosmetic artifice; it is a name for minoritarian being and beingness. As a concept, brownness is the mode of knowing, the aesthetic rationality, that correlates with this ontological condition."[39] *The Sense of Brown* invites us to engage the work of removing the blockages that keep us from sensing or being attuned to the brownness of the world. In so doing, it mobilizes Chuh's "ontological condition" and its attendant "aesthetic rationalities" to recognize and re-create the world in and through its brownness.

To prepare *The Sense of Brown* for publication, we followed a process similar to the one that was used during the production of *Cruising Utopia*.[40] We have largely left José's prose as it was at the time of his death, making silent corrections of spelling and occasional minor adjustments for syntactic and grammatical clarity and precision.[41] We did not exclude any of the manuscripts José included in his draft manuscript and have kept his sequence intact. However, we have added a few chapters that were not included in his draft manuscript—inserting them in places we found helpful for framing the project's thematic arc. These chapters include "The Brown Commons," "Performing the Bestiary," "Wise Latinas," "Brown Worldings," "The Sense of *Wildness*," and "Vitalism's Afterburn." "Vitalism's Afterburn" was the last piece of writing that Muñoz published in his lifetime. We have reproduced it here as the concluding text. Its emphasis on "after" offered a fitting conclusion for a book that must remain incomplete in the wake of José's departure. Most of these other chapters were in the process of being drafted at the time of his death, and we largely suspect that José would have included at least some, if not all, of them in some (revised) form.

"Brown Worldings," "The Sense of *Wildness*," and "The Brown Commons" existed in Muñoz's records only as talks. "Brown Worldings" was given at least once as an address at Cal State Los Angeles the spring before his death. He gave "The Sense of Brown" as an address a number of times that same year. "The Brown Commons," in turn, is a poetic fragment that Muñoz delivered at Bard College in the fall of 2013. Though it cannot suffice as an introduction to the project, which Muñoz never had time to write, it does give the reader a sense of how he was introducing the contours of the project to the public. We have included it as an opening statement to the book, though we want to emphasize that Muñoz intended *The Sense of Brown* to open with an introduction, followed by "Feeling Brown" as the lead chapter.

For Muñoz, part of the use value of the aesthetic, and of performance in particular, was its ability to function as a conduit toward this mode of attunement, its ability to function as, in the words of Alexandra T. Vazquez, "a place of fractured togetherness."[42] It was against the majoritarian sphere's visions of competition and succession, of individual identity and group dynamics, that Muñoz sketched his notion of brownness, offering a sense of the brown commons. And it is with his own description of this vision that we conclude this introduction to *The Sense of Brown*:

> The brown commons is not about the production of the individual but instead about a movement, a flow, and an impulse to move beyond the singular and individualized subjectivities. It is about the swerve of matter, organic and otherwise, the moment of contact, the encounter and all that it can generate. Brownness is about contact and is nothing like continuousness. Brownness is a being with, being alongside. The story I am telling about a sense of brown is not about the formation of atomized brown subjects. It is instead about the task, the endeavor, not of enacting a brown commons but rather about knowing a brownness that is our commonality. Furthermore, the brownness that we share is not knowable in advance. Brownness is not reducible to one object or a thing, so the commons of brownness is not identifiable as any particular thing we have in common. . . . A brown commons as I am attempting to sketch here is an example of a collectivity with and through the incommensurable.

1

The Brown Commons

1.1 Nao Bustamante performing *Given Over to Want*, Autentika (Sculpture Quadrennial Riga), *No New Idols* performance festival, Riga, Latvia, June 1, 2019. Photograph by Lauris Aizupietis. COURTESY OF NAO BUSTAMANTE.

"Brown commons" is meant to signify at least two things. One is the commons of brown people, places, feelings, sounds, animals, minerals, flora, and other objects. How these things are brown, or what makes them brown, is partially the way in which they suffer and strive together but also the commonality of their ability to flourish under duress and pressure. They are brown in part because they have been devalued by the world outside their commons. Their brownness can be known by tracking the ways through which global and local forces constantly attempt to degrade their value and diminish their verve. But they are also brown insofar as they smolder with a life and persistence: they are brown because brown is a common color shared by a commons that is of *and* for the multitude. This is the other sense of brown that I wish to describe. People and things in the commons I am rendering are brown because they share an organicism that is not solely the organic of the natural as much as it is a certain brownness, which is embedded in a vast and pulsating social world. Again, not organic like a self-sufficient organism, but organic in that the world is brown as the objects within that world touch and are copresent. The brown commons is not about the production of the individual but instead about a movement, a flow, and an impulse to move beyond the singular subjectivity and the individualized subjectivities. It is about the swerve of matter, organic and otherwise, about the moment of contact, and the encounter and all that it can generate. Brownness is about contact and is nothing like continuousness. Brownness is a being with, being alongside. The story I am telling about a sense of brown is not about the formation of atomized brown subjects. It is instead about the task, the endeavor, not of enacting a brown commons but rather of knowing a brownness that is our commonality. Furthermore, the brownness that we share is not knowable in advance. It is not reducible to one object or a thing, so the commons of brownness is not identifiable as any particular thing we have in common.

While I am narrating an expansive brown commons that traverses the regime of the human, the politics that organize this thought experiment are primarily attached to the lives of human actants in larger social ensembles. I am drawn to the idea of a brown commons because it captures the way in which brown people's very being is always a being-in-common. The brown commons is made of feelings, sounds, buildings, neighborhoods, environments, and the nonhuman organic life that might circulate in such an environment alongside humans, and the inorganic presences that life is very often so attached to. But first and foremost, I mean "brown" as in brown people in a very immediate way, in this sense, people who are rendered brown by their personal and familial participations in South-to-North migration patterns. I am also thinking of people who are brown by way of accents and linguistic orientations that convey a certain difference. I mean a brownness that is conferred by the ways in which one's spatial coordinates are contested, and the ways in which one's right to residency is challenged by those who make false claims to nativity. Also, I think of brownness in relation to everyday customs and everyday styles of living that connote a sense of illegitimacy. Brown indexes a certain vulnerability to the violence of property, finance, and to capital's overarching mechanisms of domination. Things are brown by law insofar as even those who can claim legal belonging are still increasingly vulnerable to profiling and other state practices of subordination. People are brown in their vulnerability to the contempt and scorn of xenophobes, racists, and a class of people who are accustomed to savagely imposing their will on others. Nonhuman brownness is only partially knowable to us through the screen of human perception, but then every *thing* I am describing as being brown is only partially knowable. To think about brownness is to accept that it arrives at us, and that we attune to it only partially. Pieces resist knowing and being knowable. At best, we can be attuned to what brownness does in the world, what it performs, and the sense of the world that such performances engender. But we know that some humans are brown in that they feel differently, that things are brown in that they radiate a different kind of affect. Affect, as I am employing it in this project, is meant to address a sense of being-in-common as it is transmitted, across people, place, and spaces. Brown affect traverses the rhythmic spacing between those singularities that compose the plurality of a brown commons.

My use of "brown" is certainly an homage to the history of brown power in this country that was borne out of insurrectionist student movements. I do not mean brown in the way media pundits pronounce the browning of America in relation to national electoral politics. I am reaching back and invoking the sense of brown that was the Chicano walkouts of 1968, brown as in brown berets. Turning to the past in this particular fashion makes the point that the world is not becoming brown; rather, it has been brown. The brown power movement followed black power and was joined by red power, gay power, and other movements for liberation. They were movements that attempted to articulate a refusal of dominant logics and systems of thought, an insistence on thinking and doing otherwise. The brown power movement was intimately linked to modes of knowledge production and institutional practices that would ultimately congeal as ethnic, Latino, or Chicana/o studies.

As the case of book banning in Arizona shows us, the fact that the potential and force of brownness are intimately linked to the production of knowledge is not something that escapes the notice of the enemies of brown life.[1] Draconian immigration laws that are springing up all over the country after the passage of Arizona's SB 1070 have been shadowed by simultaneous legislation that has targeted the production of ethnic studies knowledge. While it should go without saying, it bears repeating that the violent attacks on ethnic studies and the knowledge it produces are also violent assaults on brown life. Fortunately, brown thought flows through the channels of what Stefano Harney and Fred Moten call the undercommons of the academy.[2] While official curriculums and itineraries for learning are vulnerable to those who would drive them underground, brown practices of thought will—as they have always done—thrive in the realms of the intramural, the unofficial, and the fugitive.

A brown commons is pivotal to various struggles to imagine and enact a particularity that is always only salient as coterminous with plurality. Jean-Luc Nancy's notion of a being singular plural, as I suggest throughout this book, is central to my understanding of the nature of this kind of commons.[3] A brown commons as I conceptualize it would share some similarities with the grand concordance of things described by political theorist Jane Bennett.[4] Commons are never placid. Life in the commons is and should be turbulent, not only because of the various enclosures that attempt to overwhelm a commons, but also because disagreement within the commons—what Jacques Rancière would call dissensus—is of vital importance to the augmentation of the insurrectionist promise of the commons.[5] The brown commons is under siege. Brown commons are human-nonhuman collectives that are, in Bennett's words, "provoked into existence by a shared experience of harm."[6] Brown commons are queer ecologies insofar as they are not ecologies depending on nature, which does not mean that they exclude nature. The queer ecology, which is the brown commons, includes the organic and the inorganic.

Brown, it is important to mention, is not strictly the shared experience of harm between people and things; it is also the potential for the refusal and resistance to that often-systemic harm. Brownness is a kind of uncanny persistence in the face of distressed conditions of possibility. One highly illustrative example of the persistence of this uncanny brownness is Antonio Viego's "The Life of the Undead," which tracks the paradoxes informing public health discourse on Latino mental and physical health.[7] Whereas the psychotherapeutic literature concludes that Latinos suffer anxiety and depression more than any other group, the epidemiological literature concludes that they possess better physical health than any other group and live longer than would be expected considering the socioeconomic challenges they face. Brownness's uncanny physical persistence has been enshrined within the term "epidemiological paradox" invented to name it. One could invoke Lauren Berlant's phrase and say that Latinos' slow deaths are much slower than they should be.[8] As I would channel Viego, I suggest, "Latinos live long deaths." The point here is that within this brownness and all its turbulence, in Viego's analysis, public health discourse cannot help but falter in its attempt to capture brown people's persistence. This is because of how its accounts of Latino mental and physical health compete with and cross-cancel each other: the psychic and the somatic are never at the scene at the same time.

The commons is an old idea in the history of politics and philosophy. It has often been used as a stand-in for nature and for the ways in which it is subsumed by the enclosures of private property. In book 5 of *The Republic*, Plato describes a proto-communism of the simultaneous "mine" and "not mine" which reimagines relationality through a recast notion of kinship.[9] Aristotle, in book 2 of his *Politics*, upholds the idea of a traditional polis by saying that the blood of cousins is stronger in his idea of the polis than the bloodlines between father and son in Plato's *Republic*.[10] For thinkers like Locke and Rousseau, the commons eventually gives way to the formation of society, progress, and history, being fenced off as private property. Michael Hardt and Antonio Negri have suggested a rewiring of the commons, what they describe as an urban commons, or—as they put it—a commons in the metropolis. They say the city is not just a built environment and an object of capitalist production, but "a living dynamic of cultural practices, intellectual circuits, affective networks, and social institutions."[11] The city is not just an enclosure of nature but is its own commons that is teeming with potentiality for the kind of living otherwise, the kind that a full engagement with the commons might help us actualize.

The commons I delineate is a brown one. Certainly, questions of inclusion and exclusion arise. Why brown? The short answer is that the world is and has been brown and has been so despite the various blockages that keep us from knowing or being attuned to brownness. This is to argue that lives are still organized and disorganized by harsh asymmetries that systemically devalue classes of singularities, in this case those onto-particularities that adhere to a shared sense of a brown or browned world. Here we can consider John Dewey and the shared sense of harm that collates the experience of people and things as belonging to a commons, a commons that is brought into being by what Spinoza would called a shared affect of indignation that can potentially lead to a thinking and analysis that would help assemble a self-conscious and potentially insurrectionist commons.[12] Yet it is important to add that the commons I am sketching here is articulated as a brown commons for the point of describing not only a shared indignation but also a process of thinking and imagining otherwise in the face of shared wounding. It was Leon Trotsky who famously said that "active indignation is linked up with hope."[13] This hope is what I have called a critical hope or an educated desire; it is an active refusal and a salient demand for something else.[14] Critical utopianism is not borne of complacency, of an idle wishing for things to get better. It is borne of the sense of indignation one feels at the harm that is visited upon groups, individuals, cultures, ways of life, and the planet itself. The task at hand is not to enact a commons, but to touch an actually existing commons.

To imagine a brown commons, we must think about the integers and their relationship to vaster circuits as a whole. This book draws upon some ideas from what has been called speculative realism, especially object-oriented ontology as well as self-described new materialism, most prominently what Bennett called vibrant matter. Readers of Bennett will have a sense of her influence as I describe a commons that is made up of a concordance of things, both human and nonhuman. While these new approaches, reworked realisms, and materialisms that announce an unapologetic return to ontology are often cited or invoked alongside each other, there are salient disagreements between them.

Graham Harman insists on thinking about objects as existing before relationality.[15] Timothy Morton, also a proponent of object-oriented ontology, suggests that the object is "a weird entity withdrawn from access, yet somehow manifest."[16] Harman is clear that while the object does not yield access it does have allure; there is a capacity for these semiconcealed entities to speak to each other. This is related to his stand against full-blown relationality on the basis of his critique of assemblage theories, which he distrusts, insisting that these chains of relationality function as complex feedback loops, seeing as they represent—in his view—the "blurring of boundaries between one thing and another."[17] He contends that this move has "held a moral high ground in philosophy for too long."[18] Harman is interested in countering the now-standard political reflexes associated with terms like "essence" (bad) and "reciprocal interplay" (good).

While my political commitments to old materialism keep me on the side of the relational, I do get quite a bit out of this point in Harman, despite the fact that I ultimately reject his account of objects and relations. I am struck and persuaded by his warning that objects blur into each other too easily in assemblage theory. Indeed, there is much to be gleaned by contemplating the brownness (of things) before they are shuttled off into an assemblage. Bennett too is interested in aspects of Harman's proposition, specifically his allergy to post-Kantian correlationism, but in the end she is a theorist of relationality and complex systems over relational objects. Bennett wonders whether or not there is a need to choose "between objects or their relations."[19] She suggests we "toggle" back and forth between things (her word for objects) and systems.[20] Bennett points out that Harman does attempt to think about the ways in which mysterious objects, full of only semiaccessible essence and agency (that thing that for me aligns it with brownness), communicate and even commune, despite his insistence on aloof objects. It is therefore interesting that, in an essay on the work of Nancy, Harman offers some praise of the older French philosopher—who, like Derrida, is ultimately guilty of obscuring the object—specifically on the question of touching. He points out that, for Nancy, "To touch something is to make contact with it even while remaining separate from it because entities that touch do not fuse together. To touch is to caress a surface that belongs to something else, but to never master and consume it."[21] It makes sense that Harman would attach himself to this story about touching since it is indeed more persuasive than his account of the weird communications between objects.

This Nancy-inspired materialist mode of touching is also more persuasive than the dizzying shuttling back and forth between thing and complex network that Bennett calls for. Bennett leans on assemblage theory, with its choreography of coding and recoding, territorialization and reterritorialization. I have attempted, in the most disloyal of ways, to describe some aspect of a brown commons by raiding recent debates in critical theory that have shown no interest in thinking about the brownness of the sphere we dwell within, the relations that bring this commons into existence, the brown components of that world, the ways in which they manage to make contact but not be alike or recognize each other exclusively through semblance. A brown commons I am attempting to sketch here is an example of a collectivity with and through the incommensurable.

Feeling Brown

ETHNICITY AND AFFECT IN RICARDO BRACHO'S
THE SWEETEST HANGOVER (AND OTHER STDs)

Ethnicity, Affect, and Performance

The theoretical incoherence of the identity demarcation "Latino" is linked to the term's failure to actualize embodied politics that contest the various antagonisms within the social that challenge Latino and Latina citizen-subjects. While important political spectacles have been staged under group identity titles such as Chicano and Nuyorican, Latino, a term meant to enable much-needed coalitions between different national groups, has not developed as an umbrella term that unites cultural and political activists across different national, racial, class, and gender divides. This problem has to do with its incoherence, by which I mean the term's inability to index, with any regularity, the central identity tropes that lead to our understandings of group identities in the United States. "Latino" does not subscribe to a common racial, class, gender, religious, or national category, and if a Latino can be from any country in Latin America, a member of any race, religion, class, or gender or sex orientation, who then is she? What, if any, nodes of commonality do Latinas and Latinos share? How is it possible to know *latinidad*?

Latino/a can be understood as a new social movement. In this sense, I want to differentiate between citizen-subjects who subscribe to the category Latino/a and those whom the U.S. Census terms Hispanic. Rejecting "Hispanic" in and of itself does not constitute a social movement, nor am I suggesting any such thing. But I do want to posit that such a linguistic maneuver is the germ of a self-imaging of "Latino" as, following the important and pathbreaking work of the Chicana feminist Norma Alarcón, an "identity-in-difference." In this schematic, an identity-in-difference is one that understands the structuring role of difference as the underlying concept in a group's mapping of collective identity. For Alarcón, an identity-in-difference is an optic better suited to considering contemporary mappings of diversity than the now-standardized homogenizing logic of multiculturalism.[1] To be cognizant of one's status as an identity-in-difference is to know that one falls off majoritarian maps of the public sphere, that one is exiled from paradigms of communicative reason and from a larger culture of consent. This exile is more like a displacement, the origin of which is a historically specific and culturally situated bias that blocks the trajectory of the Latina or Latino citizen-subject to official citizenship-subject political ontology.

This blockage is one that keeps the Latina or Latino citizen-subject from being able to access normativity, playing out as an inability to perform racialized normativity. A key component of my thesis is the contention that normativity is accessed in the majoritarian public sphere through the affective performance of ethnic and racial normativity. This performance (of whiteness) primarily transpires on an affective register. Acting white has everything to do with the specific performance of a particular affect, which grounds the performing subject in a normative white lifeworld. Latinas and Latinos, and other people of color, are unable to achieve this affective performativity on a regular basis.

In his study *Marxism and Literature*, Raymond Williams coined the term "structure of feeling" to discuss the connections and points of solidarity between working-class groups and a social experience that can be described as "in process" yet nonetheless is historically situated.[2] Williams's formulation echoes Alarcón's explication of "identity-in-difference" as "identity-in-process."[3] I suggest that Williams's approach and a general turn to affect might be a better way to talk about the affiliations and identifications between racialized and ethnic groups than those available in standard stories of identity politics. What unites and consolidates oppositional groups is not simply the fact of identity but the way in which they perform affect, especially in relation to an official national affect that is aligned with a hegemonic class. Latina/o (and other minoritarian) theater and performance set out to specify and describe ethnic difference and resistance not in terms of simple being, but through the more nuanced route of feeling. More specifically, I am interested in plotting the way in which Latina/o theater and performance theatricalize a certain mode of feeling brown in a world painted white and organized by cultural mandates to feel white.

Standard models of U.S. citizenship are based on an official national affect. English-only legislation initiatives throughout the nation call for English to be declared the official national language. In a similar fashion, there is an unofficial, but no less powerfully entrenched, national affect. It is thus critical to analyze the material and historical import of affect as well as emotion to better understand failed and actualized performances of citizenship. May Joseph has brilliantly explicated the ways in which the performative aspects of citizenship have been undertheorized in previous discourses on citizenship. She reminds readers that within the important discourses on citizenship and participatory democracy, "performance emerges as an implied sphere rather than an actually located process."[4] Following Joseph's lead, I position performance as an actualized sphere, one that needs to be grasped as such to enact an analysis of citizenship. Citizenship is negotiated within a contested national sphere in which performances of affect counter each other in a contest that can be described as official national affect rather than emergent immigrant. The stakes in this contest are nothing less than the very terms of citizenship. It is thus useful to chart and theorize the utility and efficacy of different modes of affective struggle. This essay suggests that it is useful to look at contemporary U.S. Latina/o drama and performance as symbolic acts of difference that insist on ethnic affect within a representational sphere dominated by the official national affect.

I contend that this official national affect, a mode of being in the world primarily associated with white middle-class subjectivity, reads most ethnic affect as inappropriate. Whiteness is a cultural logic that can be understood as an affective code that positions itself as the law. The lens of Foucauldian discourse analysis permits us to understand whiteness—and the official national affect that represents its interests—as a truth game.[5] This game is rigged insofar as it is meant to block access to freedom for those who cannot inhabit or at least mimic certain affective rhythms that have been preordained as acceptable. From the vantage point of this national affect code, Latina/o affect appears over the top and excessive. The media culture, a chief disseminator of official national affect, often attempts to contain Latina/o images as spectacles of spiciness and exoticism.[6] Such mainstream depictions of Latino affect serve to reduce, simplify, and contain ethnic difference. The work of many Latino and Latina playwrights and performers operates in direct opposition to the majoritarian sphere's media representation of Latinos. Much of this performance work functions as political attempts to contest and challenge prefabricated media stereotypes with dense and nuanced accounts of the emotional performances of self that constitute Latina/o difference and survival.

The affect of Latinos and Latinas is often off. One can even argue that it is off-white. The "failure" of Latino affect, in relation to the hegemonic protocols of North American affective comportment, revolves around an understanding of the Latina/o as affective excess. I know I risk reproducing some predictable clichés such as the Latino being "hot 'n' spicy" or simply "on fire." I answer these concerns by making two points: First, it is not so much that Latina/o affect in performance is so excessive, but that the affective performance of normative whiteness is minimalist to the point of emotional impoverishment. Whiteness claims affective normativity and neutrality, but for that fantasy to remain in place one must only view it from the vantage point of U.S. cultural and political hegemony. Once we look at whiteness from a racialized perspective, like that of Latinos, it begins to appear to be flat and impoverished. At this moment in history, it seems especially important to position whiteness as lack. The second point is that rather than trying to run from Latino-as-excess stereotype, it seems much more important to seize it and redirect it in the service of a liberationist politics. Such a maneuver is akin to what I have described elsewhere as a disidentification with toxic characterizations and stereotypes of U.S. Latinos. A disidentification is neither an identification nor a counteridentification; it is a working on, with, and against a form at a simultaneous moment.[7] Thus the "hot 'n' spicy spic" is a subject who cannot be contained within the sparse affective landscape of Anglo North America. This accounts for the ways Latina and Latino citizen-subjects find their way through subgroups that perform the self in affectively extravagant fashions.

Minoritarian identity has much to do with certain subjects' inability to act properly within majoritarian scripts and scenarios. Latinos and Latinas are stigmatized as performers of excess: the hot and spicy, over-the-top subjects who simply do not know when to quit. "Spic" is an epithet intrinsically linked to questions of affect and excess affect. Rather than simply rejecting this toxic language of shame, I wish to reinhabit it and suggest that as such, it permits us to arrive at an important mapping of the social. Rather than saying that Latina/o affect is too much, I want to suggest that the presence of Latina/o affect puts a great deal of pressure on the affective base of whiteness, insofar as it instructs us in a reading of the affect of whiteness as underdeveloped and impoverished.

The inquiry I am undertaking here suggests that we move beyond notions of ethnicity as fixed (something that people are) and instead understand it as performative (what people do), providing a reinvigorated and nuanced understanding of ethnicity. Performance functions as socially symbolic acts that serve as powerful theoretical lenses to view the social sphere. I am interested in crafting a critical apparatus that permits us to read ethnicity as a historical formation uncircumscribed by the boundaries of conventional understandings of identity. In lieu of viewing racial or ethnic difference as solely cultural, I aim to describe how they can be understood as affective difference(s), that is, the ways in which various historically coherent groups feel differently and navigate the material world on a different emotional register.

To better understand affective difference, a turn to the phenomenological psychology articulated by Jean-Paul Sartre is efficacious. The methodological underpinnings of my approach have included Williams's historicization of feeling and Alarcón's formulations of an identity-in-difference. Sartre's *Sketch for a Theory of Emotions* (1939) first formulated many of the major ideas that would be fully realized in *Being and Nothingness*, the major text of the first half of his career. In that brief book, Sartre rejects a Freudian notion of the unconscious and instead insists on a Husserlian description of the "conscious phenomenon" that is emotion. For Sartre, consciousness is a conscious activity, the act of knowing that one thinks. Emotion is thus an extension of consciousness, what I would call a performed manifestation of consciousness. According to Sartre, humans comprehend the world as making demands on them. Life in this existentially and phenomenologically oriented description consists of a set of tasks, of things we need to do. We encounter routes and obstacles to the actualization of certain goals, and make a map for ourselves of the world that includes these pathways and blocks. But when we are overwhelmed by this map of the world, a map replete with obstacles and barriers to our self-actualization, we enact the "magical" process that Sartre describes as emotions. When facing a seemingly insurmountable object, we turn to emotion. Sartre concludes, "The study of emotions has indeed verified this principle: an emotion refers to what it signifies. And what it signifies is indeed, in effect, the totality of human relations of human-reality to the world."[8] I am most interested in this notion of emotion being the signification of human reality to the world. Such a theory is deeply relational. It refuses the individualistic bent of Freudian psychoanalysis and attempts to describe emotions as emotions, the active negotiations of people within their social and historical matrix.

While these ideas about the relational nature and social contingency of emotion are helpful in the articulation of this writing project, it is equally important to posit that I do not subscribe to Sartre's approach without some deep reservations. Sartre ultimately describes the emotions as regressive, explaining that consciousness can "be-in-the-world" in two different modes. One is what he calls an "organized complex of utilizable things"; the other magical way of being in the world clicks into place when the organized matrix of utensils is no longer perceivable as such, and one becomes overwhelmed.[9] Emotions describe for Sartre our relations to a world that has overwhelmed us. In Sartre's paradigm, the magical realm of emotions is something we regress into when under duress. It does not take much critical scrutiny to see that this move betrays a typically misogynistic gender logic that positions men as reasonable and better suited to deploying the world of utensils, whereas women (and men who are overly feminine) are cast as a weaker order that must regress to a magical relation with the world. Furthermore, the discussion of magic and regression resonates with an understanding of people of color as primitives who forsake reason only to hide behind jujus.

Yet the actual description of an emotion can nonetheless be useful to a minoritarian theory of affect. Sartre describes emotions as surfacing during moments of losing one's distance from the world of objects and people. Because stigmatized people are presented with significantly more obstacles and blockages than privileged citizen-subjects, minoritarian subjects often have difficulty maintaining distance from the very material and felt obstacles that suddenly surface in their own affective mapping of the world. The world is not ideologically neutral. The organization of things has much to do with the way in which capital and different cultural logics of normativity that represent capital's interests give normative citizen-subjects advantageous distance. Sartre's affective sketch is useful because it can help minoritarian subjects better comprehend the working of emotion. This mapping can potentially enable a critical distance that does not represent a debunking of emotion but an elucidation of emotion's "magical" nature within a historical web. The phenomenological aspect of Sartre's inquiry demystifies the magic of emotion, and this is, in and of itself, an important contribution to a theory of the affective nature of ethnicity.

Unlike Sartre, Walter Benjamin values the realm of affect, which he sees as a vital human resource under siege by the advent of technology. For Benjamin, the realm of affect has been compromised within the alienating age of mechanical reproduction. Though some technology (notably cinema) offers the possibility of a utopian return of affect, Benjamin longs and searches for strategies by which affect could work through (not avoid, ignore, or dismiss) the numbing alienation associated with technological modernization. Furthermore, he pursues aesthetic strategies that, as Miriam Hansen puts it, "reassess [and] redefine, the conditions of experience, affectivity, memory and the imagination."[10] Sartre's work, when considered and partially amended in relation to Benjamin, stands as a productive theoretical opening.

Within this field of contested national affect, Latina/o drama has the potential to stage theoretical and political interventions. David Román has argued that the performance of Latina/o has "been politically efficacious for people from quite distinct cultural backgrounds and ideological positions [who] meet and organize under the label of Latina/o and Chicana/o in order to register an oppositional stance to majoritarian institutions."[11] While I have stated that the term "Latino" has been politically incoherent, it has nonetheless, as Román has argued, done some important political work.[12] The performance praxis of U.S. Latinas and Latinos assists the minoritarian citizen-subject in the process of denaturalizing the country's universalizing "national affect" fiction as it asserts ontological validity and affective difference. A useful example of this theoretical/political potential is the often misread drama by the Cuban American playwright María Irene Fornés, who eschews identity labels such as "Latina." Her refusal or reluctance to embrace an uncritical model of Latina identity is a critical and theoretical act. Only a few of Fornés's plays actually feature Latino and Latina characters: *Conduct of Life* is staged in a generalized Latin American nation, and *Sarita* features characters clearly marked as Latina or Latino.[13] Even so, I contend that all of her dramatic personages represent Latina/o affective reality. Their way of being, and their modes of negotiating the interpersonal and the social, stand as thick descriptions of ethnic feeling within a hegemonic order. Fornés's oeuvre stands out from the mainstream of American theater partly because one is not easily able to assign motivation to her characters. Traditional narrative arcs of plot development are all but absent in her work, a difference that is often interpreted as the avant-garde nature of her plays. Such a reading is only half right, however. This particular mode of avant-gardism can be characterized as representative of a specifically transcultural avant-garde. Her plays appear mysterious to North American eyes because they represent a specifically Latina/o *manera de ser* (way of being). This mystery is not accidental, nor it is a problem of translation; it is strategic, measured, and interventionist.

This Bridge Called My Crack

In the remainder of this essay, I focus on a case study that I view as a left theatricalization of the affective overload that is latinidad. Ricardo Bracho's play *The Sweetest Hangover (and Other STDS)*, specifically its 1997 production at Brava Theater in San Francisco, represents a lifeworld where Latina/o affect structures reality. The excessive affect that characterizes latinidad (and excess should always be underscored in this context as merely relative) is the fundamental building block of the world imagined in this performance. I suggest that the world of Bracho's production also indexes other antinormative subcultural formations, such as the alternate economies of recreational drug use and homosexual desire.

"This Bridge Called My Crack" is a play on the classic 1981 anthology of writing by radical women of color, *This Bridge Called My Back*. I chose the word "crack" as part of a playful attempt to highlight the thematics of anal eroticism and recreational drug use; the crack is not crack cocaine but instead crystal meth, a drug that in certain vernacular orbits is referred to as "crack." It is important to note that my punning here is meant to serve more than the general cause of irreverence. I am instead interested in calling attention to the continuation of the radical women of color project by gay men of color. In the 1983 foreword to *Bridge*, Moraga comments on the shift in cultural climates between the two editions; within a parenthesis she writes, "(I am particularly encouraged by the organizing potential between third world lesbians and gay men in our communities of color)."[14] Granted, I make much of this parenthetical statement; I use it, for instance, to draw a line between the groundbreaking work of the *Bridge* authors and the cultural production of Latino playwrights like Bracho, Luis Alfaro, Jorge Ignacio Cortiñas, Nilo Cruz, and Jonathan Ceniceroz. I nonetheless connect the work of such cultural workers because I feel that they do "co-map" Latino lifeworlds where Latino affect—manifested in politics, performance, and other passions—is no longer represented as stigmatized excess. The gay male writing tradition that I am attempting to suture to this feminist tradition labors, via affective performance, to enact a powerful utopianism that is most certainly influenced by *Bridge*. Affective performances that reject the protocols of (white) normativity help map out cultural spectacles that represent and are symbolically connected to alternative economies, like the economies of recreational drugs and homoeroticism. Such spectacles and the alternative economies they represent help us in, to borrow a phrase from one of Cherríe Moraga's poems, "dreaming of other planets." The poem itself, titled

"Dreaming of Other Planets," works as something of a key to understanding the utopian impulse that reverberates throughout Bracho's play:

> my vision is small
> fixed
> to what can be heard
> between the ears
>
> the spot
> between the eyes
> a well-spring
> opening
> to el mundo grande
>
> relámpago strikes
> between the legs
> I open against
> my will dreaming
>
> of other planets I am
> dreaming
> of other ways
> of seeing
>
> this life.[15]

This theoretical formulation, "dreaming of other planets," represents the type of utopian planning, scheming, imaging, and performing we must engage in if we are to enact other realities, other ways of being and doing within the world. The play, like the poem, dreams not only of other spaces but of other modes of perceiving reality and feeling the world. While Moraga dreams of other ways of seeing, Bracho's play instructs its audience in other ways of feeling: feeling brown. For Moraga, the dream of another time and place is achieved through the auspices of poetry and the act of writing. This notion of dreaming is ultimately descriptive of a critical approach that is intent on critiquing the present by imagining and feeling other temporalities and spaces.

More concretely, another planet that is dreamed of, in the instance of Bracho's play, is a nightclub, a place called Aztlantis—a name that signifies both the Chicano lost homeland and the lost island of myth. This other place and time calls us to think about the project of imagining a utopian time and place. It is a scene of what I have referred to elsewhere as "everynight life."[16]

Nightlife is a zone where the affective dominance of white normativity is weakened. *The freaks come out at night.* The play's set is wide and spacious, organized by walls of corrugated metal, lit with flashing pinks and blues producing a frenzied nightclub aura. Vinyl shower curtains are deployed to further segment space. The freaks that populate this club include the central protagonist, Octavio Deseo, Chicano club promoter and diva extraordinaire. He runs his nightlife emporium with the help of his ex-lover, the Salvadoran disc jockey djdj. The club's frequent performers are two black women: Plum, a black female student who leaves academia at night and enters the alternative affective register of Aztlantis, and Natasha Kinky, a black transgender woman who dances at the club with Plum. The club regulars are Miss Thing 2 and 1. Thing 2 is a twenty-year-old Filipino gay man and Thing 1 is a black Puerto Rican twenty-year-old gay man. The Things, who speak in rhyme and comment on all the play's proceedings, are both Greek chorus and a reference to the Things in Dr. Seuss's *The Cat in the Hat*, little monsters who bring the house down. The cast is rounded off by Octavio's love interest, Samson, a thirty-year-old man of mixed Filipino and Chicano ancestry who works as a tattoo artist and a security guard at the club.

Bracho's multiethnic ensemble signals a new moment in minoritarian performance and cultural work in which the strict confines of identitarian politics are superseded by other logics of group identification. The play's cast does not cohere by identity but instead by a politics of affect, an affective belonging. All of these subjects are unable to map themselves onto a white and heterosexually normative narrative of the world. The protocols of theater, literature, and cultural production by people of color in the United States has primarily concentrated on black-white relational chains (which can be best described as colored-white configurations) or ethnic or racial separatist models. The fact that Aztlantis is populated not exclusively by Latinos but by different kinds of people of color of various genders suggests that traditional identitarian logics of group formation and social cohesion are giving way to new models of relationality and interconnectedness. We can understand the ties that bind this utopian nightlife community as affective ones: shared vibes and structures of feeling assemble utopia in this production.

The play's multiracial and multigender composition is mirrored in the actual audience in attendance on opening night. It seems useful to cite a theater review from the *San Francisco Examiner*, an article whose first two paragraphs focus exclusively on the play's audience and that thus stands as a unique document of the play's reception:

> Almost every opening night for a new play has something of the air of a party, given all the friends of the author and cast who turn out to show their support. Saturday at the Brava Theater Center, however, was more like attending a community celebration—perhaps crossed with the peak hour at a popular gay nightclub.
>
> The house was as packed as it possibly could be, short of putting chairs on the stage. The median age was decidedly lower than at most theatrical events and the racial mix considerably broader. The crowd, or a substantial portion of it, greeted the world premiere of Ricardo A. Bracho's "The Sweetest Hangover (& other STDs)" as if it were a celebration of a community that rarely gets to see itself depicted in any genre.[17]

The reviewer, Robert Hurwitt, discusses the racial composition of the play, which he describes as "a dramatic treatment of the world of gay people of color—Hispanic, Asian, African American; male, female and transsexual."[18] His amazement concerning the play's audience dominates the first three paragraphs of the review: he is especially intrigued by the audience's demographic relation to the characters onstage. The performative and happening-like nature of opening night and the play's subsequent extended run are worth considering since that too is part of the play's intervention. In his influential study of the Renaissance stage, Stephen Orgel explicated the importance of the actual space of the Swan Theater to the larger culture: "[The] building was the physical embodiment of both an idea of theater and an idea of the society it was created to entertain."[19] In a similar fashion, the space of the Brava Theater and its audience work in tandem with the play's actual text, representing a certain idea within the social, one that was first articulated in *Bridge*. Also, the literal space of a theater like Brava, a major venue that specializes in feminist, queer, and racialized performance, is also important to consider. Brava is the literal figuration of an ideological landscape first laid out in *Bridge*. The fact that this queer male world can benefit from and manifest itself in relation to this house, partially built by racialized feminism, is a literal legacy from that foundational anthology.[20]

The world of *The Sweetest Hangover* is a world without white people. During the play's second act, Thing 1 is feeling overwhelmed by the white people at the nightclub. He complains of what he calls "colonial regression syndrome." He wears a pith helmet, an ascot, and other items of explorer gear, and talks about shooting a film called *Paris Is Gagging—a Study in Whiteness and Other Forms of Madness*. His stalwart yet shady companion, Thing 2, suggests he get over whiteness by simply blinking his eyes and letting in darkness. This ritual thus magically expels whiteness from the play, leaving a brown world of feeling, organized by the affective belongings between people of color. In this way, *The Sweetest Hangover* mirrors and reconstructs the composition of *This Bridge Called My Back*. The play offers an ensemble of racialized and ethnic characters that, like *Bridge* and its contributors, try to reconceptualize the social from a vista that is not organized around relations to whiteness or the majoritarian sphere. In this fashion, the play offers us a profound way to think through the social, which is predicated on a break from the structuring logic of white normativity.

The play amplifies the message of *Bridge* by folding in male homosexuality (and eroticism) as well as the demimonde of recreational drug use. In the same way in which *Bridge* argued for modes of female being in the world rejected by white feminism and different modalities of patriarchy, *The Sweetest Hangover* makes a case for other ways of being in the world that are deemed outlaw and illicit. Octavio and most of the other characters are recreational drug users. The production resists the moralism that U.S. culture continually rehearses in relation to recreational drug use. In a simpler fashion, the play embraces non-couple-oriented, nonmonogamous gay male sexuality—a modality of being queer that is currently being demonized and scapegoated by gay pundits from the right. The crack that my subtitle invoked is meant to speak to both demonized identity vectors: recreational drug users and gay men who refuse to compromise their erotic life by conforming to normative and assimilationist modes of comportment.[21] While *Bridge* does not mention the antidrug hysteria that surfaced during Ronald Reagan's so-called War on Drugs or the particularities of homophobia directed at men of color, it nonetheless makes a case for antinormative and racialized ways of being in the world.[22]

The major conflict in the play between Octavio and his lover, Samson, is not Octavio's drug problem, but Octavio's refusal to conform to a drug-free monogamous ideal that Samson desires. This ideal is a modality of affective normativity. The play enacts reversal in that Samson's desire for this ideal is critiqued with the same sharp critical lens usually reserved for individuals with a "drug problem." Octavio's particular relationship to drugs and sex is not moralized against or celebrated. Within the logic of the play, drugs simply *are*. Such modes of being in the world are folded into the rich affective archive of latinidad. Obviously this is not to say that all Latinos participate in the alternative economies of homosexual eroticism or recreational drug use, but it is to imply that these demonized acts are, in part, components of some Latino experiences.

Sex and drugs are not the only horizon of Latino affective reality that the play embodies. Sound is as important to the play and the story of Latino feelings as the other nightlife components discussed in this essay. Octavio's ex-lover, djdj, has taken a "vow of sonics," which entails his refusal to speak through any vehicle other than the records he spins. Octavio asks Samson not to take this refusal to speak to him seriously since djdj broke up with Octavio by playing a song. djdj's voice is heard in a series of one-scene monologues throughout the play. Since he does not "speak," his monologues represent nondiegetic moments in the play, moments when the character speaks directly to the audience.[23] Miss Thing 1 and Miss Thing 2 function as a Greek chorus during these soliloquies, sounding like a catchy pop melody hook chorus. In the first scene of the second act, titled "[djdj] Exposes," the master of sonics exposes his affective reality by playing snatches of songs by 1980s Latin freestyle pop pioneers such as Exposé, famous for their hit, "Point of No Return." This melancholic meditation provides a moment of foreshadowing that announces the character's death later in the act. At this point in the drama, djdj has literally hit a point of no return:

> I met a man last night, and kissing him was hearing Exposé for the first time. *taking me to the point of no return.* not the *words uh-oh-oh* or the tempo *uh-oh-oh* just that time of my life. high school keggers in Excelsior, after-parties hanging with the popular girls and all the doggish jocks *and lookout weekend cuz here I cum because weekends were made for fun.* This is the mid 80's high nrg cha-cha *and six minutes, six minutes, six-minutes doug e fresh you're on-uh-uh-on* time. *Yeah it's like a jungle sometimes* getting wasted *and I think I'm going under* this numb feeling of lubes and Michelob as I dance with Michelle to Shannon's *Let the Music Play* or is it Lisa Lisa *Lost in Emotion.* Kissing him was a party in some football player's backyard where cops would come, Eddie would start with Lisa, Anita would leave to the backseat of a car, Daisy would fall in love with someone else's boyfriend for the second time that weekend. Straight mating rituals done to *the roof the roof the roof is on fire we don't need no water let the motherfucker burn.* Kissing him in the Mission, coming back from a beer run, Stacey Q singing *We Connect* and we do. But this is Collingwood Jurassic Park. 3 am and I don't know what song is on his radio. I'm kissing him and I feel the jets in my pulse.[24]

The mention of "the jets in [his] pulse" announces the next moment in the play's soundscape: the Jets' "I Got a Crush on You." This monologue is a unique interrogation of a relational chain that connects affect to memory to sonics. Music plays a major role in Bracho's play: its job is to draft an affective schematic that is particular to the emotional emergence and becoming of a citizen-subject who will not feel American in the way in which the protocols of official affective citizenship demand. The sappiness of the pop tunes registers as affective excess to majoritarian ears, but as something altogether different to the minoritarian listener who uses these songs as part of her affective archive. The sounds of popular culture and the playwright's citational practice tell a story about the way in which the resources of popular culture are deployed in a manner that is different and decidedly dissident in relation to structuring codes of U.S. national affect. djdj's soliloquy, like the whole of the play, calls on music to conjure a past affective temporality. That sonic past is important to the utopic reformulated and antiessentialist nationalism of the play.

djdj's plot line is central to the play's narrative. His death due to AIDS-related complications breaks up the affective community that held the utopic world of the play together. Plum has gone off to law school; Nat, after traveling to Thailand for hormonal injections, has found a man; Samson has fled the urban space, running from a fear of AIDS and urban violence; Octavio goes out in the world of everynightlife; Miss Thing 1 and Miss Thing 2 remain as the ruling queens of the bar stool. In the play's final scene, the rhyming queens sit at the Endup, an actual gay bar in San Francisco, Thing 1 wearing opera glasses and carrying a butterfly net. These instruments of white gentility are to be deployed for the project of installing a man in his life. The dialogue indicates that even though the world of Aztlantis has crumbled, the affective possibilities it represented are far from diffused. Thing 1 undergoes a brief crisis of consciousness on his bar stool throne, which his co-Thing talks him through.

> THING 1: Ain't no Aztlantis to go to, no djdj [crosses himself] to sweat to. Ain't no Samson to swoon over, Octavio to gag on. Last I bumped into the girls, Nat had herself a man and Plum was 'bout ready to start law school. What's there for us?
>
> THING 2: These seats. A new bar. Same old fashions, same old tired faces and tracks. Why, you looking for something else?
>
> THING 1: I need more, more than kiking with the children, making a world dark and glamorous and giving off vapors to the white girl. Something for us, instead of waiting in line to be put on their lists.

THING 2: And you got it. Cute fashions, friends in low places that are keeping you high. Major props.

THING 1: We might have it by the d.j. booth or here in welfare alley at the Endup but turn to the corner and bam! you are punk ass shit. Nothing.

THING 2: Naw I beg to differ. Being punk ass shit is not nothing. Being a punk is power.

THING 1: According to whom? Not the fellas on my corner, definitely not my folks. Power don't come in bumps or pumps, girl.

THING 2: The power of being a punk in the world comes from knowing it's your world and the rest of these sad motherfuckers live in it and need to to get to your groove. Boypussy Power!

THING 1: Yeah but how can you hear your beat with the other wall of sound, white noise. . . .

THING 2: Change the channel and stop listening to college grunge radio.

By advocating for "Boypussy Power!," Miss Thing 2 is riffing on the lessons and important manifestos of biopower made by radical feminists of color. In that instance, a line is being drawn between the feminist field of struggle and the struggles that gay men of color face. The work of these radical women of color is instructive and enabling, both for these two characters in the play and for the playwright himself. The most important advice Thing 2 gives Thing 1 is the declaration that being a "punk" is power once one understands that the world and the groove belong to the "punks." Thing 1 worries about the sound of white noise, and Thing 2 makes it clear that he must learn how to tune such sounds out. The sound of white noise is the official national affect, the beat of a majoritarian drum that defies a minoritarian sense of rhythm. Thing 2 (and the playwright) instructs Thing 1 and the audience to believe in one's own affective groove, one's own way of being, dancing, striving, dreaming, loving, fighting, and moving in the world and to never let the affective hum of white normativity overwhelm that very important groove.

This analysis has posited ethnicity as a structure of feeling, as a way of being in the world, a path that does not conform to the conventions of a majoritarian public sphere and the national affect it sponsors. It is my hope that thinking of latinidad in this way will help us better analyze the obstacles that must be negotiated within the social for the minoritarian citizen-subject. I have positioned Bracho's work as a continuation of another project begun almost forty years ago by fierce women of color who also found their way of being in the world labeled wrong, inappropriate, and insane. Many of the contributors to that volume wrote about the way in which the dominant culture made them feel crazy and wrong-minded. Part of *Bridge*'s project was to show that this craziness was a powerful way of being in the world, a mode of being that those in power needed to call crazy because it challenged the very tenets of their existence. Ricardo Bracho's *The Sweetest Hangover* continues that project, allowing us to continue to dream of other planets and to finally make worlds.

3

The Onus
of Seeing Cuba

NILO CRUZ'S *CUBANÍA*

Old Cubans say that if you walk to the very end of Key West, you will be able to see Cuba. I myself don't know any Cubans, young or old, who have actually seen the island from this point, but there is a plaque at that spot that marks it as officially ninety miles from the island of Cuba. Of course, a lot more separates Cuba from Key West than those piddling ninety miles. There is a haze that obscures any view, ensuring that one will indeed never see Cuba from that or any other vantage point. That haze is composed of certain ideological mists that we might understand as the United States' endless propaganda war against the island, the rage and melancholic romanticism of the Cubans outside the island, and the North American left's precritical celebration of the revolution. Cuban exile art thus needs to respond to the onus of breaking through the distorting cloud that keeps us all from actually seeing Cuba. In this way, Nilo Cruz's work is both admirable and necessary, insofar as it not only understands the onus of seeing Cuba but also in fact tries to do something about it. Cruz's writing practice attempts to cast a picture of *cubanía*, of Cubanness as a way of being in the world; this picture not only helps us begin to achieve a historical materialist understanding of Cuba, but it also encourages us to access cubanía as a structure of feeling that supersedes national boundaries and pedagogies.

3.1 Daphne Rubin Vega and Adriana Sevan in Nilo Cruz's *Two Sisters and a Piano*, 2000. Directed by Loretta Greco at the Public Theater, New York. Photograph by Michal Daniel. COURTESY OF MICHAL DANIEL AND THE PUBLIC THEATER.

If this play, *Two Sisters and a Piano*, were to be addressed on the level of plot, such an explication would dwell on the way in which the work attempts to interrogate a difficult and pivotal moment in Cuban history.[1] The play is set in Cuba of 1992, at the moment of perestroika. Through the lives of four characters (two sisters—one a writer and the other a musician—a lieutenant in the nation's military, and a piano tuner) a charged moment of historical transition and entrenchment is described with dense nuance. The two sisters are political prisoners who have been upgraded from penitentiary incarceration to house arrest. The house they are sent to is their now dilapidated family home, and they settle among its ruins. María Celia, the older sister, is forbidden from practicing her vocation as a writer. The other sister, Sofia, is allowed to play her out-of-tune piano for a time until that too is taken away from her. Throughout the play she trembles with desire for the outside world and the bodies of men, while María Celia longs for her husband, a political activist who has escaped Cuba, denouncing it from the outside, and who labors to get his wife and sister-in-law out through diplomatic mechanisms. María Celia is desired by Lieutenant Portuondo, the military representative who is in charge of her detainment and who enforces the restriction against her writing. His great conflict is this assigned duty and his love of María Celia's writing and body. The play's other major character is Victor Manuel, the piano tuner. María Celia treats him with suspicion as he is desired by Sofia. His major concern is the state of the family piano.

A reading that focused primarily on plot would miss some of the important cultural work that Cruz is doing. The play is about cubanía as a *manera de ser* (a way of being), and it attempts to provide an affective understanding of the world. These characters, anchored in the Cuba of 1991, are witness to a moment of world historical turmoil. They face this moment with manifold desires and longings: some desire social change, while others desire sexual and psychic liberation. Still others are invested in the state and strive for the survival of the existing system. These feelings speak to the emotional lifeworld of cubanía. The sisters are full of desire for another place and time, a then and there in which their desires will be realized. They dream through their writing and music of a moment when longing will be fulfilled. The men stand in for a certain aspect of nation. They themselves are not without ambivalence, yet they nonetheless represent an established order, a here and a now. The women represent something that we might understand as melancholic attachment to a lost Cuba and, at the same time, a utopian longing for a reformulated evolution that perestroika promised to some on the island. (We know now that perestroika and the end of Soviet economic aid did not bring a new golden age to Cuba, but instead made the island even more susceptible to the U.S. government's savage embargo and brought on an especially hellish "Special Period" of scarcity.)[2] The sisters dream of another temporality while the men are anchored to a notion of presentness.

Throughout Cruz's oeuvre, we encounter women who dream of and desire different times and places. The world they represent is familiar to anyone who has lived inside or outside of a Cuban community here or there. The playwright deploys female characters as melancholics whose affective relationship to the world is a critique of its current conditions. They are personages living outside of a national order, and whose desire exceeds the bounds of the national here and now. This strategy echoes what we can today understand as Tennessee Williams's queer ventriloquism. Through his memorable and often tortured heroines (a partial list would include Laura and Amanda Wingfield in *The Glass Menagerie*, Blanche and Stella in *A Streetcar Named Desire*, Maggie from *Cat on a Hot Tin Roof*, or *Suddenly Last Summer*'s Catherine), Williams was able to represent the affective reality of homosexual desire. While Williams was never able (and perhaps never desired) to write what we would reductively call an out gay play, the affective landscape of pre-Stonewall homosexuality was certainly represented in his work through these powerfully dramatic female conjurings. María Celia and Sofia seem like a tribute and intertextual reverberation of this particular mode of rendering emotional realities through analogy and allegory. The fact that María Celia and Sofia's desires are suppressed and literally under house arrest speaks to the revolution's problematic relationship to public displays of queer desire and ontology.

Cruz uses emotion as an instrument to see Cuba beyond a certain ideological fog. To better understand this strategy, we might compare his work to two other important Cuban American plays. María Irene Fornés's short play *Mud*, for instance, is set in an economically impoverished U.S. locale.[3] Mae, the play's female protagonist, finds herself trapped in a life where she is unable to actualize her emotional and intellectual potential. This boundedness is similar to the chains that keep the two sisters from achieving their own liberation in *Two Sisters and a Piano*. Mae's plight is meant to be felt by anyone who is sensitized to the transnational gendering of poverty, yet it speaks to a Latina/o cognoscenti in powerful and culturally specific ways. The mysteriousness of Fornés is akin to a mysteriousness that saturates Cruz's work: his characters do not conform to the strictures on character development that dominate North American theater. In other words, motivations of his characters are not available to North American viewers who are unable to see psychology and feeling outside of their own emotional confines.

It is also useful to compare the playwright's work to that of another Cuban American dramatist. Jorge Ignacio Cortiñas's *Maleta Mulata*, like much of Cruz's work, challenges the affective protocols that U.S. culture routinely prescribes.[4] The play is set in a Miami household in the 1980s. Family members struggle with the literal ghost of their Cuban past as well as with contemporary imperatives to become American. *Maleta Mulata*, like *Two Sisters and a Piano*, offers valuable insight into what I call the melancholia of cubanía. This complex affective formation, in the case of Cortiñas's excellent play, focuses on Miami-based Cubans' inability to accept the reality of a socialist present on the island. A similar melancholia characterizes María Celia and Sofia's struggle with the island's present. Furthermore, Cruz's play foregrounds the Cuban state's own melancholic longing for a pre-perestroika universe. In this fashion, María Celia's writing and Sofia's music threaten to wake Cuba up from its willful melancholic slumber, forcing the country into a post–Cold War temporality.

Cruz, like Fornés and Cortiñas, and, for that matter, a host of Cuban American cultural workers that would include and not be limited to Coco Fusco, Carmelita Tropicana, Marga Gomez, Ela Troyano, Delores Prida, Raul Ferrera Balanquet, Ernesto Pujol, Achy Obejas, Caridad Svitch, Tony LaBat, Marcos Bequer, and Felix González-Torres, all negotiate the onus of seeing Cuba, the almost impossible project of looking beyond this vision-obscuring haze to a rich lifeworld of affective particularity. Cuba and Cuban America are both obscured by this haze and, at the same moment, constructed as monolithic. If we ever hope to understand Cuba, it seems especially important to really see it at this particular moment, as multinational capital encroaches on the island and the U.S. embargo shows no sign of abating. Cruz's drama functions as an elegant and penetrating optic that may well be indispensable to the task at hand.

4

Meandering South

ISAAC JULIEN AND *THE LONG ROAD TO MAZATLÁN*

Over the last few years, Isaac Julien has completed several multichannel projection installations in triptych format. His 1999 *The Long Road to Mazatlán* is a collaboration with Javier de Frutos, a Venezuelan-born dancer and choreographer. In this essay, I endeavor to follow particular lines of thought, both formalistic and political, generated by Julien's project. Indeed, this essay is another moment in what has been for me a decade-long engagement with the artist's work.[1] In this instance, the lines of thought flow South. *The Long Road to Mazatlán* explores masculinity and its undoing. The masculine cinematic genre par excellence, the road movie, is one of many constructs that the film invokes and unmakes. The history of other takes on the precariousness of masculinity in the Western film, like Andy Warhol's *Lonesome Cowboys* (1968), exists within the film as a minihomage to the late auteur. The film even rehearses Robert De Niro's over-the-top rendition of masculinity in crisis from his 1976 cult classic *Taxi Driver*. *The Long Road to Mazatlán*'s intertextual dimensions are bolstered by formal strategies. Formalistic and thematic strategies tell us what happens when the fragile and tentative fiction we understand as masculinity goes South.

The triptych format allows the artist to explore the historical and aesthetic vicissitudes of his thematic from multiple perspectives. Stark juxtapositions that would be impossible to negotiate via a single screen are constantly animating each other. Yet the triptych format does not let the contrasting of images follow simple binary logic. Formally, the triptych always allows a third space of contemplation.[2] This third space allows for a ludic reterritorialization of masculinity. In this essay, I am interested in this multiplicity of images and the way in which the rejection of the singular or even coupled image, in favor of the triptych, functions as an aesthetic strategy that is very much in line with Julien's mode of cultural production.

Throughout the artist's work, one can detect a poetics of historical excavation that resists conventional narrative form. The turn to the past in Julien's work has never been linear: the triptych offers us multiple perspectives on what may or may not be a story of homosocial desire that vectors into the sexual. The story that is available to the attentive viewer, that is to say the viewer who accepts the challenge of making meaning of the rich visual layering that the triptych format offers, is a story about movement and desire. Gilles Deleuze, when discussing the triptych in the work of painter Francis Bacon, declares that movement is the law of triptychs: "There are so many movements in Bacon's paintings that the law of triptychs can only be a movement of movements, or a state of complex forces, inasmuch as movement is always derived by forces extended upon the body."[3] A movement of movements is endemic to the triptych. Deleuze goes on to explain that the triptych is the result of the forces of isolation, deformation, and dissipation that impact the body. Yet the triptych in Bacon works with these forces and leads to a visual format that can "incorporate coupling as a phenomenon. But it operates with other forces and implies other movements."[4] In *The Long Road to Mazatlán*, the couple form is incorporated but also undone. The movement of movements is rendered via the choreography of two cowboys, dancing a dance of desire, a dance that is imperfect, full of jerky and disjunctive movement. The dance is the dance of masculinity's undoing.

I want to propose that three copresent modalities exist in *The Long Road to Mazatlán* that contribute to what I am calling the undoing of masculinity. The copresence of gesture is rendered possible by the aesthetic strategy that, after Deleuze on Bacon, I link to the triptych. I will survey three different modalities of undoing that layer each other in the project. All touch on what I call a modality of "queerness." "Queer" is a term that has been rehabilitated in the discourse of humanities over the last several decades, so much so that it has lost much of its conceptual clarity. I therefore index Julien's project insofar as his work permits me to offer a very particular if not provisional definition of queerness. The point of this particular move is to make an intervention in queerness, to reinvigorate what it might mean in

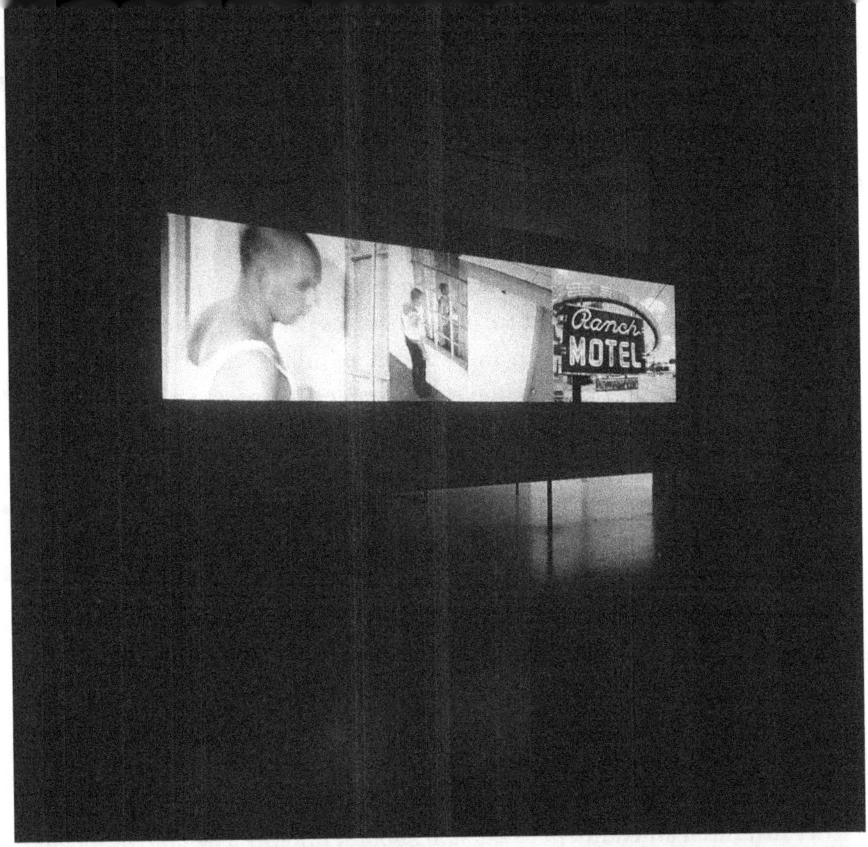

4.1 and 4.2 Isaac Julien, *The Long Road to Mazatlán*, 1999. Triple screen projection; three Beta submasters. COURTESY OF ISAAC JULIEN AND VICTORIA MIRO, LONDON/VENICE.

relation to understanding different ways of being in the world that negotiate the forces which impact the body in ways that bend it toward the well-worn roads of normative heterosexuality. Indeed, I want to suggest that going South, following *The Long Road to Mazatlán*, is a queer road less traveled.

To begin my explication of the first modality or layer of masculine undoing in this installation, I first turn to Julien's collaborator, Javier de Frutos, and his performance/research, independent of Julien, which has focused on issues of singular masculinity and its discontents, or more nearly, wounded idealities of iconic masculinity. In his own work, de Frutos looks at the figure of the loner or drifter, as manifest in the oeuvre of queer writers like Tennessee Williams. De Frutos's work dwells in the historicity of queer man as outsider. This is a romanticized and eroticized take on what the Chicano novelist John Rechy (along with the likes of the late William S. Burroughs) would identify as the gay outlaw. This gay outlaw might be related to what the psychoanalytic critic Leo Bersani has identified as the antirelationality of the "homo."[5] For my part, I am skeptical of Bersani's privileging of this singular and nonrelational homosexual as the mode in which gay men can know the self par excellence. Indeed, by considering the layering of performative meaning that the triptych offers, *The Long Road to Mazatlán* stands as a substantial amendment to Bersani's solitary homo. The cultivation and eroticization of one's outsider status are a visceral and important dimension of the definition of queerness that Julien's work cultivates, but there is something more in the horizon that we must know as being pivotal for us to know queerness. Thus, the gleaming and seductive rendering of a southern horizon on the triple screens often achieves a provisional harmony. *The Long Road to Mazatlán* is marked by big sky, a vista that is synonymous with both the movement within movements that is a southward journey and its mimetic life in the Hollywood Western. Often one figure—a figure who indexes authors of a poignant collective fantasy of the homo (Williams, Capote, Burroughs, Rechy, Genet, and even Bersani), that is, the gay outlaw—looks at a horizon that suggests that something is missing. Homoness in and of itself is not queerness, since queerness thirsts for something more than a shattering singularity.

From the first modality I move to a second in which the relational is always central to and constitutive of masculinity within a larger scope than what the homo/hetero binary would suggest. In her pioneering text *Between Men*, Eve Kosofsky Sedgwick famously outlined the porous line between the homosexual and the homosocial.[6] The homosocial certainly organizes our reality, and it secures masculinity as a site of privilege and sovereignty.

The dance South, this downward choreography, is a dance that includes a movement that I identify as queer, insofar as it puts new pressure on masculinity. The filmic text that is most recognizably resonant when considering this aspect of the text is Warhol's *Lonesome Cowboys*. Warhol himself would not fit into the homo mold that Bersani and others would claim holds sway. Warhol and his oeuvre are a fine example of queerness as a restructuring of relationality.[7] Warhol's Factory is in fact a remaking of artistic production through a reconceptualizing of kinship and belonging that is driven by a drive toward queerness. In *Lonesome Cowboys*, Warhol sends up the obvious homosexual underpinnings of the Western's foppish cowhands who do awkward dances around themselves and the one female presence in the film, superstar Viva. Sedgwick's thesis clarifies the fashion in which homophobia is often coexistent with violence against women. In *Lonesome Cowboys*, Viva is supposedly gang raped, yet that rape scene stands as a goofy farce insofar as the spoofing performances of masculinity by male superstars including Joe D'Allesandro, Eric Emerson, and Taylor Mead seems no more menacing than that of small boys playing an awkward game of dress-up. The masculinity on display in *Lonesome Cowboys* is clearly something hastily manufactured on the factory room floor. It seems to come undone. In a similar fashion, the male couple in *The Long Road to Mazatlán* comes undone at the seams. The masculinity manufactured via Warhol's 1960s mode of filmic production is not so much an open secret as it is a shared joke. I contend that *Lonesome Cowboys* is illustrative of Sedgwick's theorization of a homosocial continuum, a precarious schematic that frames masculinity as a contingent and relative phenomenon. Warhol's illustration is a ludic mirroring of Sedgwick's theory, albeit with quite a few more laughs.

The same sense of playfulness permeates the couple who meander on *The Long Road to Mazatlán*. It is a playfulness that marks a line between awkwardness and eroticism. The lovers' dance in *The Long Road to Mazatlán* includes an aquatic splash play at a pool that is reminiscent of Narcissus's pond. The psychoanalytic reference is a light joke, engulfed as it is in the dance's general logic of play and jumpiness. In a similar manner, a sexy tussle in a motel room is an exercise in Judson postmodern dance technique in which the movements of everyday life are reframed as dance. This modality, a homosexual/homosocial relational axis, is attuned to the logic of the couple. Deleuze explains the figure of the couple as most resonant on the level of rhythm. The figure of the couple is a merger of elements in Bacon's work for Deleuze, both expressed through the metaphor of sound. The figure of the couple is essentially a linkage of melodic lines and rhythm. When considering *The Long Road to Mazatlán*, we hear both this cohesion and its undoing. The piece's exquisite sound design is both aligned with and disaligned from the choreography.

This brings me to the third modality I wish to discuss in *The Long Road to Mazatlán*, a modality that I see as emblematic of the queerness that Julien's work affords us. Deleuze's prose rings with jubilance when he discusses this modality that is formally tethered to the triptych:

> With the triptych, finally, rhythm takes on an extraordinary amplitude in a forced movement which gives it an autonomy, and produces in us the impression of time: the limits of sensation are broken, exceeded in all directions; the Figures are lifted up or thrown up in the air, placed upon aerial riggings from which they suddenly fall. But at the same time, in this immobile fall, the strangest phenomenon of recomposition or redistribution is produced, for it is the rhythm itself that becomes sensation, it is rhythm itself that becomes Figure, according to its own separated directions, the active, the passive, the attendant.[8]

I cite this passage at length because this opening in perception that Deleuze comes to, through the contemplation of Bacon's triptych paintings, hums along with my own reception of the triptych in Julien. Julien's collaboration with de Frutos is indeed a dance on its own terms. The three screens offer an amplitude of visual possibility. The two dancing bodies intertwine with the flickering dance of lights, of a perpetually flowing triptych of image combinations, a phenomenon of recomposition and redistribution, not unlike the ways in which different forces bearing upon the dancer's body lead to a composing and recomposing of self. The game of corporeal distribution and redistribution is mirrored through the triptych format.

Deleuze did not link Bacon's triptych law of movement as having anything to do with biography, especially the painter's sexual life as a gay man. But the work's queerness, at least according to the definition of queerness I am attempting to enunciate here, has everything to do with this other modality that the triptych animates, this process of recomposition and redistribution of form and self. The triptych encompasses both the singular and the relational/couple, yet it nonetheless represents a multitude that is glimpsed through the triptych's formal choreography of images. That dance is reflected on the level of content and style via the performance that the installation documents and reanimates.

But other questions, perhaps more concrete ones, about what going South to a mythical Mazatlán might mean in the age of globalization and the North American Free Trade Agreement also surface. Going South connotes a certain unbecoming that is adjacent to the undoing of masculinity which I have discussed, yet it is not the same thing. In North American vernacular English, to say a venture or a project has "gone South" is to indicate that it too has become undone or has simply failed. This example is more than a North American racist tic within everyday speech. It is illustrative of what the South represents in a certain alterity, marked as negative within the purview of a North American dominant ideology of bias and projected fantasies of contagion and affective particularity attached to brown bodies from the South. When the dancer in black (Phillippe Rierra, from the South of France) poses in front of the mirror and does his best Robert De Niro *Taxi Driver* impression, he fails not only because of a certain lapse in masculine ideality but also because of what sounds like a thick Latino accent that betrays his body as not that of the one who has succeeded in taming the West or the South but, instead, as the body that has to be deterritorialized. Thus, in this final example from the installation, we see how the third modality I have discussed represents an attentiveness to a layering that happens on the ground level of the sociological field. Indeed, this is an indexical moment that resonates throughout Julien's work—race and sex as aspects of belonging and indifference that are intractable.

In this chapter, I have attempted to merge aesthetic questions with political concerns. But in this instance, the means clearly outweigh the ends. *The Long Road to Mazatlán* is a performance that invites us to "go South," which is to allow a certain decomposition and recomposition, a process that is not only queer but also of the greatest urgency.

"Chico, What Does It Feel Like to Be a Problem?"

THE TRANSMISSION OF BROWNNESS

What does it feel like to be a problem? This provocative line in W. E. B. Du Bois serves as an opening to consider the complexity of racial recognition, commonality, and belonging. Although the lines are familiar to most who have ventured to think critically about race and racial formations in the Americas, they are worth citing:

> Between me and the other world there is ever an unmasked question: unmasked by some through feelings of delicacy; by others through the difficulty of rightly framing it. All nevertheless flutter round it. They approach me in a half-hesitant sort of way, eye me curiously or compassionately, and then, instead of saying directly, How does it feel to be a problem? they say, I know an excellent colored man in town; or, I fought in Mechanicsville; or, Do not these Southern outrages make your blood boil? At these I smile, or am interested, or reduce to the simmer, as the occasion may require. To the real question, How does it feel to be a problem? I answer seldom a word.[1]

This notion of feeling like a problem jumps off the page for African Americans and non–African Americans who consider themselves problematic subjects—subjects that are coded minoritarian in my analysis. Certainly feeling like a problem is about feeling apart, feeling separate. However, in the spirit of African American studies' interest in the nature of double-voiced discourse and Du Bois's own theory of double consciousness, one can also ruminate on the ways in which feeling like a problem is also a mode of belonging, a belonging through recognition. Thus feeling like a problem is a mode of minoritarian recognition. Rather than mapping belonging through exhausted narratives of identity, there may be considerable value in thinking about the problem of feeling like a problem as not simply an impasse but, instead, an opening. Thus, I aim to take two tracks: one considers what it means to feel like a problem, while the other considers the problem of feeling itself and how it functions in relation to belonging and knowing the other through what Teresa Brennan, in a posthumous text, described as the transmission of affect.[2] More specifically, I am interested in making sense of a certain modality of what I will call intraracial empathic projective identification. The larger analysis this chapter is culled from hopefully represents an opening in thinking, an opening in theory, and, ideally, an opening in feeling.

This essay is also meant to dwell on a field of possibility, what I would call the series of relays between the affective spike of what blackness meant and continues to mean within the historical field of U.S. culture and of what brownness might mean today. This writing turns to the force of African American studies, especially the component of that discourse that participates in a larger radical black tradition. I employ that hermeneutic in the field of Latina/o studies which, in my estimation, is still emerging. While I refer to Latina/o studies inquiry as emergent, I nonetheless see it vectoring toward positivism and the empirical. Although the empirical has its place and utility, I see it as crucial that the far-reaching questions and heuristics that we invoke under the name of theory be applied to the experience and particularity of U.S. Latinas/os.

The problem of being a problem resonates within recent Latina/o studies discourses. Suzanne Oboler, in her important interdisciplinary study *Ethnic Labels, Latina/o Lives*, describes the meaning attached to the label "Hispanic": "While advertising and business concerns are actively seeking entry into what they perceive as a 'lucrative Hispanic market,' Hispanics are simultaneously being categorized as 'low-income people' who confront 'unusual unemployment.' Indeed, Latina/os are increasingly associated with high numbers of school dropouts, rising teenage pregnancies, crime, drugs, AIDS, and other social ills of this society, leading the New York State Governor's Advisory Committee on Hispanic Affairs to state, 'As the full public hearings revealed, and this report describes, the situation of [the] majority of Hispanics in New York State is extremely troubling. The same basic issues emerge again and again.'"³ In this passage Oboler is mimicking the sociological apprehension of the problematic nature of the Hispanic. There are problems on at least two levels: How can Hispanics be an ideal niche marketing target and, at the same time, riddled by crime, drugs, and AIDS? This troubling nature—this notion of being a problem—is nonetheless useful if one were to put hermeneutic pressure on the very category of Hispanic or Latina/o.

Identity is indeed a problematic term when applied to Latinas/os—groups who do not cohere along the lines of race, nation, language, or any other conventional demarcation of difference. Latina/o identity itself is thus a problem. It is perhaps within this very status as problem that we can begin to understand the particularities of the system of belonging and recognition that I am pointing to as *latinidad*. To this end, Du Bois's rhetorical parry—what does it feel like to be a problem—is worth attending to closely. I contend that feeling like a problem, and its commonality, may provide us with a better understanding of feeling brown. Feeling brown is my attempt to frame the particularity of group identification that temporarily displaces terms like "Hispanic" or even "Latina/o."[4]

Patricia Gherovici, an Argentine psychoanalyst and Lacanian clinician practicing in Philadelphia's barrio, rejects the more politically palatable term "Latina/o" for the word "Hispanic." In her fascinating study, *The Puerto Rican Syndrome*, Gherovici critiques the current mental health protocols and institutions currently in place to help disenfranchised groups in urban areas like the one she herself works with. Her thesis, that the mental health system is concerned with merely suppressing the symptomatology of larger social ills, is worth citing:

> In the barrio one finds all the hurdles one can expect when dealing with marginalized groups: urban poverty, alcoholism, drug addiction, disintegrating families, and the most extreme violence, encountered on a daily basis and manifesting itself in the most aberrant forms. This community provides a privileged context to explore how the American community mental health model can apply. In most cases, services available to the Hispanic community are geared toward simple symptom suppression. The model is functionalist, based on the idea of correcting symptoms with the goal of helping—or even forcing—the patient to comply with the model of capitalist productivity.[5]

It is therefore to Gherovici's advantage that she uses the label "Hispanic," a word that does not blend as easily into a multicultural diversity management paradigm as the concept of Latina/o. "Hispanic," as a term inflicted on communities by the U.S. Census, shows the seams of the systemic state violence that has attempted to classify groups like those she studies, and to reproduce them as proper cogs in a larger underclass service economy. I understand and admire the conceptual force behind the maverick analyst's linguistic choice, yet I resist this tactic because I find the category of Hispanic so politically repellent and I worry that it disrupts the reparative work that Latina/o studies needs to do in relation to the different communities it attempts to address.[6] But Hispanic, in Gherovici's distinct and strategic usage, does once again foreground Latinas/os' status as a problem, which is, again, the point of this particular meditation, after Du Bois and for Latina/o studies. Indeed, what does it feel like to be a problem?

Feeling brown, the idea of feeling brown, is my attempt to begin to conceptualize this mode of belonging that I conveniently index elsewhere as the concept of latinidad. But feeling brown is the phenomenon that underwrites this particular concept of latinidad that I am attempting to describe. Feeling like a problem, in commonality, is what I am attempting to get to when I cite and exercise this notion of feeling brown. The terminology I am invoking squarely indexes the quasi-militant Brown Power movement which, modeled after Black Power, peaked in the 1970s along with other U.S. civil rights struggles like Red Power and Gay Power. While the Brown Power movement is for most a historical footnote, it nonetheless captures a certain political utopian aspiration that does not cleanse the stain of feeling like a problem in the manner in which the cultural detergent of weak multiculturalism does. Feeling brown also connotes a sense of group identification that I find similarly efficacious. Feeling brown is feeling together in difference. Feeling brown is an "apartness together" through sharing the status of being a problem.

Feeling brown refers to what I describe earlier as a manera de ser, a way of being in the world. This is not the same as being seen as or perceived as brown. Similarly to the field of visual ethnic recognition, within the affective register there are indeed varied affective shadings of brownness, whether it be different national experiences among Latinas/os or types of colorism that are akin to the physical biases that exist within blackness. The visual and the affective are different identificatory routes: one can feel very brown and perhaps not register as brown as the dark-skinned person standing next to one who is involved in the endeavor of trying to feel white. The reverse is probably more common. The memoirist Richard Rodríguez has used the word as an organizing trope in his book *Brown*.[7] My project differs from Rodríguez's in several ways. Most significantly, I understand latinidad's brownness to be historically situated, while Rodríguez is at some point prepared to consider the unshaven Richard Nixon of the Nixon–John F. Kennedy debates as "the brown" candidate. Rodríguez's identification with brownness is always mediated with ethnic/racial abjection. When I invoke the concept, it is connected to a historically specific affective particularity. Brownness registers as a mode of affective particularity that a subject feels in herself or recognizes in others.

This project then calls upon some psychological stratagems to offer a heuristic that is attuned to the place and particularity of minoritarian subjects within the social. Like Gherovici, I understand the underlining problem to be a capitalist ethic that attempts to manage groups through socially toxic and racist protocols. Multiculturalism, as many have explained, is the most recent attempt to deal with what we can identify—echoing Du Bois, over a hundred years later—as the problem of the color line.

As I proceed, I should clarify that feeling brown, the theoretical hermeneutic I am offering, is to some degree an internally conflicted term since I am speaking more nearly of affect than of feeling. For example, I am persuaded by Teresa Brennan's description of the breakdown between affect and feeling. While she wrote that "there is no reason to challenge the idea that emotions are basically synonymous with affects (if more an evidently physiological subset) or that moods and sentiments are subsets referring to long lasting affective constellations," affect's valence, as opposed to feeling, has a more energetic nature.[8] This is to say that affect connotes a projection out, as one's affect is transmitted, and depletes or energizes the social sphere. Yet, feeling brown, for me, begins to get to the question of group identification, a concept that my interdisciplinary analysis strives to address. Feeling is meant to index a communal investment in brownness. Brownness is a value through negation, the negation projected onto it by a racist public sphere that devalues the particularity of non–Anglo Americans. This negation underwrites racialized poverty while supporting other asymmetries within the social. Owning the negation that is brownness is owning an understanding of self and group as problem in relation to a dominant order, a normative national affect. Brown feelings are the glue that coheres group identifications.

Brown feelings are historically situated, and while brown in this analysis is linked to latinidad, brownness in its relation to blackness is not simply about Latina/o group identification. Vijay Prashad takes another track in his book *The Karma of Brown Folks*.[9] In that text he thinks through the place of another mode of brownness, one more nearly associated with a model minority version of brownness. Like me, Prashad turns to and restructures Du Bois's question to ask, in relation to South Asians in the U.S.: What does it feel like to be a solution? Which is to say that in the U.S. national imaginary, the racist imagination frames South Asians in a radically different fashion. I nonetheless cite Prashad's different brownness to point to the way in which group identifications play a larger role in the nation-state's understanding of normative national character or affect. While these brownnesses mean radically different things on the register of difference, they both do the work of shoring up normative national affect through their deviations.

Group identification, as described by the Indian-born post-Klein theorist W. R. Bion, is crucial to this notion of feeling brown.[10] Bion's notion of projective identification, his unique elaboration on Klein's formulation, especially his description of emphatic projective identification that is almost directly oppositional to the psychotic's projective sadism, is key to understanding brown feelings. Projective identification, a concept whose initial formulation was suggested in the work of Melanie Klein, was primarily a primitive defense employed by the subject to cast off aspects of the self that were toxic. This notion in Klein, perhaps one of her most popular contributions to psychoanalysis, described the mechanism in which the infant dispelled aspects of the self, "bad feelings" (hate, envy, greed), onto the other.[11] In its initial articulation, the mechanism known as projective identification is linked to pathological practices: most specifically a sadism arising out of what is known in Kleinian thought as the schizoid/paranoid position. Most often, it has been associated with negative personality traits. In Lacan's project, one that emphasized the Oedipal in ways that Klein resisted, projection is always neurotic. Bion described another moment, a secondary moment after the abnormal and sadistic aspects of projective identification. He termed this moment normal projective identification, which he understood as being related to empathy—what he called putting oneself in the other's shoes. It is this notion of empathic projective identification that I find most useful when describing the coherence of groups and the transmission of affect that facilitates modes of belonging. There is something innately empathic about this shared affective construct that I am calling brownness, this response to a certain negation within the social that corresponds to this question of feeling like a problem.

Much has been written about *The Souls of Black Folk*'s structure of address. The text is indeed a call for white sympathy, since it addresses a white liberal subject who is potentially receptive to the idea that the color line is indeed the structuring antagonism of the twentieth century. But, following Bion and others, I read the text as performing a secondary function that is not a call for interracial sympathy but, instead, the work of elaborating intraracial empathy. That is precisely the use value of *The Souls of Black Folk* here and now and within the context of Latina/o studies and the project of imaging and elaborating a politics of black feeling. The *souls* of black folk are plural. Du Bois described blackness via the metaphor of soul—thus rendering the African diaspora as a less than corporeal entity. This depiction resonates alongside the then-nascent idea of the psychic.

At this particular moment, when, as I have argued, Latinas/os and Hispanics are described as sociological problems, it seems that imagining a psychic life that is structured around intraracial projective empathy is especially a boon. Antonio Viego's work on psychoanalysis and its potential utility for Latina/o studies is of exceptional importance on this front. In his book *Dead Subjects: Towards a Politics of Loss in Latino Studies*, Viego makes the argument that the concept of latinidad must attend to the mostly neglected realm of the psychic if it is to ever offer a useful diagnosis of the contest between self and other that structures the social and consolidates identitarian categories.[12] More specifically, Viego has argued for the use value of a Lacanian understanding of the subject that does not make the same mistakes as American ego psychology, a mode of psychology that posits the potential for a therapeutic conclusion to analysis based on the principle of a whole subject. He persuasively argues, "We need to question further the assumption that the solution to psychological trauma should be to fill out the ego more, plug up the holes, amplify and lengthen its reach. Minoritized folk, in particular, too often instantiated as lacking in the social, must learn to imagine alternative ways of making life pleasurable, tolerable—new ways of accessing the dialectical movement of desire, without being convinced that building the ego's defenses is the answer."[13] The counsel offered by this Latina/o studies psychoanalytic thinker is key to the project of imaging brown feeling. Being "instantiated as lacking" is indeed the condition of brownness, which is the condition of feeling like a problem. This status of "problem" cannot simply be projected out, dismissed, dumped on the other. Indeed, a more reparative move is required, which is holding on to the problematic, fractured, and negated status of self within the social and working through such a position, striving to find new ways of living in the world that are pleasurable, ethical, and indeed tolerable. I am not suggesting that one needs to simply disavow one's status as injured or traumatized by the state, or that one simply give up on imagining political transformation.

More nearly, I am suggesting that we be attentive to the psychic vicissitudes of our belonging in difference, which I describe as feeling brown, and work through that position, rather than grasp for an ego ideal that, as Viego explains, always leaves us disappointed.

A group investment in brown feeling requires a certain transmission as affect, and this happens through various sensory circuits. In Du Bois, the most pertinent example is that of the sorrow songs. The sorrow songs are those songs sung by slaves that, on one level, painted a picture of happy servants and the salvation promised by servitude and God. Yet, Du Bois's reading practice, which has been this essay's interpretive compass, reads these songs for meaning that is manifest not on the level of content but, instead, on the level of affect:

> What are these songs, and what do they mean? I know little of music and can say nothing in technical phrase, but I know something of men, and knowing them, I know that the songs are the articulate message of the slave world. They tell us in these eager days that life was joyous to the black slave, careless and happy. I can easily believe this of some, of many. But not all the past South, though it rose from the dead, can gainsay the heart touching witness of these songs. They are the music of unhappy people, of the children of disappointment; they tell of death and suffering and unvoiced longing toward a truer world, of misty wandering and hidden ways.[14]

I step from these lines in Du Bois and turn to my own "archive of feeling," to invoke Ann Cvetkovich's useful phrase.[15] Within my own fragmented memory narrative that I call upon to understand my connection to some of my modes of communal belonging, which are belongings in feeling, a particular moment resonates powerfully for me: an early televisual representation of brownness in the form of the television program *Chico and the Man*.

Airing on NBC from September 1974 to July 1978, *Chico and the Man*, starring Freddie Prinze and Jack Albertson, was set in the barrio of East Los Angeles. *Chico and the Man* was the story of two men from radically different cultural backgrounds who grew to respect one another. Chico, the enterprising young Chicano, was determined to go into partnership with cranky, sarcastic, cynical Ed Brown. Ed's character resonated alongside the racist humor/racist-as-object-of-humor paradigm pioneered on CBS's *All in the Family* through the character of Archie Bunker. Ed operated a small, rundown garage and spent most of his time complaining and alienating people. Chico cleaned up the dilapidated garage, making it into a functional business. He moved into a beat-up old truck in the garage. His efforts brought in new customers. Chon Noriega has suggested that the show transformed the concurrent Chicano movement into a "domestic comedy located in someone else's house-cum-business."[16]

The role of the Chicano Chico was played by the troubled Puerto Rican comic Freddie Prinze. Prinze, who eventually took his own life, grew up in poverty and struggled with drug addiction and mental illness until his death. Indeed, he perfectly embodies the figure of Latina/o as problem that I have described at the beginning of this chapter. While the show's troubling premise and Prinze's tragic iconicity shadow this, the explication of the transmission of brown affect hinges on the application of a Du Boisian sonic filter as applied to the show's theme song. The *Chico and the Man* theme song was recorded by the Puerto Rican–born folk/pop crossover artist José Feliciano. The tune functions for me as a sonic equivalent to a screen memory. The song's content, on the level of narrative, is somewhat uplifting. The lyrics echo the show's narrative premise:

> Chico, don't be discouraged,
> The Man he ain't so hard to understand.
> Chico, if you try now,
> I know that you can lend a helping hand.
> Because there's good in everyone
> And a new day has begun
> You can see the morning sun if you try.
> And I know, things will be better
> Oh yes they will for Chico and the Man
> Yes they will for Chico and the Man.

Most listeners to the spare and haunting pop tune would notice the disjunctive relationship of the lyrics to the sonic performance. Some of this has to do with context: this is a show where a white man regularly makes some racist joke about Latinas/os and a young Puerto Rican retorts with the catchphrase he popularized, "Lookin' good." *Chico and the Man* was a show about a sly Latino who charmed a constantly irritated white racist. On the level of sound, Feliciano's low voice does not bubble with the enthusiasm the lyrics suggest. Although Chico is being asked to resist being discouraged, and the promise of a new day hangs in the air, the song indexes the fact of feeling like a problem. The narrative indicates that Chico is indeed a problem that the Man does not understand. What does it feel like to be a problem, Chico? This is the question that echoes in my head, and it is one that helps us approach this question of brown feeling.

In my own memory, and in the here and now, I do not hear Feliciano's song as one of uplift, but instead as something else. I hear something that I want to identify as akin to brown feeling, this commonality in feeling like a problem. Sorrow songs are of course specific to an African American experience rooted in chattel slavery and later forms of racial violence. By discussing the mass-mediated music of José Feliciano, I do not mean to describe it as the same. More nearly, I am interested in the way in which this commoditized musical expression can be understood to function or perform its affective particularity in a fashion similar to that of the sorrow songs.

Still thinking about the blind Puerto Rican singer and his career, I turn to one particular affective spike in his life. In October 1968, José Feliciano sang a stylized version of the national anthem during a nationally televised baseball game that incited an uproar and a stream of complaints.[17] The familiar lyrics became something else through the brown singer's voice. The performance was slow and plaintive. The public responded with scorn to the browning of the national anthem, which is to say the manifesting of sorrow and disappointment that the minoritarian subject feels in relation to the normative affective protocols that make one feel brown. The song sings America in a way that neither Walt Whitman nor baseball fans ever wanted to hear: it sings America brown.

Feliciano's performance severely damaged his rising career trajectory. His style integrated rhythm and blues traditions with the folk acoustic genre. This hybridization functions on the level of soundscape. Returning to Brennan, the question of transmitting affect is especially pertinent in this instance. Brennan argues that the visual should not be considered the primary conduit for the transmission of affect.[18] Affect travels through other routes, like smell or sound. Frantz Fanon theorized that racism was often first manifest as a complaint about the other's smell.[19] One can argue that smell, like sound, is mostly a transmitter of the other's particularity.

Jimi Hendrix and Marvin Gaye were both performing stylized versions of "The Star-Spangled Banner" at roughly the same time. But their versions were not transmitted on national broadcast television like Feliciano's, and the performative effect of those performances did not disrupt the public sphere in the same fashion, nor with the same intensity. If we think about the scene of that 1968 baseball game, both visual and more importantly sonic, and look and listen beyond the scorn of disgruntled all-American baseball fans, we are left to wonder what other work that performance did. I want to suggest, echoing J. L. Austin's notion of a performative utterance, that this performance was a "brown utterance" that represented a still-nascent articulation of a particular mode of belonging-in-difference or particularity for people who feel brown—for people who know their self and recognize each other through a particular negation, a negation that is enacted by failing to conform to the affective protocols of normative cultural citizenship.[20]

I have no evidence that this belonging in brownness was anything other than the potentiality I have proposed here. Yet that lack of empirical evidence is not the point of my avowedly idealist formulation. Du Bois, who studied philosophy with George Santayana at Harvard, was, as literary critic Shamoon Zamir has argued, clearly a reader of Hegel's *Phenomenology* who employed some of the idealist aspects of the German philosopher. According to Zamir, while Du Bois was not an "upbeat Hegelian" like many other American Hegelians, he nonetheless accessed "a complex model of thinking about consciousness and history" through Hegel.[21] This Hegelian mode allows Du Bois to "conceptualize more clearly than before a sense of history and inheritance, of the pressure of the past on present action."[22] Certainly, the life of brownness requires a mode of analysis that can think about the intertwined nature of consciousness and history. Brownness is thus a mode of consciousness that responds to the pressure of the historical. Zamir describes *The Souls of Black Folk* as a psychology of history. Theorizing latinidad as brown feeling is theorizing a shared and historicized affective particularity, which is also to say, to some degree, psychology. The transmission of affect is the mode in which historical consciousness is transmitted.

In this chapter, following what I above called a Du Boisian compass, I have looked to Feliciano's musical performance as a powerful circuit of transmission for brown feelings. It is my contention that brownness can be heard in my remembrance of moments of childhood when not just another TV theme filled my parents' living room. It can be heard, more concretely, during those minutes in 1968 when a blind Puerto Rican man's mournful rendition of what is for many the national sorrow song was sung in a voice that sounded, to a nation in turmoil, like a problem.

6

The
Vulnerability
Artist

NAO BUSTAMANTE AND
THE SAD BEAUTY OF REPARATION

In the 1992 video *Rosa Does Joan*, Nao Bustamante's performance persona Rosa appears on the comedian and home shopping maven Joan Rivers's then daytime talk show. She poses as an exhibitionist who shares her sexual tales and describes her shocking proclivities to Rivers, a seemingly titillated audience, and an expert who evaluates her authenticity as an exhibitionist. This expert, a Dr. Georgia Witkins, is the author of *Passions: How to Manage Despair, Fear, Rage and Guilt and Heighten Your Capacity for Joy, Love, Hope and Awe*, and her author's blurb indicates that she has been a guest expert on over one hundred television programs, including *Donahue, The Oprah Winfrey Show, 20/20, Today, Good Morning America*, and *Hour Magazine*. A clinical psychologist, Bustamante's persona Rosa—her PhD certifies—is the "real deal": an authentic exhibitionist. Rivers describes the book that Witkins is promoting as a guide for those who cannot control their emotions, and the book's subtitle promises to help the reader with the management of emotion.

This concept of affective management speaks to a language of difference management that took hold in various spheres in the 1990s. This framing of multicultural difference as manageable deviation is descriptive of the actual problem with difference from the vantage point of corporate and state interests. Feeling, be it excessive, minimal, or just wrong, in one's affective response to the world, needs to be managed if queers, people of color, or other

6.1 Nao Bustamante as Rosa in *Rosa Does Joan*, 1992. COURTESY OF NAO BUSTAMANTE.

minoritarian subjects are to be incorporated in a larger social matrix—or so speaks the corporate ethos behind affect management. Passions are emotional manifestations that do not conform to dominant modes of comportment or expression.

In the video *Rosa Does Joan*, Bustamante becomes Rosa, a character or persona that she devises for the purpose of guerrilla-style stunt performance. This persona-style performance is consistent in all the artist's work. Rosa is part of a continuum of characters who feel too much or not enough, whose affective attachments and associations do not cohere or correspond. They thus signify a people whose affective life and subsequent comportment do not correspond to normative affective behavior. In this video, the performance artist is strangely authenticated as a problem within normative protocols of affective management. It is a stunt performance insofar as Bustamante poses as an exhibitionist, a role she does not identify as, and the talk show host, audience, and production staff are working under the assumption that she is not playing a character, but instead being herself.

For the video documentation of Bustamante's Rosa piece, she wears a black wig and heavy makeup. That look, dark hair and eyes, and the character's name announce her as a Latina. Her fictional public sex encounter with a "multigendered ambisexual" at a public aquarium marks her as a sexual deviant, or a queer. I want to contend that Witkins is indeed correct when she confirms Rosa as the "real deal," inasmuch as both the character and the artist behind her are examples of affective particularity that registers as excessive. The hoax performance is representative of a certain guerrilla-style performance that Bustamante often employs in the corpus of her work. As Rosa begins to tell Joan about her kinky exploits in various public places, she has indeed exposed herself as not being capable of maintaining proper affective comportment within the social. Rivers's now-canceled talk show (and others like it) represents a phenomenon that we can only describe as the contemporary freak show. In this instance, however, Bustamante hijacks the show and uses it as a site to insist upon an affective particularity that cannot be managed within the protocols of normative North American affective comportment. Rosa's trip to the dark continent of daytime talk shows and its subsequent documentation chart the ways in which affective difference is positioned as popular amusement in mass culture—an affective difference which, after having been consumed as titillation and recodified as a pathology, can be attended to with an over-the-counter aid, like a how-to book.

Witkins's book recommends that the reader contain what Sianne Ngai has classified as "ugly feelings" in her book by that title.[1] Witkins advocates and promotes positive feelings like joy, love, hope, and awe over "ugly feelings"—while a queer or ethnic spectator may indeed not understand how a phenomenon like exhibitionism qualifies as what Witkins marks as the passions that need to be contained. "Despair, fear, rage, and guilt" are indeed not necessarily the feelings at the center of much exhibitionist practice, for we can imagine the role her positive affects, "love, hope, or awe," play in animating exhibitionism. Yet, like other nonconformist sexual performances and practices, exhibitionism still qualifies as negative within the mediatized field of affective televisual representation. Thus, positive affects in the service of queer desire are the kinds of passions that need to be managed. Ngai describes ugly feelings as representing "interpretations of predicaments," which she delineates as "signs that render visible different registers of problems that obstruct agency."[2] Throughout this book, I discuss brown feelings as manifestations of the ways in which ethnic modes of comportment not only represent antinormative affect, but also challenge the ways in which

THE VULNERABILITY ARTIST

dominant ideology prescribes certain codes of normative comportment. Exhibitionism is a mode of comportment that insists on a certain decibel of emotion, one that like many aspects of Latino culture is considered too loud or unharmonious by normative ears. Exhibitionism scrambles the public/private dictates of normative desire. Private feelings or desires are broadcast in a fashion that calls attention to the codes of conduct that structure public emotion.

When speaking of exhibitionism and the ethnic body, it would be remiss not to cite the important work of scholars who, like Coco Fusco, locate the origins of performance as not in Dada or surrealism, but in the exhibition of captured and enslaved people compelled to perform for colonial power.[3] Similarly, Saidiya Hartman's important analysis of the performance of chattel slavery and its most sinister stage, the auction block, is an important and formative source for my analysis.[4] I will argue that Bustamante's performance is a reparative endeavor that engages the difficult "other" history of performance. By reparative, I want to call attention to the ways in which Bustamante's performance practice engages and reimagines what has been a history of violence, degradation, and compulsory performance. For a female artist of color to engage this field is not only historically loaded, but it is also extremely vulnerable making.

The broadcasting of affect makes Bustamante what I want to call a vulnerability artist. This label of vulnerability artist is meant to invoke Franz Kafka's "A Hunger Artist."[5] In Kafka's tale, the hunger artist's performances of self-imposed starvation in the village square once held the community's interest. His suffering and prone body on display was a popular amusement for a bygone era. Once his act becomes outmoded, the artist, now demoted from town square to circus midway oddity, finally dies when he loses the interest and attention of the populace. That story's tragic protagonist, a man who performed a ritual associated with a private bodily practice, fasting, is also a story about a broadcaster of affect. Gilles Deleuze's take on Spinoza's ethics and their relation to affect proposes that affect is a sign that registers on the body. For Deleuze, following Spinoza, affection indicates the state of a body affected by others.[6] Affect marks the passage of one state to another as an increase or decrease in the body's power. Thus, affect, projected onto another or by the other, affects one's agency. For Ngai, bad feelings are indicative of an obstruction of agency. By provisionally linking these two theorists' perspectives, one can see the ways in which affect that is representative of ugly feelings is indeed a predicament that obstructs agency.

Bustamante's art practice is descriptive of the ways in which ugly feelings weigh down a subject, challenging the actualization of agency. In a performance titled *Sans Gravity*, an image and sound study renders the weight of affect; in *Sans Gravity*, the artist has various assistants strap plastic bags full of water to her body. Bag is taped upon bag, and the artist begins to look like a monstrosity. She lumbers through the performance space, a gigantic watery beast, and the spectator is left to think about the burden of other people's affect on one's self. But beyond the metaphorical, the actual body is vulnerable to the point of duress. The piece also underscores this sense of alienation produced by affective projection via the work's sound component. The artist's body is also wired for sound and one hears a sloshing, submerged corpulence. All bodies are vulnerable to the affect of others.

If we are to understand the force of cultural logics like racism or homophobia, it seems that they are, at an essential level, affective constructs, which is to say feelings projected outward and inward. By gleaning such knowledge, and knowing that our affect does not simply flow out of us but instead tells us a story about our relationality to ourselves and also to groups, we feel a sense of belonging to groups that inspire a sense of unbelonging. A focus on affect potentially denaturalizes experiences like racism or homophobia. We are all weighed down, burdened, by emotions that are radiated toward us. And we all seek relief.

The drama of Bustamante's performance, and its resolution, involves the audience in lifting the artist's burden. In the literal yet poetic syntax of Bustamante's performance practice, this is done with spikes, needles, and sharp objects. The newly animated audience pokes the artist, and we see her body overwhelmed. The prods and pins that besiege the artist function as a literalized choreography of affective projection. Audience members witness the individual being overwhelmed by the group. This is worth further consideration. The hunger artist in Kafka's story disappears because his mode of performance has become antiquated and the public no longer showers him with affective recognition. Bustamante's story complicates the pop ego psychological formulation that would come from a source like Witkins, whose statements would boil down to a formulation like: *good feelings are the only affect that nourishes the self.* The artist needs the projected affect of others, visualized as spikes, to release her burden. In *Sans Gravity*, bad feelings are not automatically negatively valenced insofar as they are constitutive of subjectivity. In this way the vulnerability artist's drama is the reverse of what happens to the hunger artist. Her affective burden is ruptured by the sharp projections of the affect of others, but this conjoining of negative affect is strangely something like a reparative moment.

Negative affect, projected by the group, stabs the burdened body and soul of the vulnerability artist. But rather than destroying this object, it is saved as in the same way a bad object can be saved in Melanie Klein's psychoanalytic choreography. Touched by the other's bad feelings, the vulnerability artist is saved or repaired in the first moment. This reparation happens on a symbolic register in which the performance's resolution is arrived at in the act of liberation or extraction of self from the affective burden of ugly feelings. In a slightly later moment, she is more than saved: she is transformed from monster to human fountain, as the vulnerability becomes a strange monument to the sad beauty of reparation. The moment she is touched by the other, she projects onto the world/audience as she literally spills forth, becoming a living cascade sculpture, spilling out onto the world.

The vulnerability artist is projected upon by the world, and she also projects out. I now turn to an earlier performance, one planned as a celebration of the anniversary of the discovery of America. *Indigurrito* (1992) stages a relational drama around race and emotion. Bustamante's character in this performance is a sort of postmodern Aztec priestess/dominatrix. She is interested in addressing a negative aspect, and her character attempts to naively cleanse men of their ugly feelings, specifically white guilt. She does so by strapping a burrito to her crotch, using the harnessing device associated with dildo play. The harness matches the rest of her highly sexualized yet satirical costume for the performance. She invites white men to "absolve" themselves of historical guilt. The burrito is vegetarian. They bow before her and partake in the reparative ritual.

The supplicant in this fake ritualistic performance wants to escape the burden of negative affect that haunts racial and sexual relations. Biting the mythical phallus of the burrito, while a joke, also renders an account of affect's crisscrossing economy. The joke is centered on a wish/desire for the other to absolve us of our negative emotions with a magical gesture. Bad feelings can simply be bitten away, ingested by the other. This performance thus stages another fantasy of reparation: the white men on stage are absolving their own burden of guilt in the comical ritual, while the artist is also making her bad feelings available, prone and vulnerable.

The laughter that the performance solicits is of a highbrow nature insofar as the butt of the joke is not only white men in general, but, to a certain extent, one white man in particular: Freud. The performance she is staging is an imagined drama of castration anxiety.[7] One is reminded of seemingly

6.2 Nao Bustamante performs *Indigurrito*. COURTESY OF NAO BUSTAMANTE.

countless moments from the early days of queer theory where essays about the lesbian phallus reigned. I want to suggest that this performance is a continuation of such a project that delinked the phallus from heteronormative parameters and biological masculinity. This fantastical scene represents a further particularizing of this Oedipal script by replacing the universal (read white) penis that stands in for the phallus in crude psychological formulations with a highly racialized and particular tubular object: the burrito.

In Bustamante's harness, the burrito is not only Mexican. It is also imbued with energies that can best be described as queer. On one luxurious and arch level, it's pure camp. (Imagine! That girl straps on a burrito!) But after teaching that performance documentation to a large, undergraduate lecture class, I once had a pedagogical moment that further explicated the queerness of the piece. One young man, a first-year student, explained that the tape made him uncomfortable insofar as the men on stage worshiping the burrito were simulating fellatio. I thought this aspect of the gag was so obvious that it need not be addressed in any depth. But indeed, this playful humiliation of white men by a woman asking them to play the sodomite was a flashpoint for this student. On further reflection, I realized that this aspect of *Indigurrito* was as much about straight masculinity and its anxieties of being undone through one highly ritualized (and reified) sexual act as it was about "becoming" a homosexual. In this case, the vulnerability artist sheds illumination on the weakness in the armor we know as straight masculinity. This anxiousness about straight men blowing each other permeates this historical moment in masculinity and American popular culture. Straight male-to-male humiliation is often thematized, in various popular musical genres and the deeply homoerotic genre of industrial prison complex narratives like HBO's *Oz*, by the primal humiliation of one straight man sucking off another in scenes of situational or coerced sexuality. This too falls into the satirical scope of Bustamante's work.

In a similar fashion, *America, the Beautiful* (1994) represents another character that interestingly mirrors the hunger artist, an individual in need of public feelings, a character representing a raw need for public emotion and recognition. The protagonist in *America, the Beautiful* is a grotesquerie seeking approval, attempting to mold both her body and her comportment to be in sync with dominant maps of looking and feeling, especially looking and feeling both female and white. Her body and comportment are, by standardized expectations, excessive. Yet she seeks the approval or sanction of the normative. The piece's humor is produced by her stark and abject need for approval.

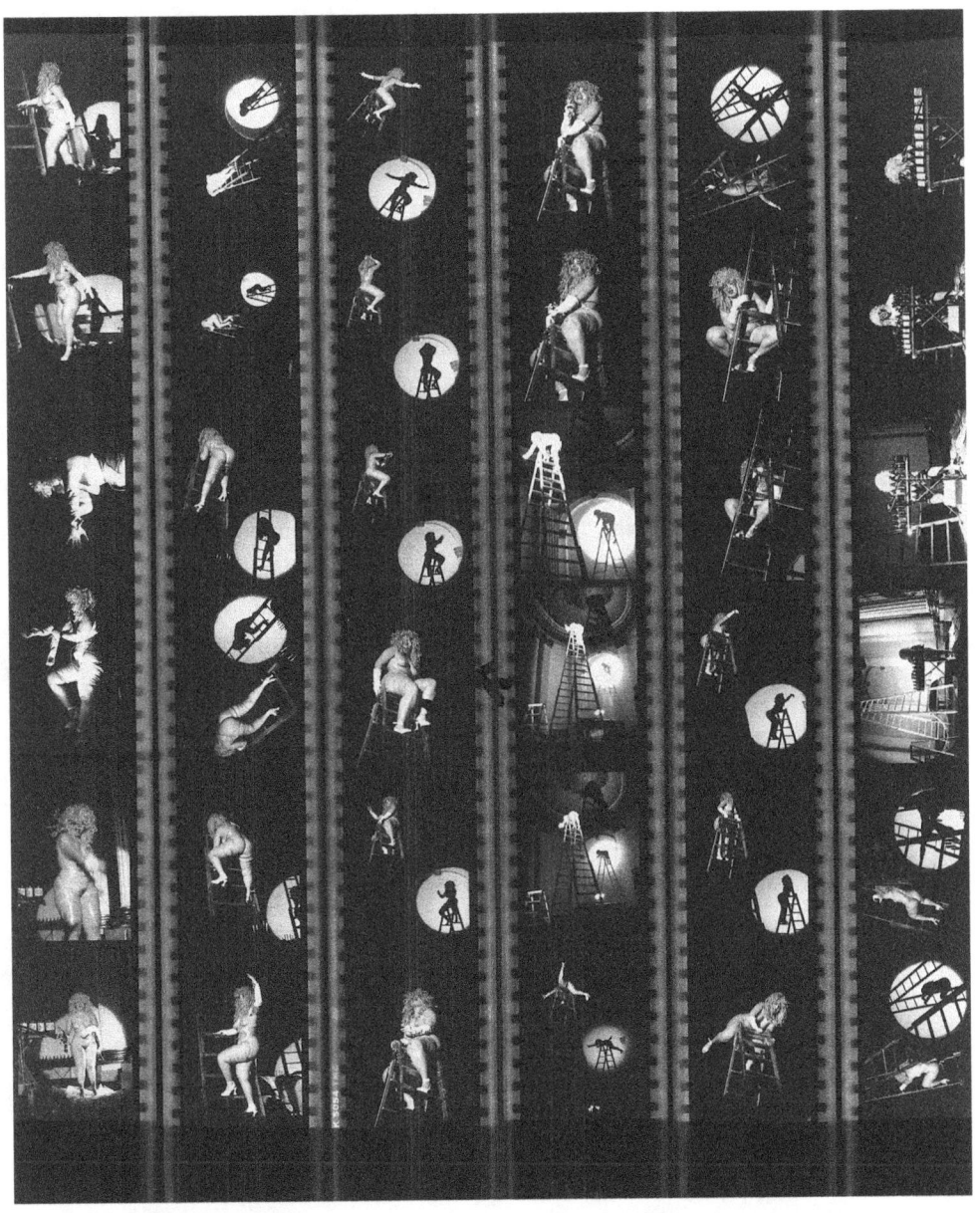

6.3 Contact sheet for Nao Bustamante, *America, the Beautiful*, 1995–98, 2002. Photograph by Lorie Novak. COURTESY OF NAO BUSTAMANTE.

America, the Beautiful commences when a nude Bustamante takes the stage and begins a performance of physical transformation. She puts a matted blonde wig on her head and coats it with hair spray. As maniacal circus music plays, Bustamante applies lipstick and face powder with great exaggeration. The wig and the face have a whitening-up effect. She then wraps translucent masking tape around her waist, stomach, and legs, and reshapes her large curvy body. Standing on a stool, she then attempts to strap on high-heel shoes. This act looks incredibly dangerous, and throughout it seems as though she will fall and injure herself. Throughout the rest of the performance, the concerned spectator feels the artist's great neediness and considerable vulnerability.

The comedy and the drama are one of both vulnerability and failure. There are two aspects of this performance that I wish to linger on: one is the way in which the body is animated by affect, and affect itself becomes, in Deleuze's lexicon, a sign.[8] In this sense, the pantomime is a language of and through affect. The bittersweet humor is in accordance with the hunger artist's desire to be acknowledged by the public, his public, a public that knows itself through shared emotion, and in such a fashion that the hunger artist loses his luster by losing an audience that is desperately needed, Bustamante's character is failing to be seen or heard or felt in a way that registers as a particularity in belonging and difference. Like the hunger artist, the vulnerability is this persona, an incarnation that craves interest and applause by the audience.

After performing several amateurish feats—stunts like climbing a rickety ladder that might crash down at any moment, and performing a weird, sonic medley by blowing into jugs—the character demands applause. She gets quite a bit of applause but is not satisfied with it. Eventually, she is still demanding applause long after the performance is over. While she stomps menacingly at the edge of the stage, she holds a bouquet of roses that was thrown to her earlier. The performance ends as the character's monstrous rage consumes her, and she begins to bite and chew at the roses in an animalistic frenzy, spitting mutilated roses at the audience. The vulnerability artist, like the hunger artist, is undone by her need of affirmative feelings. But along the way, *America, the Beautiful*'s performance of Nietzschean-like *ressentiment* clearly outlines the limits of affirmative affect, while gesturing to the ways in which agency can perhaps be accessed through exploration of the negative.[9]

A performance that generated negative affect is *Sparkler* (2001). This performance, according to the performer, elicited her first piece of hate mail.

6.4 Nao Bustamante, *America, the Beautiful*, 1995–98, 2002. Photograph by Lorie Novak. COURTESY OF NAO BUSTAMANTE.

The two-minute performance begins with a totally dark bar. At some point, a sparkler is lit, and it provides the only illumination. The sparkler of the title emerges from what seems to be her ass. She is actually holding it with her hand between her legs. The sparkler is the only illumination available. It is a torch that insists on affective difference and particularity. Bustamante's body is an affective beacon, which is to say that she illuminates a particular predicament around agency within the social: a feeling queer, a feeling brown, that is both about belonging and the failure to belong. A Latina body, a queer body, radiating a certain affective signature that is recognizable to many. This performance was met with hate mail that commented on its vulgarity. This affective sign was therefore seen as excessive: it generated bad feelings in others, perhaps challenging the normative affective comportment's seamless claim to agency. Indeed, within normative codes of affective comportment, Bustamante's performance is too much. It does transmit a kind of particularity that elicits ugly feelings. *Sparkler*'s stark simplicity and insistence on affective particularity via performance lingers in the mind of the spectator.

Antagonistic feelings, negative affect, and ugly feelings are used in the artist's work in a fashion that we can best describe as reparative insofar as negativity is not simply cleaned but viewed as constitutive of subjectivity. This performance and the feelings it generates, despite their ephemeral nature, do not disappear. The performance, its documentation via video, and my writing practice become ephemeral resources for many who are drawn to the possibilities they suggest, like moths to a flame.

7

Queer Theater, Queer Theory

LUIS ALFARO'S *CUERPO POLITIZADO*

Mapping Downtown: The Space of Memory

In November 1996, I presented a paper at a Latin/o performance conference at London's Institute of Contemporary Arts that included theorists and performers. I was to deliver a paper on Luis Alfaro and Marga Gomez. One of the major stress points of having an archive such as mine is that many of the performers and artists that I work on are very much alive and are often interested in engaging with critics who evaluate their work, and in this instance, that stress was palpable: Alfaro was in the audience. I asked him to join me onstage to read the performance monologue I was discussing.

That moment turned out to be quite interesting and powerful. Standing with me at the podium, Alfaro was no longer the object of inquiry but the coproducer of knowledge. I have always sensed that writing about artists like Alfaro was something of a collaboration and not simply advocacy criticism. Yet the centrality of this collaboration had never manifested itself so cogently to me before. Indeed, Alfaro is never merely an object of study, but an interlocutor, for he is a theorist in his own right, a thinker who helps me imagine theory and practice.[1] His work helps me intervene in queer social theory because his performances themselves carve out space for social theory making through their analysis of heteronormativity.

Alfaro presents us with views of the intersecting worlds that formed him as a queer, working-class, urban Chicano.[2] His memory performances not only help us imagine a future queer world, but also actually achieve a new counterpublic formation in the present through lived performance praxis. Thus, Alfaro's work offers an important corrective to queer theory's failure to ever truly queer its theory. That is, though queer theory's early alliance with activist movements like Queer Nation and ACT UP promised that theory making would include activism and political performance, the "theory" end of the formulation has remained rigid and traditional, adhering to predictable modes of intellectual production. Performance, though—particularly by artists who stand at multiple points of antagonism in relation to racial, class, gender, and sexual hegemonies—can function as a productive site for producing theory. The work Alfaro presented during that London conference—*Cuerpo Politizado* (Politicized body), a cross section of his solo performance work to date—is a compelling case in point.[3]

I walk into the theater at the Institute of Contemporary Arts in London and immediately notice the song that is playing: Petula Clark's "Downtown." The song paints an idyllic picture of a utopic urban sprawl, recalling a moment when downtowns were hubs of excitement and progress. In the age of financially depressed commercial zones, the song's lyrics and soft pop melody seem rife with irony. As the houselights lower, I lose myself in thought about this song and what it means today. My reveries are interrupted when a video called *Chicanismos* is projected onto the screen.

The video begins with slow-moving sweeps of downtown Los Angeles, which then accelerate. The soundtrack jumps like a scratchy car stereo from station to station while the visual montage flashes shots of low riders gliding down crowded city streets, a man in a mariachi outfit getting off work, Chicana homegirls with heavy makeup leaning against a street pole, homeless men with overgrown beards, and graffiti that reads "Shy boy is crazy." Four times, the intense visual bombardment is interrupted by Alfaro, who, playing four different characters, delivers brief video monologues between sections of the montage.

These characters—four manifestations of Chicanismo—all belong to the rich ensemble of social types that constitute Los Angeles. The first figure, a bearded and disillusioned Chicano studies professor, represents faded nationalism. He is followed by a teenage mother who, despite her love for her baby, stands for youth in crisis. Then, a hyperassimilated Gap employee inadvertently reveals the situation of young people trapped within the service industry, and, finally, an undocumented maid who identifies with her employers and declares that the United States is her home demonstrates how the most economically vulnerable are compelled to sacrifice their own nationality. These four social players map the different horizons of experience that delineate the space of contemporary Chicano LA. More than inhabiting space, these four characters are bodies that create space—the space of Chicano Los Angeles. This is a complicated relationship, as Elizabeth Grosz suggests:

> Bodies and cities are not causally linked. Every cause must be logically distinct from its effect. The body, however, is not distinct, does not have an existence separate from the city, for they are mutually defining. . . . There may be an isomorphism between the body and the city. But it is not a mirroring of nature in artifice. Rather, there is a two-way linkage which could be defined as an interface, perhaps even a co-building. What I am suggesting is a model of relations of bodies and cities which sees them not as megalithic total entities, distinct identities, but as an assemblage between subject and form linkages, machines, provisional and often temporary sub- or microgroupings.[4]

Bodies and cities define each other. The bodies represented in *Chicanismos* are the city of Los Angeles, which is to say that one cannot abstract them from the social matrix of that city. In setting the scene with the song "Downtown," Alfaro invokes a pointed irony: the song's idealistic lyrics, "Downtown, things will be great when you're downtown . . . ," contradict the downtown that Alfaro presents—one of faded dreams, poverty, self-hatred, and social subordination. But Alfaro's citation of the song reads as more than simply ironic: it evokes a memory, a dream that was never achieved, a lost ideal. For Alfaro, then, the song is a passionate act of remembering, a strategy to conjure up the romanticized images of a world that never really existed. Thus, an unfulfilled dream from the past is read in relation to a reality in the present. Alfaro starkly juxtaposes these images from two eras and realms to call for a new temporality, a new moment, one of social transformation and activist politics. Through critique of a false past and an embattled present, he lets the idea of a future emerge.

As the video concludes, the houselights go up, and a man sitting in front of me speaks loudly from his seat. He gets up and slowly walks toward the stage. He is Luis Alfaro, in the flesh. When he emerges from the audience after having been one of "us," our sense of tranquil spectatorship is displaced. The leap from performances contained within the video and the live body of Alfaro produces a stirring shock effect.

The houselights begin to dim again as Alfaro reaches the stage. The monologue he has recited since he began his migration from the audience to the stage is titled "On a Street Corner." It tells the story of a heterosexual couple walking down Broadway in downtown Los Angeles. The man says to the woman, "Shut up, bitch." She complains about the beatings he inflicts upon her, and he threatens to leave her. She pleads for him to stay by saying, "Aw, no, baby, you're the only thing I remember." The woman is so deeply immersed in this relationship that the man has overwhelmed her memory. Alfaro then accesses his own memory testimony as he reaches the center of the stage and says, "Because desire is memory and I crave it like the born-again in my mama's church. But it's hard to be honest sometimes, because I live in the shadow of the Hollywood sign. Because on the street corner known as Pico and Union, my father made extra money on pool tables, my mother prayed on her knees."

Alfaro continues to transform downtown into a narrative series of childhood vignettes. He talks about the time when Sonia Lopez slaps him after he forces a kiss on her, and he concludes that this must have been his introduction to S&M. He recalls Bozo the Clown at the May Company on Broadway, tossing presents to a throng of kids that he is part of. When a board game hits another boy in the eye, Alfaro becomes terrified that the clown will throw something in his direction.

He then slips out of the directly autobiographical register, offering other memories laced with violence. He paces around the stage as he tells the story of a woman who dances in the projects and of the husband who beats her, about the drunk from the bar who staggers home, about the man who rides the Pico bus and slides his hand under women's seats, about the glue sniffer on Venice Boulevard who watches the world in slow motion. Alfaro's pace and voice quicken as he concludes the monologue with an incantation that recalls memory and summarizes the piece: "A man got slapped. / A woman got slugged. / A clown threw toys. / A drunk staggered. / An earthquake shook. / A slap. / A slug. / A shove. / A kick." The stories condense into acts. And these acts conjure up bodies that collide with the image of a city. Indeed, these slaps, punches, and so forth constitute the social realm.

Clearly, memory is a central theme in Alfaro's work. It is structured through the violence and pain that inform much of urban Latina/o reality. Memory recalls and indexes both the affective world of U.S. Latinos—that is, their ways of being in the world that are organized through feeling—and their communal and collective construction of latinidad. The term "latinidad," a theoretical catalog of different modes of Latina/o self-fashioning, demarcates a set of affective performances that help delineate Latina/o particularity. Latinidad is not about race, region, nation, gender, language, or any other easily identifiable demarcation of difference. Rather, it is an antiidentitarian concept that nonetheless permits us to talk about Latinas/os as having a group identity, which is necessary for social activism. Thinking of latinidad as antinormative affect offers a model of group identity that is coherent without being exclusionary. Through performed memory, a deployment of rehearsed and theatricalized Latino affect, Alfaro negotiates two different temporal narratives of the self: the migrant child and the gay man of color, two affective registers of Latino experience that interrogate each other through the performer's theatrical mixing.

Alfaro has described his work as a series of combinations, "mixing gay life with Chicano life, street life with Catholic life, *cholo* life with [his] life."[5] This mixing resonates with the kind of cultural layering that queers of color often need to enact if they wish to maintain simultaneous memberships in queer communities and communities of color. Memory is not a static thing for the queer of color; it is an antinormative space where self is made and remade and where polities can be imagined. While memory is not static for anyone, it is always "in the making" for the minoritarian subject who cannot perform normative citizenship and thus has no access to the standardized narratives of national cultural memory. This dominant culture that projects an official history that elides queer lives and the lives of people of color necessitates a counternarrative that memory performances supply.

The memory performances that interest me are decidedly antinormative, which is to say that they are deployed for the purposes of contesting affective normativities that include, but are not limited to, white supremacy and the cultural logics of misogyny and homophobia. The queer of color's performances of memory transmit and broadcast affectively charged strategies of minoritarian survival and self-making, carving out a space for resistance and communal self-enactment. Their memory performances thus work as calls intended to solicit responses.

Those affiliated with Latino communities and queer communities know the ways in which so much has been lost—whether through the dismantling of civil rights discourse, the routinization of the AIDS pandemic, or other social battles. Many of us take periodic refuge in the past: the time before the AIDS pandemic; before the state and the ideological forces of dominant culture decided with renewed enthusiasm that Latinos and Latinas, along with other migrant communities, are the cause of all the nation's ills; before affirmative action was dismantled in California; before Proposition 187 in effect legalized the treatment of taxpaying undocumented workers as an underclass. Memory performances call forth an affect that predates current attempts to dismantle the citizen status of minoritarian subjects.

We need to remember this prior time not as a nostalgic escape, but as an enabler of critiquing the present. Performances of memory remember, dream, recite a self, and reassert agency in a world that challenges and constantly attempts to snuff out subaltern identities. Memory performances deploy affective narratives of self, ways of being from the past, in the service of questioning the future, a future without annihilating epidemics, both viral and ideological. Alfaro's work demonstrates the importance of memory for the politics of the present and the future. Alfaro's memory performances are the dreams of a subject who falls out of the narrow confines prescribed by the state, the law, and other normative grids. They are the frames around subjects whose affect is deemed excessive, wrong, or simply off. Such performances amplify and transmit these recitations of dreams and contribute to a project of setting up counterpublics—communities and relational chains of resistance that contest the dominant public sphere.

Between Two Virgins

Alfaro walks into a circle of light after "On a Street Corner" and prepares to tell a family story called "Virgin Mary." He commences by explaining, "We used to have this Virgin Mary doll. Every time you connected her to an outlet, she would turn and bless all sides of the room." A cylinder of light contains Alfaro, as though he too were in a glass case. The performer goes on to recount the story of Virgin Mary's origin, how she was purchased during one of his father's surprise drunken trips to Tijuana, when he would come home from the racetrack around midnight and load the entire family into the station wagon. Young Luis offers the Virgin as a gift to his Tia Ofelia when she is suffering from breast cancer.

Young Luis explains how Tia Ofelia, like everyone else in the family, was a grape picker from Delano, California. She lived on the top floor of a two-story wooden home that was flanked by high-rise projects. The bottom floor was occupied by cholos from the Eighteenth Street Gang. After Luis's aunt passes away, the rivals of the Eighteenth Street Gang, the Crips, come looking for them and firebomb the house, killing the cholos and destroying the house, along with the Virgin Mary.

Years later, Alfaro recounts, he meets a man who will become his first love. The man owns a rotating Virgin Mary doll that he bought in Mexico. Alfaro describes him as having white skin, eating broccoli, and talking like characters on a TV series. He was "every *Partridge Family/Brady Bunch* episode rolled into one." This white man teaches the young Alfaro how to French kiss, lick an earlobe, and dance in the dark. Young Alfaro's fascination with this man has much to do with the way he embodies a normative imprint that dominates North American culture. In part Alfaro desires his whiteness, which itself constitutes his normative way of being in the world, but also his taste for broccoli, his sitcom voice, and his way of dancing, all of which mark this way of being. Alfaro is crushed when this lover leaves him, and he once again finds himself surrounded by family who tell him, "*Aye mijo*, don't you understand? Blood is thicker than water, family is greater than friends, and the Virgin Mary, that old Virgin Mary, she watches over all of us." The relationship fails, in part, because Alfaro cannot perform normative white affect, and he is comforted by his past world, a world of ethnic affect. The affect of an ethnic past is thus a storehouse of resources for the minoritarian subject who strives to fabricate self in hostile normative climates.

Alfaro uses the rotating deity to forge a connection between these different layers of experience and affect. The life Alfaro describes, positioned between a straight ethnic past and a predominantly white queer present, is the kind of reality that queers of color often negotiate. One way of managing such an identity is to forsake the past, to let go of it altogether. But for Alfaro the cost is too high. Instead, he calls upon memory performance to manage identity and, in doing so, he invents a theater of memory.

While the coherent self is most certainly an exhausted fiction, a "self effect"—as Alfaro knows—is necessary to make interventions in the social and political realm. Minoritarian, diasporic, and exiled subjects recalibrate the protocols of selfhood by insisting on the radical hybridity of the self, on the fact that a self is not a normative citizen or even a coherent whole, but instead a hybrid that contains disparate and even contradictory associations, identifications, and disidentifications. Coming to power, into self, for such subjects requires that they write themselves into history. Alfaro does so by historicizing the self through theatricalizations of Latino affect that index personal memory and collective memory—the personal memory of a family of migrant grape pickers from Delano, and the collective and spatialized memory of Chicano Los Angeles.

The Moo-Moo of History

In a valuable reading of Benjamin's angel of history, the Judaic scholar and ethnographer Jonathan Boyarin writes, "Part of the importance of Benjamin's image is the lesson that we are always once again being driven out; in some sense we have always just lost paradise, hence we are always close to it. The ongoing state of emergency Benjamin also speaks of doesn't just mean we are always in imminent danger, but also that something precious is eternally being lost."[6] This reading of the storm from paradise, which emphasizes the howling gap between us and the past, and the past's proximity to us, suggests the need for a double gesture toward our past. We need to be constantly interrogating and recuperating the past, without pretending for long that we can recoup its plenitude. This double gesture, this contradictory movement of new recognitions and new distances between the present and the past, may be most easily articulated in a juxtaposition of explicit traditional and postmodern figures of multiplicity, rather than modern identity.

Boyarin's concept of a double gesture that recognizes the need to reclaim a past, while also resisting the temptation to succumb to a nostalgic and essentialized conception of it, is especially useful with respect to Luis Alfaro's memory performances. For the minoritarian subject, the double gesture of remembering and not being lost to memory leads to a powerful emergence into politics. Memory is a catalyst: it assists in shoring up antinormative Latino/a affect and enables performances of the self that contest the affective normativity of dominant culture.

Alfaro's movement along this trajectory is especially evident in a segment of *Cuerpo Politizado* titled "A Moo-Moo Approaches/A Story about Mamas and Mexico," in which Alfaro focuses on the figure of his mother. Moo-Moo connotes both his mother's large colorful dresses and her fat body, and Alfaro foregrounds his own body image as a fat man through this meditation on his mother. The segment begins with Alfaro walking up to a table of Twinkies and eating them one by one. As he literally gorges himself on dozens of Twinkies, a tape plays the story of the Moo-Moo. Alfaro's taped voice explains that when his father first came to this country, there simply wasn't enough for him, so he married Alfaro's mother, the Moo-Moo, who was, with "hips as wide as a river, . . . abundance personified." The Moo-Moo's function was to signify the family's accruing wealth and to hide their actual poverty. But the children were embarrassed by the Moo-Moo, who attended every PTA meeting and Boy Scout outing, and inserted herself in altar boy affairs at church. She was there to remind the family "how good life was en Los Estados Unidos."

She served as a protector, even threatening to kill a neighbor who called her precious son effeminate. The Moo-Moo fended off burglars with a baseball bat, chasing a man who stole the family's small television set down to the corner of Pico and Union, though she was wearing slippers on her feet and curlers in her hair. She returned home whistling a happy tune as "blood dripped off the bat and onto the downtown pavement." In sum, says Alfaro about his mother, "The Moo-Moo was serious, gerl."

As time went on and Alfaro's father felt compelled to become "American," he decided that the Moo-Moo was too much. The Moo-Moo who once represented an abundant future "was [now] no longer desirable. The Moo-Moo of Mexico represented all the problems and setbacks we had endured in America. The Moo-Moo of Mexico was too big, too fat, too much. Too much for our new American sensibility." Then the Moo-Moo, like Tia Ofelia, lost a breast. She gave up her brightly colored muumuus and began wearing simple dark dresses that she sewed on an old-fashioned sewing machine from the Deardens store on Fifth and Main.

By the time the recording reaches this point in the narrative, Alfaro has eaten at least thirty Twinkies. He continues to stuff them down his throat in a violent fashion while the tape goes on with the story of the Moo-Moo's slow suicide courtesy of "Hostess Manufacturing," as the family home is overrun with cupcakes, Sno Balls, lemon pies, donuts, and Ho-Hos. As this image of proliferating pastries invades his imagination, he reports that at night "far from the breast of the Moo-Moo, the nightmare that is the Mexico that I do not know haunts me. I clear the kitchen of all traces of my bicultural history: the Mexican telenovela and a sweetener called America. The nightmare continues, a Moo-Moo approaches."

That Moo-Moo is Alfaro's angel of history. Her face is turned to a past that is Mexico. The Moo-Moo would like to awaken the dead from a past life, another place and time, and make whole what has been shattered through relocation and migration. The forces that call the Alfaro family to assimilate are a storm blowing from paradise, coded as progress. Her back is turned to this paradise; her eyes are focused on a past that is being debased by those around her. She is tragic like history's angel insofar as she has lost control of herself. She is coming toward Alfaro like a house lifted by a tornado. She represents the nightmare that is his history, and his bicultural queer body shakes at the thought of her. He performs a ritual reenactment of his mother's slow suicide by consuming the table full of Twinkies. In doing so, he inhabits her abjected form: this effeminate queer son who was once protected by this Moo-Moo mother becomes her in an effort to rehabilitate a body and an image that have been battered by progress and assimilation. Through his performance of the Moo-Moo, Alfaro finds a place for himself in this nightmare. He identifies with this tragic Moo-Moo and with his father's will toward assimilation. His performance is an attempt to redeem what has been lost.

It is important that the vehicle for this return to the past is a powerful and embodied relationship to the gendered Moo-Moo and not to the genderless angel. Assimilation and progress are typically coded as male, and the past, ethnicity, and heritage are represented by an abjected maternal body. Alfaro metaphorically steps into the maternal position, thereby documenting this queer male activist-performer's debt to female embodiment. More than a queer cross-identification with the female body, it is in fact a call to disengage from masculine gender in an effort to rethink the social from within an expansive political frame, one that understands the structuring force of gender within the sociopolitical realm.

Primitive Latino First Aid:
The Double Gesture of Memory Performance

The double gesture described by Boyarin, with its impulse to invoke the past for a politics of the present, is evident in another moment in Alfaro's performance, when he returns to the scene of a heteronormative childhood. In this section, titled "Abuelita," Alfaro stands behind a podium in a single, ominous spotlight, wearing a black slip, which the production's prop list describes as "a cheap JC Penney slip, size 18 or up." He holds one small finger up in the air as he recalls having cut his finger jumping through his mother's rosebush—in an effort to avoid his grandmother—when he was eleven years old. In the first half of the piece, he explains how he despises his grandmother more than his fifth grade teacher, revealing the shame this second-generation Latino felt because of his grandmother's refusal to assimilate into North American culture. Abuelita insists on maintaining the quotidian reality of a Latin American woman who reads *Vanidades* and makes everyone hush when she watches her telenovelas (soap operas).

Emerging from the rosebush, Alfaro discovers a wound:

I rise out of the rosebush
and immediately plunge into
the other Latino dramatic effect,
the painful
ay yai yai.

There's a gash on my finger
and it starts to bleed
pretty badly.

Abuelita turns on the hose
and runs my hand
under the water.
Inspecting my finger she laughs,
pinches my cheek,
Thanks the Virgin
for the minor miracle,
does a sign of the cross, and applies
Primitive Latino First Aid.

She looks at me,
smiles, raises a bloody finger
to her face.
Closely inspecting
my afflicted digit,
she brings it up close
to her eyes.

I can't tell
what she is looking for.
As if holding it up close
she might find
some truth,
some small lesson
or parable
about the world
and its workings.

Her eyes canvass the finger,
probing her vision

slowly and carefully.
And then quickly
and without warning,
she sticks it
inside her mouth
and begins
to suck on it.

I feel the inside of her mouth,
wet and warm,
her teeth
lightly pulling
equally discomforting
and disgusting
at the same time.

Being in that womb
feels as if I am being eaten alive
on one of those
late night
Thriller Chiller movies
Vampira, Senior Citizen Bloodsucker.

But it isn't that at all.
This is the only way
that abuelita
knows how to stop the bleeding.

The narrative then shifts from the past to the present:

See this finger?
Cut it at work.
Making another pamphlet
critical of those
who would like
to see us dead.

The long gasp.
Four Gay Latinos
in one room
Four long gasps.

Afraid to touch my wound.
Would prefer
to see it bleed
and gush
than to question

mortality
and fate.

Could go on
about being tested,
but it seems
so futile.
As if we
don't know
that one little test
could have been wrong.

Hold the finger
in front of me
Stick it
close to mouth
Drip, drip, drip
all over the desktop
from Ikea.

Hold it close
to face.
Quickly
and without
warning,
stick it in my mouth
and I begin to
suck.

Tears roll down.
Salty wet
tears.
Down my face.
Can feel my teeth

> lightly pulling
> and I wish,
>
> I wish for an abuelita
> in this time.
>
> This time of plague.
> This time of loss.
> This time of sorrow.
> This time of mourning.
> This time of shame.
>
> And I
> heal myself.
> I heal myself
> with abuelita's
> Primitive Latino First Aid.

The prevailing tone of the poem's first section is that of shame. But the double gesture of interrogating the past, while not collapsing under the gravitational pull of nostalgia, helps us grasp its importance to the formulation of a politicized self in the here and now. We also see a deep desire for a space of identity formation here, as Alfaro calls forth a rehabilitated and reimagined Latino family, one that is necessary in the face of a devastating and alienating pandemic. Memory performance reinvents the space of *familia*, the familia made from scratch that Cherríe Moraga has described.[7] It is a hub of identity consolidation that is reinhabited through the auspices of memory performance.

Family has been much criticized in contemporary queer theory as an oppressive totality. But such a characterization from the perspective of queers of color is deeply reductive. On the one hand, it is true that not all families of color affirm their queer children. On the other hand, the generalized gay community often feels like a sea of whiteness to queers of color, and thus the imagined ethnic family is often a refuge. The family is a space where all those elements of the self that are fetishized, ignored, and rejected in the larger queer world are suddenly revalorized. Alfaro's memory performance attunes us to those enabling characteristics.

Queer Theater and Social Theory

Michael Warner's introduction to his groundbreaking collection *Fear of a Queer Planet* is one of the most important interventions in queer social theory. In it, Warner produces a sharp critique of social theory's heteronormativity and calls upon queer studies to engage with the material social and political world. He notes that "the energies of queer studies have come more from rethinking the subjective meaning of sexuality than from thinking the social."[8] Warner contrasts *ethnos* and *eros*, arguing that, as experiences of identity, sexuality and ethnicity are fundamentally distinct: "People tend not to encounter queerness in the same way as ethnic identity. Often the disparity between racial and sexual imperatives can be registered as dissonance."[9] This is certainly true for Alfaro. In *Cuerpo Politizado* he theatricalizes this dissonance, considering it as part of queer experience.

Warner takes pains to show the way in which ethnicity and sexuality are not corresponding experiences. While I agree that these categories need to be differentiated, I would suggest that his reading of the differences between queers and people of color in relation to family requires more elaboration. His reading of the role of family is informed by a particularly white queer experience. He writes, "Familial language deployed to describe sociability in race- or gender-based movements (sisterhood, brotherhood, fatherland, mother tongue, etc.) can either be a language of exile or a resource of irony (in voguing houses, for example, one queen acts as 'mother')."[10] In Alfaro's work, the family is more than just a site to run from or a source of irony. While for queers of color family can often be a place of conflict and potential violence, it is also one where ethnicity and cultural difference are produced and nurtured. Indeed, Alfaro's work returns to the space of an ethnic past in order to formulate his identity as a queer of color. In the "Moo-Moo" and "Abuelita" sequences, he specifically turns to his mother and grandmother to draw energy and critical force. While the majority of white queers can more easily fashion a break (an exile) from their childhood in heteronormative culture, since the queer community is a white normative one that would not dislocate them from their cultural formation as white people, the queer of color who cuts ties with their familial past is often also cutting ties with their ethnicity and/or race.

Alfaro emphasizes this risk in the last section of *Cuerpo Politizado*, "Orphan of Aztlan." Still clad in the black slip from the "Abuelita" segment and standing behind a music stand as if it were a pulpit, he literally preaches this last monologue, taking on the voice of a charismatic minister, one who might be preaching at his mother's church. He invokes Aztlan, the imaginary homeland that is a central organizing principle of Chicano nationalism, though his status as orphan (or exile) from this nationalist community foregrounds Chicano nationalism's inability to claim queer sons and daughters. But Alfaro expounds a more nuanced political position at this point in his performance: he sounds a militant political note in relation to liberal queer politics:

> There has been no power-sharing
> so we are power-taking
> empowered
> to march with a million
> because I am
> sick and tired
> of seeing straight people
> kiss and hold hands
> in public
>
> while I am
> relegated to
> a T-dance
> at Rage
>
> Fuck that shit!

The artist's rage rejects the politics of gay ghettoization and instead calls for a larger queering of the social realm. Alfaro calls on queers to take power and insert themselves within the national body, instead of waiting for liberal inclusion. For him, Rage is not a club holding a T-dance, but a politics. After speaking in general terms about queer politics, Alfaro locates himself within Chicano politics. He reintroduces the biography that we are familiar with from his memory performances:

> I am a Queer Chicano
> A native in no land
> An orphan of Aztlan
> The pocho son of farmworker parents
>
> The Mexicans only want me
> when they want me to
> talk about Mexico
> But what about
> Mexican Queers in L.A.?

The Queers only want me
when they need
to add color
add spice

like salsa picante
on the side

With one foot
on each side
of the border
not the border
between Mexico
and the United States
but the border between
Nationality and Sexuality
I search for a home in both
yet neither one believes
that I exist.

Alfaro beautifully captures the liminality that characterizes the experience of being queer and of color. His work brings these concerns into the foreground but does not stop there. He calls for social change:

Blur the line
take the journey
play with the unknown
deal with the whole enchilada
Race
Class
Sex
Gender
Privilege

Arrive at the place called possibility
Try once again to create a language
a sense of what it means
to be in community

I am fast forwarding
past the reruns *ese*
and riding the big wave

> called future
> making myself
>
> fabulous
> as I disentangle
> from the wreck of this
> cultural collision

Alfaro's performance and its insistence on "the whole enchilada" is a challenge to a range of minoritarian communities. Warner produces a critique of what he calls "Rainbow theory" and its weak multiculturalism. In his call to "break the frame" of a slogan-oriented politics that presupposes the interchangeability of sexual and ethnic differences, I read the implication that any subject can disengage themselves from this "frame" with equal ease, and that the mandate to critique such a position is equally relevant for all queers. I would argue that queers of color do not have the privilege of this analytical edge because different vectors of identity are mapped on their bodies and constitute their horizons of experience. The connections are thus materially valenced for the working-class lesbian of color, for instance, in ways that an affluent gay white man may not be able to grasp. He can dismiss the "Racism-Sexism-Homophobia—grasp the connections" bumper sticker with relative ease since the connections that are suggested are to some degree abstractions for him.

When queer critique calls for anatomizing of "the whole enchilada," the white normativity at the center of queer discourse becomes visible. I agree with Warner when I posit that queer politics does need a social theoretical base. Yet to stand firmly on one, we need to call attention to just what experiential archive informs such a social theory. If queer politics is ever to acquire political efficacy, the experiential and affective archive(s) that it accesses must not be tainted by the false universality of white normativity.

My critique of white normativity in queer theory might lead to a misreading that I would like to head off at the pass. Whiteness is not monolithic. For many white people, ethnos—and therefore the ethnic family—is important; for them, ethnicity cannot simply be trumped by sexuality. Italian, Irish, and Jewish American experiences, for example, complicate any monolithic understanding of whiteness. Furthermore, there are other non-ethnicity-based forms of difference, like class and region, which represent difference within whiteness. Yet all these differences are occluded by white normativity, that is, by the assumption of a universal whiteness. While it is important to stress that I am not interested in making whiteness monolithic, I am interested in calling attention to the workings and ruses of white normativity.

Warner opens his introduction to *Fear of a Queer Planet* by invoking Karl Marx's definition of critical theory: "the self-clarification of the wishes and struggles of the age."[11] This definition applies to the queer theater work of Alfaro, whose memory performance, with its focus on the production of hybrid selves and space, is in and of itself a mode of queer theory making that also functions as social theory.

Another turn to Marx is helpful in further describing Alfaro's project. In the *Theses on Feuerbach,* Marx offers an aphorism on the difference between philosophy and praxis: "The philosophers have only interpreted the world in various ways; the point, however, is to change it."[12] While this aphorism is well worn, it nonetheless speaks to the complicated relationship between theory and praxis within actually existing queer cultures: struggles between theory and praxis are central to the question of queer theater's (or any other mode of queer practice's) relationship to this enterprise called theory. Etienne Balibar has suggested that even though Marx was very young when he wrote that aphorism, "nothing he wrote afterwards ever went beyond the horizon of the problems posed by that formulation."[13] By this, Balibar means to call attention to the ways in which the concerns outlined in that early text haunt the relationship between philosophy and politics. Balibar's reading ultimately marks the ways in which praxis becomes philosophy and vice versa. By invoking *The German Ideology*'s rewriting of this formulation, a rewriting that stresses the interrelation between praxis and production, Balibar suggests that theory is the production of consciousness.

Taking my direction from Balibar, I would suggest that the relationship between queer theory and queer theater is similar to the relationship between the critic-theorist and the performer, the relationship between Alfaro and me standing together at that podium in London. In both cases, both sides of this divide contribute to a specific mode of production, one we might call the production of queer consciousness.

Alfaro's *Cuerpo Politizado* contributes to the production of queer knowledges, queer possibilities, and queer consciousness by exploring the wishes and struggles that inform a transformative politics. In the course of the piece, the audience witnesses Alfaro's migration from his past in Tia Ofelia's burned-out lot to his present—and presence—in the performance space. There, Alfaro's audience feasts on a "delicious spectacle," a performance that engenders queer Latino possibility where it could not flourish before. Queer Latino selves are called into existence through *Cuerpo Politizado*. Social space is reterritorialized through queer theater's demand for change.

8

Performing the Bestiary

CARMELITA TROPICANA'S *WITH WHAT ASS DOES THE COCKROACH SIT?/CON QUÉ CULO SE SIENTA LA CUCARACHA?*

Carmelita Tropicana can be a beast. In the past, she has been known to be a horse, pig, and even a bear. In short, we can describe Alina Troyano's performance persona, Carmelita Tropicana, as a queer assemblage. Assemblages are not simple characters or personas; instead, they are something else, something multiple. An assemblage consists of lines of articulation, strata, and territory, but also lines of flight, movements of deterritorialization and destratification. These lines represent different intensities, different speeds and textures. We can think of the assemblage known as Carmelita Tropicana as a body without organs, which is a body that is constantly dismantling the organism, causing asignifying particles or intensities to circulate differently. This queer assemblage is always becoming. Becoming is simply a constant process of flight, change, movement within the assemblage. The notion of becoming eschews notions of fixed organic unity for anticipatory formations. It's important to know that becoming is not being or even not imitating. Becoming is a kind of deterritorialization of the body itself, where stable molar identities are interrupted and new molecular formations take place. Becoming is about the interstice, about the threshold, dislocation, and destabilization. It has been described as ludic, and it is this aspect of becoming that brings one to Carmelita Tropicana and her 2004 performance *With What Ass Does the Cockroach Sit?/Con Qué Culo se Sienta la Cucaracha?* I want to consider Tropicana's work as a choreographed lesson in becoming-animal for the purpose of transcending the identitarian and nationalist ideologies that render Cubanity a molar mode of subjectivity. Becoming-animal in Tropicana's performance practice is a ludic endeavor. By ludic I mean an aimless play that functions as an opening in the face of a seeming impasse. Aimless, in this sense, is something desirable in the face of Oedipal and state logics that constrain life and often lead to mass protocols of control and dispossession.[1]

The systemic state violence that has been directed at different populations like Latinos and other people of color in the U.S. is a serious business. Often, this identity-based violence and the animalization of minoritarian populations conjoin together. In Tropicana's work, a different nonmimetic animalization takes place and disrupts the modes of territorialization that are central to the ways in which minoritarian lives are routinely devalued. *With What Ass Does the Cockroach Sit?/Con Qué Culo se Sienta la Cucaracha?* is based on the famous children's story *Perez y Martina* by the Puerto Rican author Pura Belpré (1932). A cockroach, Martina, spends her days sweeping her humble home. One day while sweeping, she comes across a gold coin and suddenly becomes wealthy. The cockroach is soon courted by the entire animal kingdom. A rooster, a cat, and a cricket all attempt to woo her, to no avail. Martina considers the rooster too loud; the cat's meow frightens her; and the cricket's chirping fills her with unbearable sadness. Instead, a Spanish mouse, named Perez, seduces her. She imagines that the Spanish mouse is some kind of noble blue blood. They have a fabulous wedding. The roach dances flamenco in honor of her spouse. At Christmas she decides to treat her spouse to an extravagant dessert. She puts sugar, almonds, and raisins in a pot of boiling water. As they cook, she leaves her kitchen to sweep outside her home. Perez discovers the steaming hot dessert. He sticks his paw in the pot, falls in, and is cooked alive. Martina reenters the kitchen and makes the grim discovery. She sings a tragic song: "El ratoncito Perez cayó en la olla y la cucaracha Martina lo canta y lo llora, lo canta y lo llora ... y hasta ahora, todavía canta, todavía toca y todavía llora para que su pequeno Perez vuelva donde ella." (The mouse Perez fell in the pot and the cockroach Martina sings to him and cries, she sings and cries ... and even today she still sings, she still feels, and cries for her little Perez to return to her.)

This children's story is known throughout Latin America. The knowledge produced by the fable is one in which different beasts produce different modes of knowledge about typologies of the human. At the center of this fable, we see the humble insect that suddenly acquires unanticipated wealth and makes a romantic choice on the perceived prestige associated with the blue-blood mouse's lineage. The valuing of this humanoid attribute in the rodent Perez is symmetrical with the devaluation of cats, roosters, and crickets, as well as the species-specific sounds (or even animal speech) they produce. In the story, it is the mouse's curiosity, not the cat's, that is his downfall. Again, we see a non-species behavior that ends up being detrimental. Thus we encounter the moral of this fable, which can be paraphrased as "be true to one's true nature." This story functions like a mini bestiary, which is a collection of medieval fables about real or imaginary animals. These stories or fables almost always contain moral lessons.

With What Ass . . . is something of a contemporary retelling of the tale. Its main point of convergence with the Latin American folktale is the central figure of the cockroach Martina. But the revamped Martina is not quite the tragic figure that the original was. This roach is a wily character who functions within the contemporary Cuban nation-state and does just what humans know roaches to excel at: survival. The beasts she encounters are the Havana-based parrot Catalina, proud representative of yesterday's oligarchical Cuba, and Carlitos, an archconservative bulldog who represents the anticommunist hegemony of Miami's exile community. The one-woman play is densely populated by other nonhuman presences, including an elderly lizard, an internet-gossiping bumblebee, and a seemingly transgender cat. Carmelita performs a becoming of all these beasts. This performance of becoming is not about realistic imitation but, more nearly, about a figural becoming of something like the animalistic figurations of this beast. Instead of being parrot, bulldog, or cockroach, she signals the animality that these beasts embody. Tropicana shifts intensities within the assemblage or bestiary that she is, oscillating between these different animalistic becomings. The transformation on the stage of INTAR Theatre during INTAR's 2004 season is as physical as it is linguistic. Her stance as bulldog is butch and defiant, her parrot becoming is represented by frenetic fluttering arms, and her movement as a roach is a scurrying zigzag motion low to the ground. Text and movement collide in these performances of becoming. Naturalistic performance is eschewed for a fantastic, humorous becoming. These acts of deterritorialization embody the ludic character of the assemblage itself.

Una Chauduri describes this mode of becoming in performance as zooësis, which she defines as "the way culture makes art and meaning with the figure and body of the animals."[2] For Chauduri, the Deleuzian becoming-animal is potentially a powerful destabilization of some fixed organic or molar unit. We might ask what is interrupted in this play. To do so would entail a description of the human drama that is at its center, which is to ask: What work is zooësis doing in this production? To explain that aspect of the performance, I need to narrate the historical/political movement at the play's center. To read my description thus far, one would think that Tropicana's performance is a fable about the Cuban condition as rendered through figurations of the animal. This is correct, but there is also greater specificity. The play considers the animals' perspective on important events in Cuban human history, especially the case of Elián González. González was the five-year-old boy picked up in an inner tube off the coast of Florida in 1999. The boy's mother had died tragically at sea while fleeing Cuba. González was taken in by his cousins in Miami and was subsequently claimed by his father in Cuba. The custody battle for the child became nothing short of an international scandal. Mass protests erupted in both Miami and Havana. The case was eventually concluded when U.S. attorney general Janet Reno ordered González to be returned to his father in Cuba. The media was saturated with images of the child being seized from his Miami relatives' home. The Cuban American community who protested in favor of keeping the boy in Miami bitterly objected to his removal.

This incident ended the state of exception Miami Cubans had experienced thanks to the Cold War and its residue. Until that point of mass media attention, Cubans had resisted being included in the anti-Latino scapegoating protocols of U.S. popular culture. Before the Elián crisis, white Cubans in the very insular city of Miami had seemed to be able to imagine themselves as somehow set apart from the anti-Latino bias that so many other U.S. Latino groups of all races had been encountering. Cold War policy offered Cuban immigrants easier immigration regulations and a series of readily available small businesses when the first wave of Cuban immigrants arrived in the 1960s and early 1970s. U.S. national media culture had cast Cubans as heroic anticommunist freedom fighters. This image began to erode during the mass influx known as the Mariel boatlift, during which the Cuban government cleared out its prisons and mental hospitals and had inmates join average Cuban citizens who wanted to leave the communist island for Miami, the fabled land of plenty (in the play, Elián refers to the city as the "United States of Miami").

All of these historical factors granted Cuban Americans a weird kind of exceptionalism. This so-called Cuban exceptionalism began to erode during the Mariel boatlift of 1980. But it remained mostly intact. During the 2000 media-generated immigration crisis set off by González's rescue, however,

U.S. popular opinion turned against Cuban Americans. For various reasons, including the perceived rights of a father to claim his son, as well as a more nefarious anti-immigrant resentment that was now being directed at the almost-majority Cuban American population in Miami, U.S. public opinion was firmly against the loudly protesting Cubans of South Florida. This was evidenced in 2000 in the hundreds of satirical flags that were flown in South Florida by North American residents in Miami who claimed to be exhausted by what they perceived to be the Cuban American community's bad behavior during the González incident. The flags were emblazoned with the words "The republic of Miami, Dade County Florida." The words were flanked by two bunches of bananas. Of course, the phrase "banana republic" is used as a shorthand for tropical antidemocratic dictatorships. And that certainly is the manifest meaning of these satirical flags. But of course, there is another racist logic that is connoted beyond bad government. Bananas are the food associated with apes, indeed the fruit constantly associated with their image. Flying this image was an animalizing turn in relation to the dominant cultural framing of the Cubans in Miami, who had been described in the media culture as irrational and affectively primitive. Indeed, Cubans were all but directly being called beasts. Furthermore, the resentment of the "beasts" of Miami was because they refused to conform to the law.

Metonymically linking a population with the specter of animality is primarily about the dehumanization of life itself and specific groups in particular. Certainly this was witnessed in the United States in general after the election of Barack Obama. Racist humor in the form of cartoons and drawings that figured the first family as primates circulated widely through the internet circuits of American racists. Indeed, the practice of animalizing communities of color is a central tendency in the history of U.S. racism. So what does it mean, in the face of this racism imagery and history, to take on an animality that is often projected onto one? What does the performance of becoming-animal as enacted by Carmelita Tropicana mean in this context?

Humor is a key term here. As I have argued above, animalization is one of the central moves of racist humor. The racist desires and conjures images of people of color as living a life that is less than human. Indeed, the logics that conjoin real animals and people of color are a devaluation of life that is often an excuse for violent treatment and cruelty. Certainly, humanist defenses against the animalization of humans remain an important civil rights strategy, but we see another move in Carmelita Tropicana's play: instead of insisting on humanity in the face of a racist imaginary, she makes another kind of argument on behalf of the human and the nonhuman. We can easily decipher the move to become the fanciful beasts in her plays as simply a goof or gag, but I would suggest that such a reading would miss something important. In reviewing the play, the *New York Times* critic Margo Jefferson reminds us that anyone who has read animal fables from La Fontaine to Joel Chandler Harris "knows how efficiently another species can be used to observe or mirror human life."[3]

Indeed there is mirroring in Tropicana's performances of becoming-animal, but I would like to push this interpretation further and suggest that there is something more than mere mimesis or imitation at work in these becomings. Tropicana's ludic performances of becoming-animal are more than the deployment of animality for discovering truths about the human. Something else is happening, and we are instead offered a vaster perspective on life itself that eschews the organic unity prescribed by the logic of segmented and separate species. The humor in the play, like the children's tale, is derived from a mode of interspecies contact that suggests the importance of the mingling forms of life as a large assemblage and not discrete unities. Let us think of Tropicana's entire oeuvre as an intermingling menagerie/assemblage. She was the coveted pig raised for slaughter during the Special Period in *Milk of Amnesia*. In that play, she was also the conquistador's horse who witnessed the slaughter of indigenous people during the colonization of Cuba. Similarly, her play *Chicas 2000* casts actress Rebecca Sumner Burgos as a butch lesbian bear. The animal is always linked to the story of mass and individual dispossession. The image of the bestial is something that is often deployed against collectives and individuals who have been systemically dispossessed. People of color are not animals, but I would also suggest that no people are not "not animal." This is to say that the human need to visualize the human apart from the animal is often a justification of violence and cruelty to the other. What then does it mean to not fully resist while not simply acquiescing? One thing we can clearly track in Tropicana's deployment of animality is a process I have described elsewhere as a disidentification with the animal. The becoming-animal is not being-animal or human-playing-animal. The becoming-animal is the flux and engagement that I view as disidentification's imprint.

Menagerie, bestiary, and assemblage: I have employed all of these terms to describe Carmelita Tropicana's performance of an expansive sense of life that interrupts the logic of human ascendency. A tragedy like the story of Elián González, one that is so very very much focused on the relationship between two nation-states and two nationalities, is reterritorialized in

Tropicana's performance of zooësis. A pivot from the Deleuzian paradigm to the thought of Jacques Derrida seems most helpful in this instance. In his seminars from 2001 to 2002 at the École des hautes études en sciences sociales in Paris, the philosopher presented a series of lectures titled *The Beast and the Sovereign*.[4] Part of his larger deconstruction of the human, these seminars call attention to a parallel between the sovereign and the beast. Derrida brings into focus the unique state of exception that characterizes both the monarch and the animal: neither is subject to the law. The sovereign is of course above it (while often calling it into existence) while the beast is below the law. Both positions thus offer a unique perspective. *With What Ass . . .* is a performance as subterranean fable that offers the spectator a radically different perspective on the human and its tribulations. Our main set of eyes is the cockroach, who is the avatar of a sly subaltern civility. Gone is the tragic and doomed Martina of Belpré's tale. Instead we have Tropicana's Martina, who found herself in all sorts of trouble. She accidentally falls into the suitcase of the parrot Catalina's companion, the famous Buena Vista Social Club singer Ibrahim Ferrer, which leads to her movement from Havana to Miami. The cockroach encounters all sorts of animal and human threats—be it sadistic twin teenage boys, ideologically dogmatic bulldogs, or the larger story's human protagonist, the six-year-old González. In one of the performance's most intense moments, Elián discovers the insect that spends her life trying to be outside and below the radar of the human. González puts his finger on the roach's antennae. Martina is left with the task of talking her way out of this potentially deadly encounter:

> A shadow all around—what—oh my antenna, hey kid your finger on my antennae is killing me, what you're a good boy so you gotta kill me because no one likes roaches in the house? Roaches are dirty, who told you that? That's a lie! You are a good boy and you don't lie and you play with the tourist children in the hotel where your father works. The tourist children have bigger better toys than your power rangers and suc's But you got a rock and a stick and they are magic because they can fly—what a smart boy, and you like to help your daddy wash his car, so by, by dirty roach I kill you! Nooh no, kid I'm clean so clean I'm friends with the queen. What queen you ax? What's your name? Elian Gonzalez. Eliancito. The queen of Spain. Did you see the queen on TV? You love TV too. Take your finger off and I tell you about the queen, no I won't run.

In this monologue, the child and the roach weirdly merge. The cockroach does what we associate cockroaches with doing or performing. In the quotidian lexicon, the roach is *resolviendo*, which literally translates into "resolving" but in the context of Cubanity means the act of making do, problem solving in relation to limited resources and state bureaucratic obstacles. Interestingly, Martina seduces the child by telling him the story of her own encounter with Spanish royalty. Recall that in Martina's previous incarnation, she chose the mouse Perez because it was rumored that he was of noble birth. In this retelling, the mouse is displaced by the actual Spanish queen. Here, we see Derrida's pairing of the beast and the sovereign. The child grants the roach a reprieve from a death sentence. She is suddenly granted a new lease on life because of a speech act that metonymically associates her with the queen and exceptionality from above.

In the story within the text, Martina tells the story of how she once again escaped obliteration at a restaurant by affixing herself to the queen of Spain's clothing. While the restaurateur discovered the roach during the queen's visit to his establishment, he was unable to kill the beast because she cagily latched onto the queen herself without coming to her royal highness's attention. Not wanting to call attention to the presence of the insect that was clearly in his view but not in the queen's, the proprietor was forced to spare the roach. This one act then doubly performs in that its performative retelling saves Martina a second time. This making do, working through, working out, is the becoming-cockroach, which Tropicana brings into view.

The performance title is an Afro-Cuban proverb. The answer to the question "With what ass does the cockroach sit?" is of course "none." The cockroach does not have an ass; it does not sit. In the aphorism, the cockroach is the lowest of the low, and the question is meant to call out the listener who may be putting on airs, acting pretentious, or being holier than thou. The saying puts them in contact with the roach, who doesn't even have a backside to sit on. But the fact that the roach doesn't have human anatomy is important. The point of the story is that there is no being-cockroach. No metaphor of transcendence. There is only the endeavor we know as becoming. To think of becoming and not being offers us another take on the identitarian logic of unity and fixity. Our turn to the animal helps us extract us from the logic of the human that is predicated on the devaluing of some lives within and outside the realm of the human. I want to suggest that there is something very brown about this becoming, this insistence on not being a foreclosed and often disposed identity, and instead participating in new and potentially emancipatory lines of flight.

9

Performing
Greater Cuba

TANIA BRUGUERA AND THE BURDEN OF GUILT

Sitting in a Lower Manhattan bar with two dear Cuban American friends in the spring of 2000, we found ourselves somewhat overwhelmed with the psychic and political ordeal of simply being Cuban at that particular historical moment. We fumbled for the proper word to describe what we were feeling at that vexed time. We had spent weeks compulsively tracking the case of Elián González, the six-year-old boy who was rescued by fishermen off the coast of South Florida in November 1999. The irony that this was happening almost exactly on the twenty-year anniversary of another infamous Cuban immigration scandal, the Mariel boatlift, did not escape us. By this point in the ordeal, the entire nation was familiar with the boy's tale: his tragic flight, the death of his mother at sea, and various magical realist details that punctuated the case, like the account of benevolent dolphins keeping the boy afloat on the inner tube and the manifestation of the Virgin Mary in the contours of a cracked mirror in Elián's bedroom in his Miami relatives' home. Miami Cubans rallied around the boy's Miami kin, who fought for his custody. Cuban leader Fidel Castro, not one to miss the challenge of any symbolic war, pressed for the boy's return. As the situation escalated, the comportment of Cubans seemed odd and fantastic to non-Cuban viewers. Despite media representations to the contrary, Cuban Americans are not a monolithic bloc of right-wing zealots. There is in fact a Cuban American Left, networks of people and individuals who believed that the boy should be allowed to return to his father and who furthermore—and even more scandalously—do not demonize the revolution but instead view it ambivalently.[1]

That night, at the bar with northern Cubans, I realized that we felt a structure of feeling that I can only call communal guilt. I realized that perhaps this structure of feeling linked Cuban Americans and Cubans. Certainly, my right-wing relatives feel a sort of survivor's guilt in relation to those Cubans on the island whom they perceive as living in the shadow of a tyrant in a communist inferno. Cuban children in the United States are scolded for being wasteful and reminded of all the material possessions they have compared with their cousins who are deprived of capitalism's trinkets. As a Cuban American who believes in the importance of materialist analysis, the ultraconservative dominance of the community I grew up in has been a source of shame and guilt for me as an adult. As a proponent of pan-Latino coalition politics, I feel this familiar structure of feeling in relation to the historical preferences and advantages Cuban immigrants enjoy in relation to the state-sponsored harassment that other Latino groups such as Mexicans, Dominicans, and Puerto Ricans encounter. Guilt envelops the Cuban American tradition. Guilt, according to the theorist of affect Silvan Tompkins, is a subcategory of shame.[2] Guilting other people is akin to shaming others, and guilt itself is one way in which we introject shame.

In this chapter, I wish to use this commonality of guilt to do decidedly different taxonomical work than I did in the above paragraph. Rather than differentiate between various kinds of Cuban Americans—us and them, myself and the Other Cuban—I want to consider the way in which there are structures of feeling that knit *cubanía* together despite different national pedagogies and ideological purchases. Furthermore, I am interested in putting pressure on the inside/outside Cuba binary that has become so central since the revolution. By focusing on guilt's relation to all of *cubanidad*, I am attempting to render an analysis of what I will call, after the film theorist Ana López, Greater Cuba. López uses the term to talk about cinematic cultural productions by Cuban Americans outside of the island in relation to work from the island. Her expanded rendering of *cubanía* functions as a challenge to Cold War rhetorics that are interested in a strict binarization of *cubanía*. While it is important in the case of other Latin American immigrant histories, such as that of the Chicano, to differentiate between over there (Mexicans) and over here (Chicanos), I am arguing that this is not axiomatic for all Latino groups. Since the antagonisms that Chicanos have faced are remarkably different from the lesser state-sponsored obstacles that Cubans have overcome, it is safe to conclude that both cases are decidedly divergent. This makes different protocols necessary to properly understand different Latino groups, groups that nonetheless potentially work in coalition formation as *latinidad*.

It seems that thinking past the stultifying rhetorics of what Gustavo Pérez-Firmat has called "life on the hyphen" will lead us to a more nuanced understanding of the affective contours of what it means to be Cuban in the extended and somewhat pretended geography that I call Greater Cuba.[3] (This map would include the island and South Florida but also other hubs of Cuban production in New York and New Jersey, as well as spots in California and elsewhere in the Americas.) This geography is calculated in relation to affective considerations of space. I propose that Cubans live in guilt, and that an affective geography of cubanía, built on this analysis of guilt as a structure of feeling, is particularly important at this historical moment. To this end, I consider the work of Cuban national artist Tania Bruguera.

Bruguera came to my attention after her work had been censored by the Cuban state in 1994. The offending art object was a journal that had the format of a newspaper and was titled *Memoria de la postguerra* (Memory of the postwar) that included Cubans on and off the island expressing their feelings on the Cuban state at the moment. The government in turn did not invite her to perform at the 1997 Biennial. Bruguera nonetheless performed at her own residence during the exhibition as international visitors and local neighbors watched. Though Bruguera graduated from the Art Institute of Chicago in 2001, she considers herself to be a Havana-based artist: she returned to the island to inaugurate a Performance Studies Department at the Instituto Superior de Arte (the Havana Art Institute) in 2002. I consider her performance work, especially a piece titled *El peso de la culpa* (*The Burden of Guilt*), as a greater Cuban intervention that meditates and theorizes guilt and the Cuban condition.

Introjecting Guilt

The Burden of Guilt, a performance that debuted in 1997 in Havana, is part of a series of performances that Bruguera calls *Memoria de la postguerra*.[4] The artist's own description of the themes she is attempting to foreground stresses a history of guilt in relation to the nation's foundation:

> In this piece I specifically refer to the collective suicides of indigenous Cuban people during the Spanish occupation. The only way that some

Año I, No.2 La Habana, CUBA, Junio de 1994

EL POST-EXILIO Y LA POST-GUERRA
Iván de la Nuez / Juan Pablo Ballester

1. Hay una diferencia radical entre un viaje y un exilio. La experiencia al respecto de los artistas cubanos lo confirma de un modo absoluto. De un viaje el regreso es habitualmente victorioso, con el recuerdo de los buenos tratos, la exaltación de los egos y la sensación maravillosa de haber vivido los 5 minutos de gloria decretados por Andy Warhol. Estos minutos hacían casi tangible el sueño de convertirse en Madonna, Beuys, Harrison Ford o, para variar, Jürgen Habermas. En un exilio, donde los "extraños" - nuevos bárbaros, según la sociología de moda- han llegado para competir por un lugar bajo el sol, los sueños y las posibilidades sufren ligeras variaciones. Las acotaciones del terreno colocan el tope de las aspiraciones en unos paradigmas que se llaman Celia Cruz, Wifredo Lam, Andy García o, para no variar, Guillermo Cabrera Infante. Así, los 5 minutos de gloria de Warhol se nos convierten en 5 minutos de Gloria...Estefan. Y es que los cubanos, como todos los emigrantes, navegan su exilio por los mapas y territorios que se han codificado previamente. Al punto de encontrarse con un mundo de inscripciones que lo obliga a vivir en una hiperrealidad delineada por las postales turísticas. El juego que han conseguido estas "marcas tropicales" obedece a unas determinaciones imprecisables. En realidad, nunca sabremos si Cuba vende la imagen que Occidente prescribe, o éste recoge los dictados que a la isla convienen. En cualquier caso, lo importante no son las jerarquías del origen del juego, sino el juego mismo.

2. Si bien las circunstancias del viaje han sido experimentadas por muchos artistas de la isla, estos desconocen casi todo lo que implica un exilio (que por cierto, suele ser más complejo que una galería, un catálogo o un anuncio en Art en América). Los guettos de "afuera" son complejos, diversificados y se enlazan con diferentes canales de circulación. La, así llamada, vanguardia cubana de los 80 -que fue algo más que "eso: años...y nada más"- ha arribado a distintos países y, aunque siempre ha morado en los ámbitos prefijados, en cada uno se ha implicado de un modo diferente. México, por ejemplo, funcionó como un guetto cultural que insertaba su producción intelectual en espacios e instituciones dedicadas al "problema cubano". Miami continúa como el espacio por excelencia de la gratificación económica, pasado por el agua, el encuentro con un mundo retro tan obsesionado con su "cubanidad" como poco acostumbrado a la estética de la plástica cubana de los 80. Mientras en la Europa de Maastrich, inhóspita con los extraños y embelesada con los nacionalismos,

continúa pág. 10

AÑORANZAS POR CUBA
Emilio Ichikawa Morín

A mis amigos, los que están desde México
"Las piedras de la isla parecen que van a salir volando", dice un verso de la poetisa cubana Dulce María Loynaz, dueña de un premio Cervantes de Literatura y, a demás, de un silencio tan hablador como el de Sor Juana. En la isla las cosas son leves, y sus definiciones, a veces, parecen bromas; es decir, les falta gravedad: sus ríos son delgados, sus montañas menudas y sus bosques más próximos a los jardines que a las selvas.
Cristo es roca, y Cristo mismo parece que va a salir disparado Quizás por eso el nuestro, macho y marino, se encuentra en Regla, margen insolentemente izquierdo de la bahía desde donde zarpan los barcos.
Las criaturas de la Isla son como sus piedras y también como su Cristo. Parladoras y rumiantes, circulan un aviso que, a fuerza de repetirse, más parece indicar un sentido destinal que un accidente: irse del país. A pesar de las ficciones de algún propagandista, irse es una ficha recurrente en el juego de cualquier cubano y, conste, aunque duela, uno no acostumbra a irse del lugar donde las cosas le van bien. En buen chucheroo: irse es una ficha guardada para cuando el dominó se tranque.
Hasta el idioma quiebra bajo el peso del hábito. Cuando a usted le dicen que fulano se quedó, no le significan que dejó, por ejemplo, una vida bohemia por un nido de hogar o que echó raíces en Escobar, la calle más cálida de la Habana. Nada de eso. Quedarse es dejar, es abandonar, que es, también -y eso lo saben quienes se quedaron- la nostalgia por regresar. Nostalgia cada vez menos culpable, pero culpable aún.
El problema radica, para ellos y para nosotros, en que de Cuba uno jamás puede irse, sin darse cuenta de que no hay lugar en el mundo para refugiarse de ella.
Esa escapada desgarradora ocurre en diferentes grados. No estar desde Londres, así se sea un escritor de sensibilidad sin par, es de un extrañamiento más intenso que no estar desde Miami. No estar desde México es, por otra parte, una forma bastante peculiar de ausencia. Tal y como fluyen los acontecimientos, México D.F. llegará a ser, sin dudas la tercera ciudad de los cubanos.
Estar y no estar, irse y quedarse, es la tensión que signa a la gente de la isla, de esta isla, y eso se define en cualquier sitio, dentro o fuera. Sin embargo, ese doble signo se potencia, ora en su extremo, ora en el otro, y es esa potenciación la que llega a hacer distinguibles a algunos cubanos entre sí. Es una distinción de acento, no de cualidad; pero, y esto es lo que quiero advertir, es una distinción que existe.
No estar, irse, es una condición posible. De hecho, hay quienes se fueron y el exilio cubano es una realidad, tenga la textura que tenga. No están o están lejos, porque esto de aquí -ahora no es un ente sino un algo-contingente que permuta todos los días. Cambio acelerado que es capaz de pasmar al

continúa pág. 18

9.1 Tania Bruguera, *Memoria de la postguerra*, 1994.
COURTESY OF ESTUDIO BRUGUERA.

of them could rebel—as they didn't have any weapons and they weren't warriors by nature—was to eat dirt until they died. This gesture, which remained with us more as a historical rumour, struck me as hugely poetic. In a way, it speaks to our individuality as a nation and as individuals. Eating dirt, which is sacred and a symbol of permanence, is like swallowing one's own traditions, one's own heritage, it's like erasing oneself, electing suicide as a way of defending oneself. What I did was take this historical anecdote and update it to the present.[5]

The basis of this performance is a mythological origin story of Cuban guilt. The factual nature of this origin is partially relevant. We do know that Spanish colonization of Cuba was especially genocidal in relation to indigenous people. Nearly all indigenous people were wiped out during the shock of the colonial encounter. The eradication of the indigenous is the condition of possibility for Cuba's foundation. Bruguera describes the foundation of Cuban national consciousness as being formed by guilt over colonial brutality and mass killing. Guilt thus organizes and forms this particular origin narrative of Cuban consciousness. Bruguera's foregrounding of this tale calls on Greater Cuba to understand its formation in this scene of racialized violence. Stressing the tragic shock effects of the colonial encounter pulls Cubans away from the problematic and shortsighted understanding of the 1959 revolution as the crowning or central moment in Greater Cuba's history. Bruguera's work offers an expanded timeline of cubanía. Such an expanded historical mapping (which is also an affective cartography) displaces the 1959 revolution's central and organizing position, offering a more productive mapping of Greater Cuba.

The performance titled *El peso de la culpa* was performed in, and modified for, various sites. The first version of the performance was staged at the Sixth Havana Biennial (1995). While Bruguera was not officially allowed to perform during this Biennial, she nonetheless staged an alternate performance inside her house in Havana. In this version of the performance, Bruguera awaits her audience inside her house. Behind her is a large and expansive Cuban flag that the artist has made out of human hair. She wears the headless carcass of a lamb like a vest of armor atop a white outfit. She is barefoot. There is a pot of Cuban earth in front of her, along with a deep plate of water and salt. She bows in front of the containers in a slow, mechanical fashion and carefully mixes the dirt and the salt water in her hand. She proceeds to eat the dirt slowly. Bruguera continues to eat dirt for about an hour. Eating dirt slowly in a ritualistic fashion is a performance of empathy where she identifies with the lost indigenous Cuban. The consumption of earth is an act of penance that connects the artist with the actual island itself. The salt water signifies tears of regret and loss. She consumes this charged symbol, too.

In this performance, the lamb is less a symbol of Christian cosmology and more nearly signifies syncretic African belief systems like Santería, where the goat or lamb is a ritualistic creature of sacrifice. "For me," she states, "the relation that exists with the Afro-Cuban religion is that the lamb is charged with energy rather than just symbolism. But I also play with the socially saturated sense in which the lamb becomes a Eurocentric, and hence 'universal,' symbol of submission. In other words, it's less local in its intent than it might seem. A sheep or lamb as everybody everywhere knows, lies down, just like the Cuban indigenous and like Cubans in the island."[6]

The flag that hangs behind her is made out of the nation's actual body, or at least a part of that national body. Bruguera's work literalizes the metaphors of national identity and nationality. The function of this literalization reveals the material and corporeal weight of metaphors. As the case of Elián makes clear, the symbolic is routinely deployed within the rhetoric of Greater Cuba. Elián became a symbol for both the Cuban government and Miami-based Cubans. The boy's welfare and actual physical well-being were overwhelmed by the abstraction of becoming a national symbol. Bruguera's insistence on corporeal literalization makes us cognizant of the actual stakes of making people and bodies mere symbols. The stakes, as the performance's title suggests, are weighty.

If we consider the attachment of symbols of guilt to the body and the actual consumption of these symbols—native soil and salty tears—through the lens of psychoanalytic theory, we can determine a significant reversal that contributes to an understanding of the interventionist nature of Bruguera's performance. When considering the question of guilt in a reading of classical Hollywood cinema, Slavoj Žižek explains, "In psychoanalytic theory, one talks a lot about the transference or projection of guilt onto the Other (the Jew, for example); perhaps, we should rather reverse the relationship and conceive the very act of assuming guilt as an escape from the real traumatism—we don't only escape from guilt as we escape into guilt, take refuge in it."[7] Cubans across the nationalist divides of the island and exile project guilt on each other and constitute each other as what Žižek would call the big Other. Certainly, Fidel Castro has been continually constructed as the big Other of Miami-based right-wing Cuban American rhetoric. Similarly, the *gusano* (a derogatory term used for Cubans who left Cuba after the 1959 revolution; literally "worm") is construed as the revolution's Other. Bruguera's work dramatically renders a challenge and political imperative to resist the urge to project guilt out on the Other, and instead understand guilt's incorporation into Greater Cuba's disparate body. Elsewhere, I have claimed that Cuban Americans live in memory. While I do not recant that particular formulation, I would layer another analysis: Greater Cuba, whose spatial geography is an affective one, is also fractured by crisscrossing projections of guilt. But guilt is in fact the very affective terrain of the Cuban and not something to simply be deployed against the phantasmatic big Other. Bruguera's performance is a form of materialist critique that asks us to feel the weight of guilt and understand it as something incorporated into the Cuban body and the nation's body. Indeed, I would amend my previous statement by suggesting that Cubans also live in guilt.

In another performance, *The Burden of Guilt II*, part of the same series of work but performed in Santa Fe, New Mexico, and Antwerp, Bruguera kneels nude on the floor before a dish containing lamb's fat. She slowly and methodically wrings the animal fat through her hands. At first it appears as though she is washing her hands with the substance, and then it begins to look as though she is actually rubbing the strong-smelling substance into her skin, giving one the sense that she wants to incorporate the substance into her physical being. She next kneels behind a lamb's head. She is positioned behind the neck of the animal: she bows in the direction of the animal's head and, as her head recedes into her body, the animal's head appears to look out into the audience. The sacrificial beast's head is now her own, and she is becoming this creature, or at least suturing the symbol onto her own body. In this instance, we hear Žižek's suggestion that we not project guilt out but instead understand the need for the introjection of guilt, to see the way in which guilt is always already inside us, and furthermore, a Kantian condition of possibility for the current situation of cubanía.

Psychoanalysis is useful as a heuristic tool. It narrates stories about subject formation that we can potentially harness to discuss group formations. Such a tactic is not always effective or even compelling. There is nonetheless a time and a place for such inquiry. Take for example Jean Laplanche and J. B. Pontalis's useful description of the psychoanalytic project known as projection: "In the properly psycho-analytic sense: it is an operation whereby qualities, feelings, wishes or even objects, which the subject refuses to recognize or rejects in himself, are expelled from the self and located in another person or thing. Projection so understood is a defence of very primitive origin which may be seen at work especially in paranoia, but also in normal modes of thought such as superstition."[8] This definition is useful to understand how the individualistic psychic process is relevant to larger formations within the social. The above explication, for instance, seems an especially apt definition to bring to bear on issues of ethnicity or affect. Affect not only is located in a particular sense of self, but is often projected onto the world. When affect, such as shame and its offspring, guilt, are projected onto a world, this contributes to a large social imbalance that can be described as a mass paranoia. Eve Sedgwick talks about a particular imbalance in many of our critical practices, one in which paranoid readings have taken precedence over other interpretive strategies. Sedgwick instead calls for reparative readings.[9] A reparative reading is a mode of analysis that is not simply concerned with unveiling conspiracies and the secret (and seemingly always nefarious) mechanisms of power. Reparative readings are calibrated to call attention to the ways in which individuals and groups fashion possibility from conditions of (im)possibility. Reparative readings are about building and potentiality. People of color and other minoritarian citizen-subjects must continue to call on paranoid readings—some modes of paranoia are well-founded while others are simply rote and by now stale critical reflexes. Sedgwick is not calling for a simple reversal of critical methodologies; she is instead making a case for a diversification of critical approaches. Such a diversification seems equally true for the emergent body of knowledge that we can tentatively call Greater Cuban studies. Bruguera's performance signals a potentiality for a new formation, another understanding and sense of cubanía that is not organized by routine and predictable antagonisms. Bruguera's work signals another way of working with and through guilt that is not simply a cleansing of that affect or of its traditional paranoid projection.

Holding Guilt: Bruguera with Albita

Ricardo Ortiz, one of Greater Cuba's most dynamic critics, has written about guilt in relation to the music of famed Miami-based recording artist and cabaret performer Albita Rodriguez. Ortiz explains that Cubans are fueled by particular addictions—*café* and *culpa* (guilt). He writes, "That one's Cubanness should become the marker of one's guilt, the incontrovertible sign of one's culpability, results precisely from the necessity of bearing that mark, of confessing to one's Cubanity outside Cuba."[10] This formulation is produced in relation to an astute textual analysis of Rodriguez's lyrics, especially the third track on her album, "Qué culpa tengo yo." I have often heard that sentimental anthem in a room full of Cubans, noticing how it stirs and unites groups of listeners. There is a certain force behind lines like "Qué culpa tengo yo que mi sangre suba / Qué culpa tengo yo de haber nacido en Cuba? [What fault is it of mine that my blood rises? / What fault of mine to be born in Cuba?]" This invocation of Cubanness and guilt, in my experience, hits a note and accesses a structure of feeling. While Albita is older than Bruguera, they both came of age in communist Cuba and are now newly internationalized and performing within the sphere of Greater Cuba, a testament to the guilt that permeates cubanía. But any comparison between the way in which both artists negotiate cubanía and guilt is limited.

In fact, Albita and Bruguera negotiate the affect of guilt quite differently. Ortiz explains how the song soars beyond self-torturing guilt. His expert reading of the song is worth citing: "Instead the tone of the song is pure defiance: to be Cuban is in part to love freedom, to bear adversity with optimism. It is also to bear in oneself a kind of blood that pulses and rises, that both captures one and sustains one at a level of passionate corporal intensity equal to the demands and challenges of having been born Cuban in this historical moment."[11] This song of defiance is extremely powerful and effective. Its affective stance does indeed surpass simple self-inflicted and tortured guilt. Ortiz adroitly connects this defiance around cubanía to Albita's lesbian defiance. He reads the culpa of cubanía alongside the culpa of homosexuality.

While I agree and am persuaded by Ortiz's argument, I am not certain that having one's blood rise under such particular terms helps cubanía surpass that impasse around guilt that I have described. While Albita's lesbian defiance seems especially necessary on either side of Greater Cuba, where queer possibility and visibility are often met with phobic antagonism, this defiance of the guilt of cubanía seems to not really function as a break with divisive Cuban nationalisms. I would suggest that Albita, who never fully comes out in the press or media, uses cubanía as an analogy for queerness. The genius of the song has much to do with the way in which it speaks queerness differently and potentially undermines homophobic ideologies. She addresses these Cubans by speaking to them of a shaming they think they know. But, like many analogies, this rhetorical move does present some dangers. What sort of defiant and perhaps unthinking nationalism does Albita reproduce through this analogical move? Perhaps when it comes to the culpa of cubanía, we should do more than simply deflect it with the force field of a defiant posture. Perhaps it is important to actually hold onto the guilt that shadows cubanía and not simply cast it out through a process of projection. What would it be to hold guilt? What knowledge of historical positionality avails itself to us when we attempt to know, interrogate, and actually hold the burden of guilt?

Toward a Politics of Introjection

Bruguera's performance practice entails just such a holding. It is a critical retention of shame instead of a more familiar and routine Cuban negotiation of shame: rejection, outward projection, or cleansing. To hold shame looks very different than the defiance that Albita performs. A survey of Bruguera's performances that predate *The Burden of Guilt* is instructive when trying to understand the critical moves she makes. *Cabeza abajo* (Head down), for instance, also displays a posture that is different than those of direct or simplistic rejections of shame. This performance, staged in December 1996 at the Espacio Aglutinador gallery, began with an invitation to local artists and critics. The participants were asked to lie down on the floor. Bruguera was dressed in a white robe of artificial wool fabric and covered with a white Kabuki-like makeup. She carried a red flag on her back, like those used in Japanese feudal wars. She walked on top of her prostrate participants. Potato sack trenches separated the audience from the participants, further instilling a sense of battle, warfare, and conquest. The artist proceeded to mark her participants with red flags. Revolutionary anthems from the 1960s and '70s played.

In an interview, Bruguera describes the performance as being about the relationship between artists and power and as a general statement about the art world.[12] This performance was staged at a moment in which the state was particularly interested in censoring any art that could be construed as antirevolutionary. At that point, Bruguera's journal/newspaper, *Memoria de la postguerra*, had been already censored by the state. Each body becomes a colonized territory. But certainly other meanings can be deciphered if we attempt to understand the affective dimension of the performance. The art world denizens are conquered by an imperial specter. In the highly metaphoric field of Greater Cuba, this scene can potentially be read as depicting the colonizing force of the United States, Miami, or Castro, depending on one's particular ideological position. But that aspect is left open. The work does not target any one culprit; it is instead interested in unpacking a particular affective scene. Her work is a study of the ways in which Cubans are confronted by colonizing exterior force. Like the Indians invoked in *El peso de la culpa*, the participants in *Cabeza abajo* are not taking on a posture of defiance but are instead performing a passive resistance. This performance

9.2 Installation view of costume from *Destierro* in Bruguera's 2017 exhibition *Talking to Power/Hablándole al Poder* at the Yerba Buena Center for the Arts in San Francisco, 2017. COURTESY OF ESTUDIO BRUGERA.

can be seen as a rehearsal of sorts for the affective stance that Bruguera embodies in *El peso de la culpa*. In *Cabeza abajo*, the whitened artist plays the embodiment of power from above while her participants embody the passive masses. It would be a mistake to see this position as simple passivity. *Cabeza abajo* is a descriptive performance, rendering the ways in which a people survive their historical situation. The performance is not prescriptive. It does not suggest that the performed behavior is desirable; instead, it illustrates how Cubans withstand particular conditions of possibility by assuming certain poses.

Another performance, *Destierro* (Displacement), depicts a further representation of the Cuban condition, this time in the form of an object associated with the Congo religious roots of Cuban Santería, the *nkisi nkonde*.

The mythical figure is a mystical object in which believers invest their hopes and desires. The object has a powerful performative nature. The objects are performative insofar as they can perform as a speech act, according to J. L. Austin's definition of the term. For instance, two dolls tied together can function in the same way as the linguistic speech act, "I now pronounce you man and wife," insofar as it contractually joins two entities. Not every *nkisi nkonde* object is anthropomorphic: at times it may simply appear to be a pouch. The contents of the pouch may spell out a subject's name or some other aspect of their identity.

The object in Bruguera's case does represent a human form. The object's performative nature has been transformed in the diaspora, and it is not uncommon to hear stories of people investing certain desires and wishes in the object; for example, someone who may wish to win the lottery could very well sew money into the doll's lining. The object thus becomes a receptacle and a symbol for projected desires. When Bruguera wears her *nkisi nkonde* outfit, a massive uniform made of wooden and metal nails and a mud-covered Lycra material, she represents an aspect of Cuban syncretic culture. Each nail represents a desire hammered into the object's form. In this massive costume, Bruguera tours public spaces as part of the *Destierro* performance. She confronts Cubans and tourists as she tours old Havana's most historic sections. In the dilapidated beauty of rustic town squares, the figure of Cuba's syncretic nature confronts its populace. Those inside the object's epistemology recognize it and quickly form an identification to it that is calibrated by their own relationship to the belief network, while for others outside that loop it appears to be some ancient musty relic come to life, perhaps a Caribbean mummy emerged from a hidden tropical crypt.

When confronting the *nkisi nkonde*, those in the know can perhaps understand each *clavo*, or nail, as a desire that has been literally introjected into the object. While introjected into the object it is still visible, a desire that is literally worn on the sleeve. Perhaps the desire that is made visible on the figure is one of flight, or maybe a wish for the island, a desire to stay. It is significant that this performance was first staged on Castro's birthday, a holiday that calls the nation to embrace its leader and his status as a literal representative of the nation. For those who believe in the revolution's infallible glory, Castro almost functions as a *nkisi nkonde*, a symbolic figure in which the populace invests its hopes and desires. For those who denounce the leader, he is the fetish, the juju, the ultimate Other, also potentially represented in the performance. Again, Bruguera's performance explicates the ways in which Cuban people, arguably on and off the island, participate in an economy of projection, investing desire and guilt in outside objects rather than understanding the potential transformation available through a politics of introjection.

What would the contours of this politics of introjection be? What possibilities could this politics suggest? What potentialities avail themselves? To this end, it is important to pick up the psychoanalytic thread that this chapter produces. It is equally important to be explicit about this thread, its nature, and exactly what it is not. The psychoanalytic inquiry I am attempting to compose here is decidedly non-Lacanian, or rather it represents a turn away from a particular North American reception and utilization of Jacques Lacan's project. In Lacan's paradigm, there is an overarching and indeed terrible otherness to the other. Lacan develops the thematic of projective identification, a motif first located in British psychoanalyst Melanie Klein's work, and uses it to describe the rage that develops when the infant realizes she cannot break through the mirror and instead that her own image is merely refracted upon her. In Klein's theory of introjection, the ego consumes the lost object or ideal through a process of introjection. Once introjected, the ego cannibalizes the lost object, and it is lost anew. The story of introjection that Klein tells is called into question by French psychoanalytic theorists Nicolas Abraham and Maria Torok, who take issue with Klein's assignment of introjection as a primary process. For example, on the fashion in which Klein positions fantasy, Abraham and Torok state, "We are astonished Melanie Klein sees fantasy—a product of the ego—as predating the process, which is the product of the entire psyche."[13]

Abraham and Torok are also attracted to a notion of introjection. They note that introjection was first invented by Freud's collaborator Sándor Ferenczi, who described it as a process of broadening the ego. The psychoanalytic duo explain that the process of introjection first manifests itself when the child discovers the emptiness of her mouth in relation to the presence and then absence of the breast. The oral void, once discovered, is filled with language and words. Eventually, words replace cries, and the pleasure and satisfaction of the breast give way to the satisfaction of possessing language. They explain that the transition from a mouth filled with the breast to a mouth filled with words occurs by virtue of the intervening experiences of the empty mouth. Language would not exist without the satisfaction of the breast. Abraham and Torok then take a rather poetic turn when they discuss language itself as the communion of empty mouths. Thus, a politics of introjection would be something like the communion described above. If we introjected feelings like guilt, things that we too easily project, these feelings would not reductively fill a void, but the process would make us cognizant of our shared affective nature, the empty mouths of cubanía. Only when we acknowledge that our mouths are empty, that neither ideal—here or there—can permanently replace our loss, can we begin the absolutely necessary process of communion.

To do this, it seems important to visit other spots in the firmament of psychology and psychoanalysis that are not the reified dialectics of negation that dominate Lacanian paradigms.[14] Abraham and Torok tell us a story of a collective negation that we can, following the work of Laplanche, describe as allogenic as opposed to what he has described as autocentric(ally) eschewed theories of relationality for circumscribed theories of the self. According to Laplanche, the latter have imposed their hegemony on all of metapsychology, both clinical and theoretical. He calls for the revision of our approaches to the question of the psychic when he proposes giving a full place in metapsychology to a process that is irreducible to an autocentricism: those whose subject is quite simply the other.[15] This allogenic assertion certainly speaks to the communion of empty mouths that Abraham and Torok describe. It is also relevant in a recent turn to the psychic in critical race theory that Hortense Spillers calls for.[16] Spillers justifies her own escalating interest in psychological approaches to the social by describing them as potential intramural protocols. They are intramural insofar as they may shed light on our relationship to each other within communities of color: again, each other, and not some little other out of Lacan.

Bruguera's performances are also intramural exercises, allogenic acts that let us see beyond the self-resisting to project. I have explicated the ways in which Bruguera's performance eschews autocentric cubanía for a Greater Cubanía, which returns me to the scene at the bar, and my friends, sharing our shame and guilt about Elián, finding ourselves speechless (an infrequent phenomenon for Cubans in general), and perhaps finding ourselves in our speechlessness. Which is to say, we were taking comfort in the communal nature of empty mouths, wishing and desiring a moment when Greater Cuba discovers its own communion of empty mouths.

10

Wise Latinas

U.S. Supreme Court Justice Sonia Sotomayor's nomination to the court in May 2009 was met with great skepticism by the North American right. When Republicans went through her public record, they came across a speech she had given at a few universities. Sotomayor and Obama's enemies had attached themselves to the quote, "I would hope that a wise Latina woman with the richness of her experiences would more often than not reach a better conclusion than a white male who hasn't lived that life."[1] Republicans decried this quotation as an example of reverse racism. Their objection, it would seem, had much to do with the idea that a jurist who did not claim universality in the fashion in which white men could was an invalid adjudicator. I contend that the sensationalist ire the term generated was in no small part due to her use of the term "wise Latina." It would seem that the term "Latina" and its linkage to a word like "wise," which is usually associated with more universal subjects, was precisely the site of provocation for her conservative enemies. We are left to conclude that "wise" is a word reserved for subjects who claim a more objectivist mode of knowledge production and knowing.

This essay focuses on what I would like to describe as the "otherwiseness" of brownness. By "otherwiseness," I mean to render the production and performance of knowledge that does not conform to the mimetic coordinates assigned to both the designations "wise" and "other." I want to sketch another, more subterranean route to the production of knowledge. To do this, I cast an odd Puerto Rican predecessor to Justice Sotomayor: underground screen legend Mario Montez. This essay meditates upon Montez's embodied production and performance of knowledge during select moments from his work with Andy Warhol and Jack Smith. I turn to Montez's performance as an important and indexical moment that allows us to imagine a brown otherwise. The cinematic/performance moments I consider display Montez's performance of an affective particularity that displaces much of the coercive mimesis that structures North American understandings of Latino particularity. This essay draws a zigzagging line between Montez and Sotomayor and contemporary performance artist Nao Bustamante for the purpose of a brown mode of knowledge production and knowing-beyond-knowing, of otherwiseness, which gives us a richer account of feeling and being brown in America.

I will narrate the parallel tales of Montez and Sotomayor's star-turn performances, especially the staging of both of their big auditions for career-making cameras as well as the way in which Bustamante, like Montez and Sotomayor, found affective and other immaterial resources to stand tall in the face of hostile fire. The linkage between feeling brown and being brown is crucial to the larger sequence of writings that this chapter belongs to. No simple idea of Latino ontology makes any sense unless it is linked to a phenomenological field. We often know *latinidad*, or brownness, through its affective contours, which is to say the set of collective and often contagious responses to one's historical and emotional situation. This relay of responses is once again knowable to us as a kind of affective performativity, a kind of feeling which is a mode of doing. Certain collectivities, like those that provisionally cohere under the sign brownness, share historical trajectories of negotiating particular sets of material obstacles within the social, which include, but are not limited to, uneven distribution of resources; systematic race-, nation-, and language-based bias; unjust and phobic immigration policies; and a general tendency to be scapegoated during a nation-state's moments of economic or cultural instability. Thus, I am interested in a mode of affective particularity that I am describing as brownness, and this focus leads me to the project of describing particular performances of brown feelings that produce knowledge about singularities and pluralities that do not conform to anticipatable notions of reason. But these alternative and often-subterranean paths to knowledge production and reception are, I want to insist, not reason's other. The simple rejection of reason as a majoritarian project seems too easy and indeed counterproductive. Such a move simply shores up simplistic dyads of cognition and emotion that need to be interrupted. More nearly, my aim, through the route of affect, is to chart a provisional de-universalizing of reason for the express purpose of imagining and describing multiple modes of being, feeling, and knowing in the world. This knowing brownness of the world is, more nearly, participating in a shared sense of brown.

The uproar over Sonia Sotomayor's now-infamous line, one she repeated in a few academic contexts over a span of about five years—the assertion that she hoped that a "wise Latina woman" might reach better conclusions than white males without the same experience—points to calcified opposition to the convergence of particularized (in this case gendered and ethnic) experience and wisdom and its loose cognates, knowledge and reason. For many of us who have been toiling in the fields of race, sex, and other minoritarian modes of knowledge production, the right's rancor reads as a strange validation of the resonance and significance of our shared project and the potential disruption and challenge it continues to represent. A partial de-universalizing around wisdom, a particularizing of reason, was a very controversial and exploitable proposition. Certainly, it cuts to the core of so many debates that structure our political moment. The conservative attack suggested that a Justice Sotomayor would rule from a position of empathy and experience, the realm of the affective, and not the law with all its nominal claims to objectivity and universalism. While critical legal studies may have handily dismantled legal discourse's objectivism as a system, the juridical still authorizes itself as blind to particularities of being-in-the-world like race, class, ability, or sex.

Within the right wing's framing, empathy, emotion, and the particular are wisdom's other. Briefly reading within the right's protocols of argumentation, I want to think about the epistemological circuits that Latinas and other nonuniversal subjects participate in as a kind of otherwiseness. This idea of the otherwise is partially indebted to the work of recent theoretical interventions in critical race theory such as Kandice Chuh's framing of an anti-identitarian Asian American studies based on a mode of critique that eschews the subjects and calls for a collective understanding of ethnic particularity through the project of imagining otherwise.[2] Equally important is Rey Chow's notion of a "coercive mimesis" that understands ethnicity itself as a captivity narrative, one that is compelled upon the minority subject within capitalism.[3] Legal theorist Richard T. Ford understands this phenomenon in terms of a minority subject's "compelled performance" before the law.[4] Both Chow's and Ford's paradigms are grafted onto a Lacanian analysis in Antonio Viego's important *Dead Subjects: Towards a Politics of Loss in Latino Studies*.[5] Through Viego's lens, the affective performances of Latina otherwiseness represent what he would call the hysteric's discourse, a discourse that potentially interrupts the compelled performances and coercive mimesis that structure reality for racialized subjects.[6]

The conservatives' attack fell short, and Justice Sotomayor's nomination was approved 68 to 31. This essay considers Sotomayor's performance on the stand and, concomitantly, the performance of those Republican senators who questioned Sotomayor. The event that is Sotomayor's confirmation is one in which two different performances of public affect collided. My interest in the Sotomayor case is not based on sustained interest in legal or court history. Disappointment did not overwhelm me when Sotomayor proved not to be a particularly progressive juror, since I never estimated that her accession to the court would prove to be a radical challenge to the normative forms of subjectivity produced by U.S. law. In my estimation, the Sotomayor confirmation hearing and eventual confirmation did nothing to loosen the binds of coercive mimeticism that tie Latinos to flattened-out regimes of identity.[7] None of this is to suggest that the Sotomayor confirmation was not a laudable event. Indeed, it is mostly a good thing when segregationist barriers are broken, but such modes of integration can too easily be celebrated as a disordering of institutions of power when that is simply not the case.

Instead, I look to this case in an oddly comparativist fashion by looking at a slightly unpredictable precedent to Sotomayor's interrogation, Andy Warhol's *Screen Test #2*. I turn to this avant-garde precursor to the major court case for a few reasons. Chief among them is an impulse to link Latino popular culture and politics with aesthetic traditions that intrinsically challenge the coercive mimesis that so hampers Latino and ethnic studies. Mario's mimesis, her performance of affective particularity in the face of playwright Ron Tavel's show-business grilling, tells us another story of brownness that is not a heroic fable, but, instead, an account of a canny performance of otherwiseness in the face of majoritarian scrutiny. I also want to stage this clustering of historically unaligned examples to offer a sense of brownness as sprawling and vast; the sense of brownness I am writing through is an account of different pieces, across space and time, touching but not fusing.

When asked by Gerard Malanga to name his greatest superstar, Jack Smith named Mario Montez. When asked why, Smith responded that it was because the drag superstar "immediately enlisted his audience's sympathy."[8] Montez was a central figure in the New York avant-garde of the 1960s. He was born René Rivera in 1935. Legend has it that Montez was a

10.1 Screen capture of *Mario Banana*, 1964. Directed by Andy Warhol. 16 mm film.

Puerto Rican, a sometime civil servant who was born into an extremely Catholic family. Montez met Jack Smith, the mother of the New York underground. Montez and Smith were briefly involved. They shared a love of Hollywood B movies. Their great icon was Dominican spitfire María Montez, who was most famous for her exotic over-the-top persona and movies like *Cobra Woman* (1944), which have become official camp classics. Smith selected Montez's name as a tribute to the screen goddess. Montez met Warhol through Smith, and the drag superstar went on to make several films with Warhol.

One of those first films, *Mario Banana* (1964), represents a conflation of tropicalism, sexual innuendo, and musty glamour.[9] The piece speaks beautifully to a mingling of the quotidian and the exotic, the everyday rhythms of life, where the ordinary (eating a banana) and grand extravagance collide. Both trashy and avant-garde, the film renders Mario Montez's particular art drag persona. Mario inhabits the over-the-top style of the already exaggerated spitfire, lovingly reimaging her way of being in and out of the world at once. Mario's look is equal parts glamour girl and clown. Her act of eating a banana is equal parts lascivious and corny. The viewer's eyes are drawn to the glimmering brooch on the diva's headpiece, its luster, reflective and absorbing. The short film tells a story, like Mario's face itself, of another style or mode that is not just outdated but maybe partially out of time, albeit also off key, like the singing Maria Montez did on stage and screen. These are all aesthetic pulsations from the realm of a brown otherwiseness where so many people and things actually linger and dwell. It is portrait of life as the virtuosity of not really being virtuoso.

This leads us to the film at this essay's center. *Screen Test #2* was made in 1965 and featured Ronald Tavel, the founding playwright for the Theatre of the Ridiculous, interviewing legendary drag performance diva Mario Montez.[10] Tavel is never on camera in the film, but he is constantly heard as he auditions Montez for the role of Esmeralda in a proposed remake of *The Hunchback of Notre Dame*. It is telling that Tavel sets the stage for Montez's performance of affective particularity as he begins his inquisition by asking the diva how he feels.[11] He responds breathlessly, "I feel like I'm in another world, a fantasy ... like a kingdom meant to be ruled by me, like I could give orders and suggest ideas." Montez's opening gambit is a dreamy insistence on feeling otherwise, a certain belonging to a world where he is not subordinated because of his position in the social, but instead exists in a sphere that is "meant to be ruled by [him]" and where he gives orders and has ideas. Some would describe Montez's lines as a merely delusional fantasy of escape, but such a reading would be missing something in the drag diva's breathy structure of address. He knows his historical condition but chooses to perform and act otherwise, insisting on inhabiting a fantasy and making escapism not an act of avoidance but the signaling of an otherwiseness.

Tavel indulges this vibe for quite a while, lauding Montez's performance oeuvre in films by Jack Smith and Ron Rice. Things eventually turn ugly when Tavel insists that Montez repeat after him, "For many years I have heard your name, but never did it sound so beautiful until I learned you were a movie producer, Diarrhea." The juvenile gag plays on for a while as Tavel attempts to get Mario to repeat the word "Diarrhea" as many times as possible. Montez, always in ingenue mode, plays along. As the drama progresses, Tavel directs Mario to pretend he is a female geek who has bitten the head off a chicken, to show how he will seduce her male costars, dance a gypsy dance while sitting down, scream in character, display how he can be both sad or evil using only his eyes while half his face is covered by a veil, and repeat a story about choking his pet python. Montez weathers the verbal indignities that Tavel fires upon her. He responds to all these prompts with her face alone. All of this abuse is within the game. Tavel disrespects and ridicules, and Montez responds by performing a kind of spacey obliviousness while playing along. A line is seemingly crossed when Tavel orders the starlet in training to lift his skirt. He is next instructed to unzip his fly, stare at his penis (which is never shown), and comment upon it. Montez seems not to be enjoying this treatment but never stops playing along. The whole film leads to a fantasy bubble almost, and yet never quite, bursting. Mario never stops being Mario; if anything, she becomes more brazenly himself by never losing "herself." Tavel oscillates between flattery, supplication, and mean hectoring.

One can see this as a familiar tale: it is like the tale of a transgender working girl who tolerates her exasperating john. Tavel's producer is like the john who might like a transgender sex worker who might like what we can describe, in a euphemistically somewhat hackneyed fashion, as something extra down there. Montez plays it not so much as a deluded transvestite but, instead, as a knowing professional who understands just how to follow his script, which always includes the reluctant revelation. Despite or maybe because of the general force field of hostility projected onto Montez, he emerges a radiant superstar, one who has dramatically, despite Warhol's minimalist framing and Tavel's performance abusiveness, emerged as the survivor. It's said that everyone loves a true survivor, and Montez seems to be cognizant of this fact.

My plot summary is based on my own notes from two viewings of the film and, importantly, on Douglas Crimp's careful reading of the film in his essay "Mario Montez, for Shame!" Crimp's article initially appeared in *Regarding Sedgwick*, an anthology of essays that employed Eve Sedgwick's critical writing to address different research sites and projects.[12] His article is also part of his monograph *"Our Kind of Movie": The Films of Andy Warhol*.[13] The aforementioned essay employs Sedgwick's important work on shame and queer performativity that was ultimately published in the volume *Touching Feeling*.[14] Crimp marks Montez's performance of shame and its central and formatting force in regard to queerness. The essay works with the Sedgwickian (via cognitive psychologist Silvan Tompkins) framing of shame as affect that is located in both the self and other. The theory of shame shows us how the other can so easily flood one, especially if one is a shame-prone person. Crimp identifies the somewhat tautological framing of the shame-filled person as someone who knows shame by having been shamed. Thus, Crimp gives an account of the shame that floods the viewer who watches Tavel's rough treatment of Montez. Crimp explicates: "Shame is both productive and corrosive of queer identity, the switching point between stage fright and stage presence, between being a wallflower and being a diva, so too it is simultaneously productive and corrosive of queer revelations of dignity and worth."[15]

This description is reminiscent of Sedgwick's description of Warhol's own affect, in her essay "Andy's Shyness, Andy's Whiteness," where she narrates Warhol's shyness as the kind that could paradoxically fill up a room.[16] Mario's shaming at the hands of Tavel floods Crimp, according to his account of his own spectatorship. He suggests that this film's narrative speaks profoundly of our most universal encounter with otherness. That particular moment, the moment when affect "floods us" as a powerful and formatting force, is what I find most useful about Crimp's account of *Screen Test #2*. Crimp's reading offers a specific case of shaming, that of a Puerto Rican transgender performer, in order to offer a general account of how shame functions.

In *Cruel Optimism*, Lauren Berlant describes her own relation to case studies as one in which a specific case is used to speak to the general, what she describes as an interest in "generalizations," an interest in "how the singular becomes delaminated from its location in someone's story or some locale's irreducibly local history and circulated as evidence of something shared. This is part of [her] method, to track the becoming general of singular things."[17] Berlant goes on to discuss how after case studies become "delaminated" and generalized, they hopefully resonate across multiple scenes of the specific. Crimp's reading is only a partial becoming-general insofar as it functions as a pretty specific evidencing of queer shame, yet the specificity or singularity of a Puerto Rican subject's racialized shaming is not reflected upon. This is one of the reasons why Crimp's reading of the film has not been without controversy. Latino studies scholar Lawrence La Fountain-Stokes denounced Crimp's reading first in an open letter to Crimp distributed on the internet, and later in an essay in the anthology *Gay Latino Studies*.[18]

I wish to comment on this controversy while clearly demarcating why I bring up La Fountain-Stokes's pointed criticism of Crimp. I am not interested in championing Crimp or La Fountain-Stokes in this debate. I am indebted to Crimp's reading and, in general, to his crucial research on Warhol. Yet, as the reader will see, my reading diverges from his in that I do not fully subscribe to his shame reading and wish to offer an alternative. I certainly feel an affinity with many of the political impulses that animate

La Fountain-Stokes's reading of *Screen Test #2*, yet I also want to offer an alternative to his reading. I will briefly narrate this clash between critics not because I am choosing a side, but because I intend to call attention to what I see as the neglected question of what I will describe as the affective performativity of *Screen Test #2*, which is to say, the affective doing that the film accomplishes. La Fountain-Stokes's criticism of Crimp happens in the frame of a larger misgiving about the trend in queer theory to theorize queer shame. La Fountain-Stokes is deeply skeptical of the potential utility of queer shame as a category for queers of color, who, in his opinion, must pursue validation in the face of the systemic social harm directed at them. Queer shame, in his estimation, is deeply antithetical to both queer of color critique and the lived politics of racialized sexual minorities. (He describes my own writing on the topic of queer shame as "slightly jaded," but he goes on to blast Crimp, Michael Warner, Sedgwick, and the organizers of a queer shame conference held at his home institution, the University of Michigan.)

I have some disagreements with La Fountain-Stokes on the topic of queer shame, a concept that I have found useful in my own writing about race and sex, yet nonetheless I feel extremely simpatico with the politics that fuel his writing. I disagree with him on the "difference" that shame makes. La Fountain-Stokes attacks Crimp for not dwelling on Montez's particularity as a Puerto Rican or, in Berlant's terms, for moving toward generalization at the expense of specificity. For La Fountain-Stokes, the approach to Montez through the route of anything but pride and uplift in the face of adversity can only be seen as disappointing. I, more in sync with Sedgwick, find queer shame to be incredibly descriptive of the affective contours of queer of color and brown particularity. What I am calling brownness includes the ways in which brown people endure, strive, and flourish in relation to systemic harm. Brownness's conditions of possibility are the ways in which brown folks harness the shame directed at them, at one moment rejecting it in favor of shamelessness, and at different moments occupying shame as a copious and generative affective register. Crimp's analysis is doomed to disappoint La Fountain-Stokes's project due to the Puerto Rican scholar's deep investment in the positive affect that is associated with a particular queer Puerto Rican identitarian pride. I find the choreography of radical otherness that Crimp traces in Montez and Tavel's stylized, macabre dance to be illuminating insofar as *Screen Test #2* is a story about Mario's evanescence and weird brilliance under duress. From my perspective, the account of queer relationality that the Warhol text and Crimp's explication of it provide is instructive and useful, especially in the rendering of otherness that it makes possible. The deployment of shame as a category of analysis is antithetical to political and scholarly agendas that demand positive affect and the continuous rehearsal of rigid identitarian framings.

While shame as a category might disappoint some linear political projects, it nonetheless provides a vivid and useful description of the affective and quotidian reality of queers of color and brown people who actualize their singular and plural senses of the world through, with, and against shame and shaming. Shame can be and often is generative of desires, erotics, pedagogies, survival strategies, and striving skill sets that are evidenced daily in the actually lived experience of queers of color and other brown people. Yet shame has its limits. In Crimp's reading, "poor Mario" is overwhelmed by shame and affectively beaten down. The shaming of Mario fills Crimp with shame in the same way it fills La Fountain-Stokes with anger. Both of these responses to the film are equally valid. When considering the working of affect, it is important to remember that it is always in flux. Shame transforms to anger and then to pride faster than the blink of an eye. The reverse order is equally true. While pride in one's singular and pluralized experience of the world is nothing like a bad thing, it is certainly not the only thing. Describing any scene or situation as being dominated by one affective signature risks missing out on the possibility of offering a nuanced account of art or life. This aspect of my critique then extends to Crimp's reading too. Insofar as I agree that shame and shaming are deeply formatting of queerness, they are not the singular or even privileged affect node. We need to cast a fuller picture of affect's volatility in relation not only to spectacle but also to the quotidian. If we revisit Berlant's methodological point about the specific, we are able to consider the ways in which Crimp's reading of the case of *Screen Test #2* disappoints as a theoretical generalization for La Fountain-Stokes, because it is unable to resonate with other specific scenes of gay Latino shaming.

Then there is the question of performance. Crimp describes the feeling of shame that floods one while watching *Screen Test #2*, and La Fountain-Stokes insists that the correct affective response to the film would be anger, an anger that is directed at both Tavel and Warhol, the exploitative white males he perceives to be film's authors. (In my estimation, author effect in Warhol's films, especially the *Screen Test* films, is much harder to account for since the mostly improvisational performances captured by the camera shape these films much more than acting shapes traditional narrative films.) While I see the work that shame does, I think it is important to foreground that Montez and Tavel are performing their roles. Certainly, these roles may mirror their lived relationship to some degree, but it would be folly to think it is their actual relationship. Crimp discusses how Warhol described the Montez/Tavel interaction as being very "real." But let us consider what the performance does. It certainly may feel very real, and Tavel's forcing Montez to reveal his biological gender is certainly a tense and dramatic moment. This moment is, nonetheless, about a set of twice-behaved behaviors:[19] the process we are watching is a form of performative mimesis. It is real in that it is really interesting and compelling. If mimesis is the imitation or representation of aspects of the sensible world, especially human actions, in literature and art, and if coercive mimesis is a form of mimesis that conforms to a fixed and set repertoire of behaviors often associated with ennobling narratives of uplift and pride, then the drama staged in *Screen Test #2* by the three people whom I think of as being the three collaborators on the piece (Warhol the unconventional director, Tavel the scenarist and off-camera voice performer, and Montez the improvising on-screen performer) is one that interrupts the narrative protocols associated with a static understanding of identity. It is a performance of dreaminess and indignation.

Indeed, I think performance is exactly the language to discuss what Montez is doing. I want to assert that while Warhol's films, like Jack Smith's cinema, stand as invaluable filmic texts, they also serve as wonderful documentations of many performance practices that would otherwise be all but lost to us. So while they are not live performances, they are crucial documentations of the live. Mario performs a kind of affective otherwiseness that is conveyed as a mimesis that resists the coercive strictures of normative gender, and in doing so allows the viewer to consider the perfomativity of the performance, which is to say the kind of doing that performance accomplishes. In my reading of Tavel and Montez's engagement with each other, I see them both performing a kind of excess that is rich with agency. This excess might be something that we can preliminarily describe as camp. At one moment in Miss Montez's audition, Tavel asks her to scream in the way that Esmeralda would. Montez screams for quite a while, even after Tavel attempts to hush her. When we think of these screams, we can begin to associate them with a tradition of screaming and shouting as musicality. Mario's scream is the diva's scream, and as such it is revelatory of the ways in which sonic performance might shatter the strictures of an objectifying mimetic protocol. Fred Moten discusses a tradition of female blues improvisation as signifying what he calls "the resistance of the object."[20] This resistance of the object is the central move in what Moten calls a black radical tradition. Of course the object need not scream to resist. Sometimes the object resists by vamping and camping in the way that Montez does in so many of both Warhol and Smith's films. Let me add that I do not mean to view the performances as resisting the filmmakers so much, since I see both Warhol and Smith as, to call on the colorful language of addiction, enablers par excellence. What I think is being resisted in these avant-garde films by these odd queer men is the kind of compulsory performances of sex and race that annihilate people every day. What the films and the performances show us, in part, is how to live and feel these scripts differently. We can view *Screen Test #2* now and see it as a counternarrative for being and feeling brown, both in the face of whiteness and on its own terms. Montez's performance of affect displays a kind of sly agency that would not be visible or desirable to a certain scholarly or activist lens determined to see the world in black and white. I posit that such a black-and-white agenda does little for the project of brownness or brown feelings.

As I suggested at this essay's onset, I saw a lot of Montez and Tavel in the summer of 2009, during the Senate confirmation hearings for Sonia Sotomayor. Certainly, it can be said the Republicans made her speak quite a bit of diarrhea. They made a point of having her sell out her own sponsor, Barack Obama, by saying that empathy had no place in legal judgment and that only reason and the law should ever be applied instead. This split many on the left. I am myself of two minds on the question. The skeptic in me saw this speaking of diarrhea as the quickest and safest path to confirmation, while the idealist in me felt that there was something profoundly wrong about selling out empathy and the world of emotion and particularity it represents. It's important to note that Sotomayor has been a moderate justice whose rulings have not especially pleased the various left constituencies that lobbied on her behalf. Thus the point is not to lionize Sotomayor but, instead, to understand the performances at the heart of her confirmation hearings and connect them with the brown performances of otherwiseness I have discussed in relation to Montez and will go on to link to the work of another wise Latina performance artist.

When asked about the judge's impending nomination, the Republican senator from South Carolina, Lindsey Graham, said Sotomayor would be confirmed if she avoided a "meltdown." Meltdowns have traditionally been the province of women and ethnics, even though the last few years of public culture have been replete with fascinating white male meltdowns. (It seems that women and people of color no longer own that.) Pledging allegiance to feelings is dangerous. In a *New York Times* op-ed regarding the confirmation hearings, Maureen Dowd wrote that "any clever job applicant knows...

you must obscure as well as reveal, so she sidestepped the dreaded empathy questions even though that's why the president wants her."[21] Watching those hearings, I could not help but think of Montez and Tavel's mock interview and the very real one being televised. Many of us who felt any commonality with the judge understood that the game being played was like the dynamic between trans hustler and the john who knows but doesn't want to know. In both cases, the players kept to the script. The trans hustler and john script is a consensual fantasy that saturates popular media and lived cultures of public and commercial sex. In the case of Sotomayor and the hostile senators, a weirdly analogous fantasy of knowing and not knowing was being enacted on a national stage. For some political observers, the proceedings did not entertain. Frank Rich, another *New York Times* columnist, declared that as political theater the confirmation hearings "tanked."[22] Rich was looking for drama to rival the Clarence Thomas/Anita Hill affair. I would bet that Rich would not get Warhol's films either.

The Sotomayor confirmation hearings, with all the Republicans' bumbling attempts at getting her to reveal a true self, were a kind of theater of the ridiculous. The flattest of the jokes was the senator from Oklahoma's bad Ricky Ricardo impersonation when he addressed the judge by saying she had some "'splaining to do" in relation to her reasoning regarding gun control legislation. Sotomayor's response to the flat-footed and ethnically disparaging comment was minimalist. Unruffled, she briefly laughed at the senator's joke and quickly picked up her testimony again. She maintained a slightly bemused smile throughout, refusing to take any of the bait during the hearing. This not taking the bait was the performance of insisting on enacting another world, a world where she is allowed to "give orders and have ideas," which is, of course, the world that her adversaries were actively working against. It is a performance of coolness or even iciness in the face of adversity. Like Montez, Sotomayor refused a performance that her inquisitors were attempting to coax out of her. Instead, she did something else, in much the way Montez did decades before the confirmation hearing of 2009.

How does a wise Latina respond to that kind of ignorance cloaked in power? I think that remains an open question. But certainly a case worth studying is Sotomayor's icy performance, her refusal to be intimidated or to have a meltdown. Looking at Sotomayor's interview, we notice a weird resonance with Montez's performance of an aloof spaciness; that is not to say that iciness and spaciness are the same thing, but that they both represent an antianticipatory response to dominant affect, a feeling, a performing and being otherwise. And thus I offer the cases of Sotomayor and Montez as examples of the performance of otherwiseness, which is to say the sort of wisdom in and through feelings that can potentially enable us all to negotiate many of the hostile interviews that life offers us. These examples of otherwiseness are manifestations of an ontopoetics of brownness as an alternative sense of the world that perform an alternative mode of sharing.

As an epilogue of sorts, I want to quickly turn to Nao Bustamante's most recent performance project, *Personal Protection*.[23] The project begins, on a very immediate level, as Bustamante's response to her participation in the 2010 reality show *Work of Art*. Following the model of other reality competition shows like *Project Runway* and *Top Chef,* a sequestered cast of contestants participates in weekly competitions wherein they are gradually eliminated based on their performances. Each week, cast members/contestants who are deemed by a panel of "expert" judges to have underperformed are sent home. While *Work of Art* was supposed to feature new, emergent artists, the face of Nao Bustamante was familiar to many interested in queer and Chicana performance art. Bustamante is an established artist whose work has been written about by many queer cultural and performance theorists. Her participation in the show seemed to be a performance of infiltration, not unlike that of her older video *Rosa Does Joan*. In *Rosa Does Joan*, Bustamante inserted herself into Joan Rivers's TV talk show of the early 1990s as the character of Rosa the exhibitionist. In this most recent infiltration, however, Bustamante was instead playing and competing as herself. From week to week, Bustamante was competing against mostly younger artists, and it became clear to many that the show was interested in "discovering" the next great art star. It also became increasingly clear that this would be a young, naive, "natural" talent ready to be molded. The judges finally settled on Abdi Farah, a young African American artist from Philadelphia. Bustamante was the favorite contestant of many who were familiar with her work and with queer Chicana aesthetics. Her aspirations of winning were thwarted in the fourth episode when Bustamante was cut in a surprise double elimination round along with the show's only out gay male contestant.

Work of Art went on to become a much straighter affair after the elimination of Bustamante. That fourth episode featured famed censored Latino artist Andres Serrano, who joined the regular panel of judges, all of whom, unlike Serrano, represented middle-of-the-road art world sensibilities and tastes. It is telling that Serrano was the only judge who appreciated Bustamante's installation—a strange, abject piece that featured the artist in a makeshift, dilapidated hut-like structure and a costume that oozed primal-looking brown fluids. The piece visualized what could perhaps be imagined as a rendering of wounded subjectivity. During the judging of contestants segment of the show, Bustamante, half in character and refusing to take off her disturbing costume, was eliminated by the regular judges, who could not get the artist to spoon-feed them a description of her work that appealed to their commercial sensibilities. Like many shows of these types, editing practices attempted to identify contestants with certain tag lines. Bustamante's was taken from a response to one of her previous judging sessions where she explained that she was "not responsible for [the judges'] experience of [her] work." Of course not being responsible for their experience of her work set the stage for her eventual elimination. Bustamante came off as sullen, slightly resentful, and unwilling to please, unlike winner and model minority Abdi Farah.[24] Bustamante was literally mired in the ooze of a seemingly primal, festering wound that she refused to let go of. In this way, we might think of her as Wendy Brown's resentful queer, female, or racialized subject who is desperately caught in *ressentiment*'s web.[25] But such a reading would be wrong insofar as the television show was a singular appearance in Bustamante's performance practice.

Her follow-up to her appearance on *Work of Art* is an ongoing piece titled *Personal Protection*. *Personal Protection*'s first manifestation is as an object: it is a handmade dress composed entirely of the supposedly bulletproof polymer Kevlar. The dress is fashioned to look like the kind of gown worn by femme Mexican resistance fighters. It includes multiple layers of Kevlar fabric, a flower-like corsage adornment made of the fabric, and an extra apron layer adding to the piece's matronly look. The dress represents the manifest desire to be bulletproof in relation to the harsh interviews and evaluations the minoritarian subject must constantly endure. The garment is the literalized veil of otherwiseness that insists on another mode of being and feeling in the world. It is not difficult to imagine Mario Montez slipping into a version of the gown or Sotomayor sporting a Kevlar robe on the bench.

In a video that is the project's next component, Bustamante and a local upstate New York gun enthusiast "test drive" the dress in an open, snow-covered field by shooting it with rifles and ammunition of different calibers. Bustamante plays with the gun hobbyist, getting him to talk about the fantasy of shooting Mexicans. But it is important to remember the dress is not meant to simply be a target; it is meant to perform a certain kind of resilience to threats and obstacles that punctuate existence for so many. The dress perhaps signifies something like a previous wounded attachment to female Mexican resistance fighters, and also a response to the symbolic violence visited on Bustamante by *Work of Art* and its judges.

10.2 Installation view of Nao Bustamante, *Soldadera*, 2015, at the Vincent Price Art Museum. Photograph by Monica Orozco. COURTESY OF NAO BUSTAMANTE.

Wounded attachment is a phrase that I lift from Wendy Brown, not to evidence it or shore it up, but instead to offer a critique of Brown's formulation. Brown famously argued that "politicized identity thus enunciates itself, makes claims for itself, only entrenching, restating, dramatizing and inscribing its pain in politics; it can hold out no future—for itself and others—that triumphs over this pain."[26] Are the spectacles of Montez getting berated by Tavel in *Screen Test #2* and of Bustamante being shot at by a gun nut examples of minoritarian subjects basking in the political impasse that is their "wounded attachments"? What about the national drama of Sotomayor's televised confirmation hearing? Is *Personal Protection* a ressentiment-laden piece of art that dramatizes the injuries of Latina women within the social? Brown offers a structural account of all the ways in which attempting to think about the singularity of particular struggles within the social can never get to the point of a politically salient generalization. Like Berlant, I contend that work that starts out in the key of the particular—let's say art and media that signals the abuses that Latinas and Latina femininity endure within North American culture and politics—can become more generalized without ever losing its resonant specificity. This ability to resonate is key, and in this way we can once again understand the difference that affect makes. The structural booby traps within the social that Brown warns us against are fueled by a belief in a pervading feeling of Nietzschean ressentiment dominating not only the actions but also the strategies and tactics of social actors who do not automatically displace the particular or the singular for the general or universal.

Brown's theory of the impasse that she describes as wounded attachment depends on a belief in a stable and rigid affective field. But certain affective responses, especially unanticipatable ones, performed through the modes of comportment and behaviors that I have described as the wise Latinas' repertoire of brown otherwiseness, inherently suggest something else. They suggest another kind of response to social wounding than the repetitive and unthinking attachment that Brown diagnoses as the problem plaguing the politics of many people, many of them brown, who reject an aspirational universalism. The example of Bustamante's dress, one associated with her Mexican heritage, being repeatedly shot at again by the gun enthusiast, may visually cohere to some aspects of Brown's theory of wounded attachment, but it differs in some crucial ways. Bustamante's performance aesthetics play with the idea of being a perpetually wounded subject trapped in the impasse of what amounts to a stalled singularity. But the artist's work symbolically breaks off from Brown's idea of wounded attachment through her unpredictable response to this wounding. Bustamante goads the shooter to keep on firing. After the dress has been shot up, she inspects the bullet holes and gleefully reports that the Kevlar has caught the bullets and that she would probably have survived if she had been in the dress. She engages the visibly confused marksman, who reluctantly agrees that she probably would have survived.

Bustamante, like Montez and Sotomayor, the otherwise Latinas I have discussed, refused to take responsibility for the experience of those who would pass judgment on her. Her work represents the refusal of the compulsory mimetic performance that is often thrust upon the minoritarian subject. Otherwiseness is a performance of affective noncompliance that is intrinsically linked to a sense of brownness that Jean-Luc Nancy would describe as simultaneously being singular and plural.[27] Our sense of singularity is only knowable in relation to the sense that is produced in relation to the plurality of singularities that constitute the world. Feeling brown is an aspect of a larger sense of brown that is simultaneously singular and plural. It is through feeling that we know, or more nearly sense, the brownness of the world and each other.

11

Brown Worldings

JOSÉ RODRÍGUEZ-SOLTERO, TANIA BRUGUERA,
AND MARÍA IRENE FORNÉS

This chapter circles around three sites of what I want to call brown worlding. Performance has been described as an opening to other worlds, a passage to alternative realities, as a way to build worlds that are contestatory, oppositional, or merely alternative. These ideas of the world-making capacity of performance are ones I have engaged in, contributed to, and certainly do not want to reject *tout court*. I have used the idea of queer world making as a way to discuss the ways in which queer performance enables projects to construct and fabricate queer worlds in the face of an almost universal impulse to snuff out queer potential. But in this book, I suggest that the world is brown, albeit a brownness that has been obscured from us. Within the contours of this argument, I suggest that performance is a mode, a protocol, a path toward an attunement to the brownness of life and the world. To that end, I want to talk about three performance projects that have attuned us to the brownness of the world in a copious and expansive fashion. These three performance vignettes are not laid out as culminating examples that prove an argument. Instead, they are meant to touch and resist a certain archival impulse to master them. They are examples of what I am calling brown worlding in that they give us insight into the brownness of the world.

To become attuned to the brownness of the world is to see what is here but is concealed. It is a sustained practice of seeking, finding, and, again, touching an aspect of being with and in the world. Naturalism and realism are modes that falter in their attempts to depict or describe the brownness of the world, because that attempt at capture, at mimetic rendering, is always incomplete, but rarely owns its incompleteness. Realism or naturalism are too direct in their aim to take the measure of the brownness of the world. I am therefore interested in an attunement to brownness, its atmospherics and affective vicissitudes. This attentiveness is not undertaken in the spirit of what mastery might yield, but is, instead, an attunement to brownness as partial, incomplete, and not organized in relation to a hermeneutics dedicated to foreclosure. It is about the unfolding of a particular sense of the world that performance promises. Knowing brownness is not about mastering data, though data itself can be an aspect of brownness, but it is instead to sense the allure that is the brownness of the world. Thus, I offer three shards of a larger and continuous world of what I understand as the performance of brownness, calling on three works that barely resemble each other but nonetheless belong to brownness.

Burning Brown

LBJ was a performance by José Rodríguez-Soltero, a Puerto Rican–born New York avant-garde filmmaker and artist. The event took place at the Bridge, an experimental theater located in New York City's East Village, on April 8, 1966. Rodríguez-Soltero's performance, while not exactly an act of queer failure, was more of a shambolic queer spectacle. Rodríguez-Soltero appeared on stage carrying a live chicken, which he hung upside down from the beams above the stage. The artist then ordered a reluctant audience to abandon their seats as he and his performers, many queer downtown artists associated with the famous Theater of the Ridiculous, prepared to hop the rows of seats, mimicking soldiers storming barricades as they reached the orchestra. Audience members who had been reluctant to vacate their seats jumped out when Rodríguez-Soltero screamed that he would not be responsible for the audience's safety unless they got up. As the lights went out, the invading drag stars began their march through the seats. This act was scored to the year's top pop song, "Ballad of the Green Berets," Staff Sergeant Barry Sandler's musical ode to invading American troops. Rodriguez-Soltero also rushed the stage carrying a flag. Once on stage, Rodríguez-Soltero taped an old forty-eight-star American flag, with the letters LBJ written across it, to an asbestos screen. After several failed attempts, he was finally able to light the flag on fire. It was reported that a man in a dinner jacket stood up and denounced him as a "Pinko Fag" while others took clear delight in this very camp yet strident queer protest art. The performance was roundly denounced in the press, and the eighty-eight-seat Bridge theater had its license revoked for flag burning, which was, at the time, a federal offense only in Washington, DC, but was still in violation of lesser state and city ordinances in New York City.

Rodríguez-Soltero's *LBJ* is an example par excellence of the kind of queer performance I dwell upon in my writing. Certainly, it's a moment of chaotic queer experimentation, the staging of an alternative contestatory being in the world. It's an experiment in unrepentant pinko fag ridiculousness that is not content to think about atomized and provincial sexualities and instead enacts vaster commons that are insurrectionist in their orientation and aspirations. This highly theatrical queer and brown performance is more than a war protest if one considers its various components: a chicken positioned for sacrifice, representing a tropicalized imagining of Santería and other syncretic Caribbean religions; an old flag representing the nation before Hawaii and Alaska's incorporation; the burning in effigy of the U.S. president most associated with the atrocities of the U.S. visited upon the Vietnamese people; queer actors storming the stage to a militaristic pop tune. I do not want to read this event strictly as queer performance. I want to read it as performance manifestations of what I am calling a sense of brown. Thinking about Rodríguez-Soltero and his work as brown pulls from queer critique and postcolonial theory to understand the expansiveness of a world that is deeply brown in divergent and convergent ways.

Let me try to describe my usage of "brownness." I have felt some dissatisfaction with the term "Latino" and all its permutations, including, but not limited to, Latino/a with the slash or the sometimes popular but, for me, graphically displeasing Latin@. Instead, I have opted to do the work of Latino/a studies under the sign of an old and vague term: brown. Deb Vargas has recently noted many scholars, including Curtis Marez, Ralph Rodriguez, and myself, using brown as an alternative to Latino. Vargas herself uses it. Brownness makes one think of the brown power movement or brown berets, and I do want those connotations to remain intact. But brownness is more than those particular histories and the identities that are congealed to them. It is important to clarify that my uneasiness with Latino or adjacent designations like Chicano, Nuyorican, or hyphenated terms like Cuban-American is not simply a post-structuralist rejection of identity. The fact that identity is one of the primary conceptual vessels we travel life through, in all its frustrations and pleasures, despite its obvious incoherencies and undeniable resonances, is not in dispute. Instead, I want to describe something that I am calling a sense of brown for a few different reasons.

I want to think about a capacious sense of brown that is, in its very nature, methetic. "Methexis" is the aesthetic term that describes how the particular participates in a larger form; in Greek tragedy, it literally means group sharing, accounting for the way in which an audience takes part in a drama, adding to it, augmenting it.[1] Brownness is an efficacious alternative because it permits us to think about how some people's sense of brownness may potentially touch other people's sense of brownness. Brownness is not so much a singular understanding of self as fundamentally additive, knowing that singularities are always part of vaster pluralities.

With this stated, I do not want to muddy the particular sense of brownness that might touch the edge of meaning associated with another sense of brownness. There are certainly connections between brownness and mud that are actually exhilarating to think about. (I will get to the brownness of mud later when I discuss María Irene Fornés's short play *Mud*, a work that also arrives at a rendering of the various modes of violence that punctuate brown life in North America, but through a set of different dramaturgical itineraries.) The brownness of people over here and over there is not converging. I do not suggest that people are equally brown, but that they can productively be conceptualized as being beside each other. Vijay Prashad, when describing the predicament of South Asians in the United States, revises Du Bois's title into *The Karma of Brown Folk*.[2] Instead of conflating the brown folks that Prashad writes about with the brown forms of life I want to describe and write on behalf of, I want to think how different kinds of brownness touch but do not fuse. Brownness as a grounded experience, for a brown commons, is often borne out of what we could call a shared sense of harm, following John Dewey. But it is not just harm; it is also the shared flourishing that transpires and unfolds despite and in the face of systemic harm.

Brownness in my thinking is one opening among many, different circuits that are not there for the purposes of forming some grand assemblage. These circuits are copresent, and an attentiveness to them might offer us an alternative sense of the world, a sense of our being with brownness which is ultimately the sense of brownness. The ways in which my sense of brownness converges with what I have defined in *Cruising Utopia* as a queerness that is not ontologically fixed are many. But there is one crucial difference for me. I suggest queerness is in the horizon, forward dawning and not-yet-here. Brownness diverges from my definition of queerness. Brownness is already here. Brownness is vast, present, and vital. It is the ontopoetic state not only of people who live in the United States under the sign of *latinidad*, but of a majority of those who exist, strive, and flourish within the vast trajectory of multiple and intersecting regimes of colonial violence.

In her review of Rodríguez-Soltero's performance, Nancy Weber, an assistant editor at the amusement desk for the *New York Post*, wrote that she was "[physically], spiritually, morally and aesthetically oppressed."[3] The multiple modes of oppression that Weber registered in her response to the performance could certainly describe the experience of Puerto Ricans in New York City then and today as they experience disproportionate poverty and widespread racial profiling programs like the NYPD's notorious stop-and-frisk program. But the kind of oppression that so shocked Weber must have also described the experience of planetary recipients of U.S. foreign policy both in the 1960s and today. Weber's personal injury and the language she chose to represent it might help us understand the weird efficacy of Rodríguez-Soltero's spectacle as an act of brownness. In this performance, a queer Puerto Rican artist set an old American flag on fire in a stuttering theatrical spectacle and through that act asked the audience in attendance (and those who experienced the event through its performative reverberations) to think about the ways in which one queer act across decades and continents might acknowledge and even signal a provisional mutuality, a productive friction, and an incomplete touching, that all add up to the sense of a brown world.

The Brownness of Poverty

The world of the brown is not collapsible with the reality of those whose lives are marked by diminished life chances within capitalism. Yet those who suffer and attempt to survive under such circumstances raise the question: Can one touch poverty from the space of humanities and not attempt to master it, to know it completely, to resist the Marxian axiom of total illumination, which brings every social relation into sharp and cutting focus? The mode of touching I am suggesting is not full contact or full mimetic capture, but instead, an attempt to access a sketch of a life or lives and acquire a sense of those on the other side of one's outstretched arm. It is a truism for me that poverty is racialized. More specifically, the world of migration that new residents find themselves in is a hostile one where their legality and legitimacy are always questioned, and the life chances they are able to access are, for most, marked by poverty. My approach to brownness is a comprehension through surface touching, a mode of partial knowing as opposed to mastery and masterful knowing. My refrain in this chapter is that "the world is brown" and our challenge is to attune ourselves to this aspect of worldliness. I don't mean brown at the expense of other resonant propositions around blackness, Asianness, indigeneity, sexuality, or gender. Certainly there are many white worlds. But the syntax of my statement, *the world is brown*, is meant to insist on a version of the world that is occluded with regularity. In part, I make the effort to say the world is brown to respond to the loose lips of the punditry that saturate our mediatized sphere of cognition. One in four Latinos lives in poverty according to the census, and we are of course left to wonder about the various undocumented U.S. Latinos who did not fill out their census forms. Poverty is not an effect of a brown world. The brownness of the world is partially known through the poverty that partially engulfs it (this is some of the data that is also of brownness). John Dewey contended that groups often find cohesion through a shared sense of harm. While brownness's cohesion is not only formatted through a real sense of harm, a question lingers as to how we can think and do otherwise, how we can touch across brownness considering all the impediments that are anchored in place.

The great Marxist thinker Cedric Robinson makes an interesting argument about Marx's rejection of an older socialist tradition. Robinson wrote, "Where once dispositions of power, property and poverty had been viewed as affronts to God's will and subversions of natural law, for Marx they were the issue of historical law and personal and class ambition. Thus, though Marx was familiar with heretical rebelliousness (Martin Luther, the Anabaptists, etc.), in his economic work he more frequently drew upon secular dramatists (Dante, Shakespeare, Goethe) and pre-Christian literature (Sophocles, Thucydides, Plato, Xenophon, Aristotle) as source[s] of ideas contrary to bourgeois thought."[4] Robinson closes his book by suggesting that Marx's work would have been different if he had taken seriously the socialist and often utopian thought that came before him. The thinking he rejected might have better oriented him toward describing the material effects of racism, imperialist excess, and the abrogation of the rights of women. Marx makes his point clearest in "The Poverty of Philosophy" where he takes apart Pierre-Joseph Proudhon's idea of "utopian socialism."[5] For Robinson, Marx's turn toward a citational practice that leaned on theater and drama over more avowedly philosophical texts that eschewed any mysticism, much less mysteriousness, led him to an economic theory that would, for instance, dull his understanding of imperialism. Robinson's proposition is an interesting one, suggesting that Marx's turn to a scientific reason was too eager to cast out a notion of divinity or vitalism that would have functioned better, at the very least, as a partial engine for contemporary socialism. Robinson's argument is persuasive, but I think Marx's scientism and his rejection of previous utopian lines of thought is not a product of his turn to drama and poetry. Indeed, it is just the opposite: a certain turn to the ways in which performance attunes us to the world is potentially an opening, not a closing.

Certainly, so many enemies of the most basic socialist principles cling to a religiosity that they have twisted into a shape that undergirds their own social world. Robinson is a thinker in a radical black tradition who contemplates what our materialist thought would look like today if scientism had been avoided and other, older investments in the collective, in being-with, a different kind of communism, had been taken up. His thought instructs me when I consider the poverty that is so tethered to brownness.

Cuban-born artist Tania Bruguera is an acknowledged art star. Her work has been on display at many biennales, art fairs, and museums all over the world and can partially be described as a performance of institutional critique. One poignant example of her brand of institutional critique was her August 27, 2009, performance in Bogotá, Colombia. The performance was part of the Hemispheric Center for Performance and Politics, a semiannual *encuentro* sponsored by NYU and funded by noted U.S. funding agencies like the Rockefeller Foundation. Audiences who entered the packed studio encountered three speakers, all political dissidents, representing three different protest factions. They spoke in academic panel formation. The speakers' lectures at first disappointed most of the audience, who were expecting edgier work by the controversial artist. Her public's disappointment soon dissipated when an assistant walked around the audience with a large platter full of cocaine. Soon the audience divided. Many spectators sampled the narcotics, which were deemed "very good," according to some participants. Some denounced the artist, the performance, and audience members. Bruguera appeared on stage only once to thank the Colombian people and shut down the performance. The artist was attacked in *El Tiempo*, the national paper, and accused of illegal acts. She soon had to vacate the country before formal charges were issued. The conference itself was hijacked. Almost every panel and working session became a meeting about Bruguera, giving most people multiple opportunities to denounce the artist. For her part, Bruguera explained that her larger statement was being lost. Her piece was in part about the drug trade that decimates Colombia.

But she also wished to address a fractured right-wing political system. It was meant to speak to the hypocrisy of how narco-economies and official state economies are often aligned. It also was a critique of the conference itself, which imported U.S. students to Colombia for a ten-day event that used Colombia as a political backdrop. This brief description of the Bogotá performance is meant to offer a sense of the artist's work and the international controversy it generates.

One of her subsequent projects generated a decidedly different interest. This project was titled Immigrant Movement International and was a collaboration with Creative Time and the Queens Museum of Art and ran from 2010 to 2015.[6] Bruguera used her grant money to open an international headquarters for Immigrant Movement International, where she and her paid staff offered workshops and events to the local community that included, but were not limited to, human rights film screenings, English language classes, and free legal clinics. She lived on minimum wage in Corona, Queens, with a group of other artists. She authored an immigrant rights manifesto and a contract. As one can imagine, this work was met with great skepticism, especially from people who actually provide these services to immigrants on a full-time basis. In the *New York Times*, Andrew Friedman (who works for an immigrant advocacy group in Queens) was quoted as saying that he was "kind of allergic to the heroics" the project represented.[7] Bruguera took all her skeptics seriously: she freely admitted that the project had a 99.9 percent chance of failing, that there were so many pieces and that so much could go wrong. In *Frieze* magazine, Kathy Knoble asked Bruguera if she worried that she was creating "a kind of theatre out of someone else's existence."[8] Her response was terse: "This is not theatre. I am making the private realm public." She continued, "The focus should be on the conditions these people are forced into because of their status as immigrants. It is very hard to lose one's privileges, but maybe if more artists practiced that once in a while we might have better art."[9] Statements like Bruguera's inspire anger in many, perhaps not in the same way the cocaine performance did, but certainly with the same kind of passion. Bruguera describes her work as *arte util*, roughly translated as "useful art," and concisely described by art historian Claire Bishop as denoting "a conjunction of political action and illegality—understood here as pushing against the boundaries of what those in power describe as legal and acceptable, and being willing to embrace the criminal if necessary—so that [it] might achieve something in the social field (be this civil liberties or cultural politics) as well as taking a position within the long history of such artistic gestures."[10]

Friedman described Bruguera's project as containing an escape button. When the project is over, she will most likely take on the vestments of privilege that she has forsaken for a few years. But is that enough to delegitimize Bruguera's work on its own? It may be too easy to align her work with a more orthodox and rational scientific socialism, but perhaps it makes sense to contrast it with a different mode of brown artistic production that attempts to address poverty. This address, central in Bruguera's arte util, imagines an art project that may be at times indistinguishable from practice. Bruguera labors to imagine a response to the injustices, or shared feelings of harm, manifest via the drug economy and the abuse of immigrants, through a mode of performance that attunes us to the feelings of harm that render the world brown not only as shared harm and suffering.

The Brownness of *Mud*

As a way toward a conclusion, I want to briefly discuss the work of María Irene Fornés, who, like Bruguera, was born in Cuba. Fornés is considered a great American playwright and less often thought of as a brown or Latina one. Indeed, Fornés was never very comfortable with being thought of through rigid logics of racial or sexual identity. When I make a case for the brownness of Fornés or her play *Mud*, it is not dependent on the facts of her identity. There is something brown to Fornés's language. It may be her resistance to the capture of Anglo-American theater's prevailing discourses of realism and naturalism. But I think of her language, which is both strangely minimalist and excessive, as a kind of illegitimate speech, to invoke Jacques Rancière. Illegitimate speech is a theoretical scandal where every event, among speakers, is tied to an excess of speech in the specific form of a displacement of the statement. It is "an appropriation 'outside the truth' of the speech of the other . . . that makes it signify differently."[11] This speech is clearly on display in *Mud*, a two-act 1983 play that featured three characters: Lloyd, a seemingly neurologically damaged man who is married to Mae, a woman who relentlessly irons and goes to night school to acquire literacy and basic math, and Henry, the man who displaces Lloyd in her bed. Henry is a literate man who lets Mae imagine an outside to the quagmire of poverty and illiteracy that she dwells within. Henry allows Mae, for a time at least, to imagine and feel something else. Mae soon discovers that her new love is as dishonest as her former lover, who continues to share a shack with them. Mae's main motivation to move out of the mud that surrounds her is the sense of constraint and limitation she feels while tethered to both these parasitical men. She desires something else; she needs to move beyond. Mae imagines a life outside of the ramshackle muddy world of the play. When yelling at Lloyd, she makes sure to tell him that he will die in the mud while she will die wrapped in white, in a hospital, cared for. Her aspiration, the good life that beckons to her, is the good life of a white death, lifted from a brownness that is no longer sustaining. Mae wants out of the mud and squalor but meets a predictable and sad death as she attempts to flee, to turn her back on her problematic lovers. Her final speech, the play's last burst of dialogue, goes like this: "Like a starfish. I live in the dark and my eyes only see a faint light. It is faint and yet it consumes me. I long for it. I long for it. I thirst for it. I would die for it. Lloyd I am dying."[12] Mae's speech renders a picture of what it means to be lost in a brownness, to feel isolated and not in sync with the brownness of a vaster brown commons. *Mud* is not a story of being with but, instead, a story of being without.

Concluding with *Mud* makes the case that attunement to the brownness of the world is an attunement not only to the striving of Rodríguez-Soltero and the protest of Bruguera, but also to the suffering of brownness and the ways in which persistence can and does falter. Taken together, seen as touching, these examples of brown performance open us up to seeing and perceiving the different ways that the world is brown.

The Sense of *Wildness*

THE BROWN COMMONS AFTER PARIS BURNED

I commence this chapter with some reflections on the conceptual and historical dimensions of the philosophical and historical story of a particular sense of brownness that emerges today: what I am calling the moment After Paris Burned. To make this case, I open with a consideration of trans in a recently translated book of feminist queer trans theory. I move from those textual speculations to two events that offer a prehistory of *Paris Is Burning* and its subsequent historical legacy.

"Transgender" has become a key word for many. It describes various quotidian transmigrations of being and body. Transgender speaks to both new and historically recoded biopolitical struggles. Surely, there is a need for accounts of transgender experience writ large. With that said, it seems important to state that this is not what Paul Preciado offers in the book *Testo Junkie*.[1] This is not to say that Preciado does not contribute to the understanding of the newness and historicity of transgender life, but that the book does so through different, frequently enthralling, yet never direct routes. *Testo Junkie* is a call for what Preciado calls a "new pornopunk philosophy . . . [which would allow us] to think about doing something while we are on the way out, undergoing mutation or cosmic displacement."[2] Such a philosophical endeavor is necessary for what Preciado calls the pharmacopornographic regime in which we strive. The pharmacopornographic regime comes on the heels of a disciplinary order: control no longer comes from external technologies of subjectification. Instead, in this new moment, the technologies that shape life become part of the body, and dissolve into us like the testosterone gel that *Testo Junkie*'s narrator dissolves in his skin. But the point isn't that the body in this regime is without resource or potential. That's not the case insofar as in each body, there is a resource of orgasmic force. Preciado describes it as the power to produce molecular joy, and therefore a productive power. This is akin to labor power, which Marx described as potential or ability. According to *Testo Junkie*, today's mode of laboring, which he locates most resonantly at the contact zone between the global porn and pharmaceutical industry, is not immaterial labor, as Operaismo's inheritors would have it, but it is instead a kind of uber-material labor. As Preciado colorfully describes it, "Let's stop beating about the bush and say it: in a porn economy, there is no work that isn't destined to cause a hard on, to keep the global cock erect."[3]

Testo Junkie can be thought of as a diagnostic account of the history and futurity of trans in the age of savage porn punk capitalism. The book tells this story through wild oscillations between philosophical meditation, sociocultural history, and memoiristic writing. At times, it's a breathless history of the mutually formatting categories of "sex" and the "pharmaceutical" since the 1950s. At other intervals, it is an arresting story of loss; the book's structure of address is mostly predicated on a beloved and beguiling dead friend. *Testo Junkie* is a story of being-with: being with testosterone, being with an at times omniscient object of desire, named VD and described as an Alpha Bitch Femme, but it's also about being with one's bulldog Justine. The dog's name is an ode to the Marquis de Sade, and the book is certainly influenced by Sade. But it is, indeed, a story of being-with, and there is something of a frenzied politics and ethics to Preciado's book.

Gilbert Simondon, the philosopher of ontology, technics, and collectivity, described ethical action as a mode of amplification. Ethical comportment is to act with the self-knowledge that one is "a singular point in an open infinity of relations."[4] This is to construct what Simondon commentator Thomas LaMarre described as "a field of resonance for others' acts or to prolong one's acts in the field of resonance for others; it is to proceed on an enterprise of collective transformation, on the production of novelty in common, where each is transformed by carrying the potential for transformation for others."[5]

The "trans" of *Testo Junkie* is the fact of this mode of transformation, but not exactly an invitation to transformation. It is a call to an attunement to our transformation. In the penultimate chapter, Preciado does not call for recognition as much as attunement, an understanding of one's process of transindividuation in relation to others and objects, especially pharmaceutical objects that abound in every aspect of contemporary life: "My ambition is to convince you that you are like me. Tempted by the same chemical abuse. You have it in you: you think that you're cis-females. But you take the Pill; you think you're cis-males, but you take Viagra; you're normal, and you take Prozac or Paxil in the hope that something will free you from your problems of decreased vitality, and you've shot cortisone and cocaine, taken alcohol and Ritalin and codeine.... You, you as well, you are the monster that testosterone is awakening in me."[6] Here, again, I read Preciado with Simondon, to get to a very specific idea of being-with that I think is essential to both the terms "trans" and "brown," as I am working with them. After a stage of metabolistic preindividuality (Simondon takes much of his language from the natural sciences), a moment of transindividuation comes into play. For Simondon, the transindividual is defined as the systematic unity of interior (psychic) individuation, and exterior (collective) moment. This formulation, the transindividual, like the subject and its others, its ecological fields, its lines of object relations, resonates with what Simondon calls a real collective.[7]

Simondon helps us give an account of a being-with that is intrinsic to both trans and brown, consisting of objects, human and otherwise, that are browned by the world, or taken up by the discourse of trans, in what Preciado calls the cold pharmacopornographic era. This is to imagine a brown commons, transrelationality, and what Simondon would call the real collective. The brown commons is predicated on a certain mode of methexis, a word derived from ancient philosophy, that accounts for modes of doing and participating and group sharing that follows mimesis. Methexis is not the opposite of mimesis. Mimesis being the representing or imitation of life, methexis calls attention to a different procedure, a different component. It is a moment in which partition between the performance and the audience lifts or frays and a kind of commons comes into view that is not made by the performance. Methexis is often roughly translated as participation, of which a common example in Plato is the way that the beautiful object participates in the larger category of beauty. Certain objects, be they human actants or nonhuman and inorganic ones, including objects that are considered immaterial, like sounds, for example, be they musical or distinct accents, participate in what I call brownness or the sense of brownness. The brownness of a commons, its very nature, is the response to salient forces that have rendered circuits of belonging and striving within the world brown.

The work of Wu Tsang has become a touchstone for me in thinking about contemporary art practice that follows a queer methexis, which is one important path to what I am calling a brown commons. In this chapter, I will arrive at Tsang's work after considering some thoughts and performances that orbit around the brown commons that I see Tsang so elegantly illustrating. To do so, I first want to travel back to an event, a performance, which resonates as queer, transgender, brown, and so many other things.

It's 1973, four years after the Stonewall Rebellion. Sylvia Rivera takes the stage at a rally in New York City's Washington Square Park called Gay Is Good. Rivera was famously there the night of the riots when she, along with other transgender bar patrons, mostly black and Latino, resisted arrest during a routine raid on gays in the West Village bar. This story, the tale of gay power's revolutionary impulse, in its desire to see and be something else, is a poignant one that is canonical in LGBT studies—so much so that Stonewall was mentioned in the same breath as Seneca Falls and Selma during President Barack Obama's 2013 inaugural address.[8] Despite its status as a now-iconic site of uprising, the fault lines at the base of the gay movement were always in place, and Rivera always made a point of bringing them into a view. An early video camera captured moments from the Gay Is Good rally and displayed the fractiousness of gay politics and gay life at the time. Approximately four years after Stonewall, Rivera holds the stage during the rally and lashes out at those in attendance who choose to neglect the plight of queer and transgender people in prison, people who routinely experienced rape and other forms of violence. Rivera wears a snug body suit and clutches a hand-held microphone that she has pulled off a stand in an awkward gesture. She paces the stage in a restless fashion. The primitive black-and-white video footage decomposes during several moments of the activist's speech, as though the early technology could not capture Rivera's rage, her righteousness. The camera momentarily shifts to the audience of assembled queers, who at first attempt to shout her down. Some demand that she shut up. But Rivera is unrelenting. She will not cede the stage; she will not be silenced. Rivera makes demands not for her own sake but for the sake of others. Her words are a clarion call, not in that they bring a commons into existence, but in that they call on an already existing commons to do something, to take action, and to also expand their ability to attune themselves to the world.[9]

Rivera speaks of the weekly letters she and her group, STAR (Street Transvestite Action Revolutionaries, founded in 1970 by Rivera and Marsha P. Johnson), receive from incarcerated queers who suffer and experience a heightened level of systemic harm while incarcerated. She demands that the assembled gay masses acknowledge those who belong to a queer commons that is coming into view but is not fully visible. Certainly, scenes of dissent and contestation are critical to the task of knowing our commons. Rivera's speech can easily be understood as a statement that emerges from this moment within a burgeoning gay power movement. But it is also a moment when a brown commons comes to know itself. Fanon famously wrote about how one is blackened by the world.[10] Both adjacently and often coterminously, people are browned by life. The logic of Fanon's argument is resonant with John Dewey's assertion that groups are called into existence by a shared sense of harm. A commons is not an assemblage: it includes various things or pieces of things gathered into context and bringing about multiple effects. What I am describing as a brown commons exists, but we are not always attuned to it. Or sometimes we only encounter it within the register of the singular. This singularity, as Jean-Luc Nancy crucially argues, cannot be properly apprehended independently of its plurality.

I do not invoke Sylvia Rivera and her public performance of 1973 as an example of how Latinas and other people of color have been at the center of the gay liberation movement. That is an argument that was powerfully made by Gloria Anzaldúa more than twenty years ago.[11] It is evident that queers, or *joteria*, are at the center of liberationist movements. It is also important to know that Rivera's performance is more than a mass dressing down, more than the public shaming or calling out of the privileged white middle-class mainstream. Instead, I am positing Rivera as a thinker and activist who labored tirelessly to unconceal the profundity of our being-with. When you listen to Rivera's words, you can hear her demand that her audience think and that they open themselves to the understanding that there is something expansive to the commons, that they, those in attendance, are only a segment of something vaster. Yes, harm organizes their compresence with each other in the park, but they are part of something more capacious. The audience seems to be with Sylvia as she growls the letters that spell out gay power. Certainly those who are with her have drowned out the voices asking her to shut up. But they are only allowed this moment of methexis, this moment of group sharing and belonging, after they have thought of the commons that includes those beyond a proximate presence. Rivera was often known to chant, "Power for *all* the people." Rivera must amend the slogan "Power to the people" because "the people" as a construct often allows for the forgetting of many who belong in and to commons, people who are obscured or jettisoned because their being in common is less palatable. This commonness is less knowable in advance. To think of a brown commons is to imagine a commonness that does not always avail itself in advance, a commons that has been concealed by its browning in the world. This methetic brown commons represents a joining, but not the joining that is most easily apparent—let's say the being-in-common of that predominantly white audience facing that stage under Washington Square Park's large white arches that afternoon in 1975. It is about imagining one's singularity in relation to a plurality that includes bodies being incarcerated and brutalized on Rikers Island, two miles from the island of Manhattan.

To think of the brownness of the commons is not to think in terms of the equivalent. Within a commons that is organized by a shared sense of harm, people do not experience the same degree of harm. Indeed, if harm is that thing that collates our experience of being-in-common, then not all people are equally browned within the world. This book has given an account of brownness from the perspective of Latinos in North America who have been browned by law, browned by migration, browned by diminished life chances within capitalism. (It should go without saying that all racialized and poor populations face diminished life chances.) The sense of brownness is larger than something like *latinidad*. Indeed, it is planetary in its vicissitudes, and a full account of it is hard to imagine. Within brownness there is something that is shared, incommensurable, yet common. Brownness is not queer, as the example of Sylvia Rivera shows us. Brownness and queerness, like other vectors of particularity, such as blackness, indigeneity, Asianness that also structure my theorization, all comingle, are adjacent, sometimes provisionally interlocking in situational commonness. Attuning ourselves to the brownness of things that have been occluded is worth considering because it allows us to see the fullness of our commons, both singular and plural. Much has been written about the queerness of Sylvia Rivera, but so much less time has been spent attending to her brownness in the world and what it meant and did.

Rivera's work has been taken up with zeal by a younger generation of thinkers and activists like Dean Spade, who helped found the Sylvia Rivera Law Project, a group that provides invaluable assistance to many transgender people who often fall out of more popular narratives of queer group belonging, often because of the ways in which the world has blackened them or browned them. I am drawing on the work and activism of Tourmaline, a black queer transgender activist intellectual who liberated the tape of the

1973 rally from the Lesbian Herstory Archives. (The tape was originally posted to her Tumblr.)

Wu Tsang's work can be considered alongside the work of Spade and Tourmaline, all queer artists, intellectuals, and activists challenging queer thought to follow the lines pioneered by Rivera and Johnson when they founded STAR. These thinkers in the tradition of STAR (later Rivera would reconstitute STAR, changing the name from Street Transvestite Activist Revolutionaries to Street Transgender Activist Revolutionaries) are committed to a new methetic turn in queer and transgender work that strives to offer a more expansive consideration of mainstream sexuality politics. This generational cohort's work always strives to transmit the brownness of queerness's commons.

Wu Tsang, along with her friends Ashland Mines, Asma Maroof, and Daniel Pineda, started a performance party at the Silver Platter in Los Angeles's MacArthur Park section in 2008–10. Later, that event, the founding and running of the party and the director's aspiration to make it a safe space for transgenerational transgender contact, was documented in Tsang's film *Wildness* (2012). It tells the story of an art project that attempted to catalyze what I would call a brown commons within the metropolis. I use the word "catalyze" in that last sense quite intentionally. I mean catalyze as in start, commence, bring something into action. *Wildness* the film resists many of the protocols of realist documentary. It narrates the story of Los Angeles's Silver Platter, a long-standing Latino gay bar that catered to the local gay community and featured old-school trans and drag performers. Tsang and her three initial collaborators, all younger queers of color, punks, and artists, took over the bar's less populated Tuesday night slot and hosted a party featuring edgy queer performances by the likes of Nao Bustamante, Dynasty Handbag, Zachary Drucker, and countless other performers. These performers would otherwise most likely never perform in that space, which has been dedicated to a different kind of transgender performance. The documentary tells the story of the Silver Platter through interviews with the bar's proprietors, regular patrons, and those who would become Tuesday night's denizens. The film includes talking heads and performance documentation, but it also attends to the larger urban ecology that surrounds the space by including adjacent histories of anti-immigrant and queer violence. *Wildness* also features the bar itself as a speaking persona who narrates the ebbs and flows of brown life that traverse its walls.

The film opens with a shot of LA streets and traffic, not the glamorous Los Angeles of television and movies but the Los Angeles of workaday life.

The opening visual is shot from a car; streets are lined with minor plots of commercial space; small businesses fill out these little strip malls, lined with the seemingly ubiquitous Los Angeles doughnut shop; a blue neon sign announces "carnitas" over one restaurant. A mysterious voice-over has been narrating these first opening images to a heavy and ominous-sounding drum-driven score. In Spanish, the voice says, "Time is borrowed and it changes everything. Faces, relationships, and neighborhoods. There are not many like me left. And I wonder what will become of me?" Viewers eventually realize that the throaty feminine voice is not that of a person but of a place which holds and shelters brown life within its walls: the Silver Platter. The camera slows down long enough to focus on the back of the head of a figure walking away from the camera. Another cut, and we encounter the filmmaker/artist Wu Tsang's face, looking up at some source of illumination. Long before humans begin to take primary roles in the documentary's unfolding narrative, we witness a commons of lights, shadows, places, commerce, buildings, trees, and more. It is not until a brown commons is visualized as street, ambience, light, and movement that the documentary's protagonist can come into view. Viewers encounter the bar's glimmering sign, its luminous old-school beauty suggesting another time and place. The first three shots are scored to throbbing *cumbia* as the space erupts with dancers. Nicol is at the door charging covers, stamping arms while drinks are poured, and people circulate within the spaces. The film cuts to the world outside the bar. Gone are the glittering lights of an alternative everynight life, and instead people are shown standing around on a corner outside the establishment. Then a cut to a gorgeous shot of the emptied bar, where smoke and lights twirl, giving the space a beautiful otherworldly effect. Then the viewer encounters the women of the Silver Platter, who introduce themselves, tell us where they are from, describe life at the Silver Platter, and generally revel in the spotlight.

The Silver Platter's voice and Tsang's self-narration tell the story of the bar. It is interesting to note that their narratives are rarely aligned. Tsang makes observations about her experience of the space and their stories. She talks about desires for opening up the bar as a place that could potentially link generations of queer and especially transgender people. Tsang's narration, as we will see, also worries over the potential pitfalls of a project of actualizing the expansive potential of the Silver Platter. But with that desire to expand comes a possibility for danger, the chance that the bar's status as a safe space that accommodates many could perish. Tsang worries a great deal about the potential traps in this venture, and the bar counters her concerns by debunking the idea of a safe space, insisting instead that no one person can simply decide who and what is included in a vibrant historical common space like the Silver Platter.

The logic of the safe space does not easily hold to a place and a situation like that of the Silver Platter. The Silver Platter is a space of encounter and swerve, and it has always been so. The Silver Platter is a meeting place for many kinds of people. Its materiality is a turbulent thing. One figure in the film, Betty, discusses the ways in which the onset of the Wildness party was met with great disapproval by many of the regular patrons, who felt neglected and ignored by the new attendees. She and many of the regulars refuse to call the night Wildness and just call it *el martes*, Tuesday. Betty thinks that the crowd looks like kids from the university, boys and girls whom she describes as American and white. Nicol, the doorwoman, has a very different response. The new crowd excites her. She explains that mingling with people outside her immediate community gives her a vaster sense of belonging to the city and the nation. She remarks that despite their differences, they share something, perhaps sexuality.

There is no consensus. The commons is not a space for that. To be of the brown commons is not to be in sync, or to be lined up; conflict and disagreement are central to the commons. The film attempts to document a larger art project: the staging of a party by Tsang and three other younger queer artists of color, at least one of whom identifies as transgender, attempting to forge coalition with predominantly working-class or poor Latina transwomen. Certainly, the artists are not wealthy, but they do manage to do that thing that many cash-poor but well-educated young artists do—they live a life beyond their actual financial capital because of the other forms of capital (chiefly cultural capital) at their disposal.

The rich urban ecology of this brown city is highlighted by shots of the faded neighborhood. The Silver Platter herself explains that MacArthur Park has many layers. She discusses how the economy collapsed in the 1970s and 1980s and how the influx of Latin American migrants and political refugees influenced the environment. Despite urban revitalization projects, the rents are still cheap, and that is what brings Tsang and her friends to the area in the mid-2000s. Once arriving in their new neighborhood, the young artists meet Gonzalo, Koky, and Javier, the men who work at the bar daily. Gonzalo inherited the bar from his brother Rogelio, who had owned it for decades. The three men are supportive of the Tuesday night party, and the influx of new visitors is financially beneficial.

Tsang explains that at the Silver Platter she finds the sisterhood she was searching for in the bar. She seems to form an especially meaningful bond with Erika, with whom she does not share a language. Erika is a small person with a dreamy look in her eye. Tsang explains, "I can't explain what I felt with Erika. My dad never taught me to speak Chinese." She describes how this lack of language was always a missing piece and how it is now the way she feels closer to people. It is this thing that is missing for Tsang, knowable as inability to communicate one's situation and history, a certain muteness in the face of one's history that draws her to Erika and the Silver Platter in general. It is for this reason that the force of a kind of brownness beckons. Tsang and Erika do not fuse. They feel each other's allure. Their relationality is not predicated on a complete and uncomplicated being in common but instead on a mysterious being-with. During the voice-over about their bond and inability to communicate through conventional means, Tsang and Erika are shown hanging out, rolling around in bed together, much like the title of Cherríe Moraga and Amber Hollibaugh's famous dialogue of 1981, "What We're Rollin Around in Bed With: Sexual Silences in Feminism," wherein the authors discussed their differences along lines of butch/femme, race, and class.[12] Moraga and Hollibaugh discussed the silences that saturate butch/femme, cross-race, and cross-class dyke sex and relationality, a language of commonality through sex that is displaced by a second-wave feminist discourse that eschews the language of power differentials among women. In the case of Erika and Tsang, language cannot capture their communication, their allure, as two transgender people communing and being in common without the linguistic fusion of a full-blown dialogue. An iteration of the film was shown as part of the 2012 Whitney Biennial and titled *The Green Room*, an installation that attempted to re-create the Silver Platter in the art space. That installation featured an enhanced perspective on Tsang and Erika's communication. That two-channel video, *Que pasa con los martes?*, offers deeper insight into Tsang and Erika's weird relationality. Tsang sits in bed with Erika and some other women, bodies wrap around each other, and looks are exchanged. On one channel, Erika recounts her treacherous migration to Los Angles and describes the life she encountered at the Silver Platter. Glamorous Erika wistfully reflects on her life in LA, but the installation juxtaposes the treacherous trail she has traversed and the dangers she has encountered. Tsang's installation keeps these stories in dynamic tension. Her own mysterious being-with Erika is not permitted to elide the real material experience of dangerous and fraught border crossing.

In a conversation after a screening, Tsang talked to me about how she once used the term "brown" to describe what was happening at the space on an internet forum, which led to criticism in the comments section for using that word. She was sarcastically asked if "Asians are brown now." I hope I have made it clear that in my deployment of the term, Asian can potentially be just that. Not in a way that inhibits our thinking of a critical Asianness or even a yellowness; but a brownness that is a copresence with other modes of difference, a choreography of singularities that touch and contact but do not meld. Brownness is coexistent, affiliates, and intermeshes with blackness, Asianness, indigenousness, and other terms that manifest descriptive force to render the particularities of various modes of striving in the world. Brownness is larger than the U.S. Latino-centric rendering I am offering. Latino lives are one portal into this attunement to the brownness of world I am calling for. Brownness is certainly larger than the sets of experiences that some groups of Latin American immigrants and their children experience in the U.S. as racialized minorities. Thinking brownness is not an easy path; it is most certainly a contested, debated, and productive route. We cannot foreclose the brown commons' reach or its potential.

The *Wildness* project has one gleaming intertext: Jennie Livingstone's *Paris Is Burning*. Tsang completed a performance for camera that was commissioned as part of the Performa biennale in 2012. In preparation for *For How We Perceived a Life (Take 3)* Tsang researched Livingstone's 1990 film at the UCLA archives where interview transcripts, negatives, and outtakes are stored. The artist considered the camera one of the performance's characters. The performance is not the documentation of a live event but a performance for camera. Tsang imagined the performer troupe as doing a kind of séance that was summoning the ghosts of the film's past. *For How We Perceived a Life (Take 3)* was shot on 16 mm, the same format as *Paris Is Burning*. The duration of the piece is exactly the length of a 400-foot roll of film. Tsang attempted to create the effect of continuous reality emerging out of a fractured one; thus the piece was shot as a single take with no editing. She used take 3.

The film plays continuously on a 16 mm loop (the head is spliced to the tail). There are very specific installation instructions for the piece: the projector is behind a visible wall, and it projects through a hole that is cut out of the wall. At one point in the film, one hears the reperformed voices of Octavia St. Laurent, Venus Xtravaganza, and a very angry Crystal LaBeija.[13] The dancers converge in a huddle on the floor, displaying a touching and being in common that at first may look like an indeterminate mass. However, it soon becomes clear that they do not fuse; instead, they switch roles, swap positions, fall in line, disassemble, confront each other, and practice soliloquies that so many young queer and transgender people must have memorized at home somewhere once they stumbled on the film online, at a video store, or maybe even in a classroom. It is important to remember that *Paris Is Burning* is a canonical film for queer studies. Everyone from bell hooks to Judith Butler has something to say about it. It is curricular. It is taught regularly.

Coming of age, Tsang and the generational cohort I mentioned above were familiar with the film, as many queer people today are. Numerous queers watched *Paris Is Burning* because it promised a world, glimmering and glamorous, tinged with criminality and discord, haunted with the specter of tragedy. So many learned the word "shade," as in "throwing shade," from that film, and while that phrase is not new, its descriptive force has not waned when discussing contemporary queer of color life. It is also true that it is another tragedy of the commons. But in the case of the commons of black and brown bodies that the film represents, it was not a vague civilizing enclosure that threatened the queer ecology of the commons. It was, instead, something else, a story of pandemic and poverty that enclosed and nearly snuffed out this queer world.

The voices and words in Tsang's film are familiar for those who have lived with *Paris Is Burning*. The ball circuit now exists as an international phenomenon in many cities throughout the world, in no small part due to the distribution of Livingstone's canonical queer text. Tsang's film is the story of a brown commons (which is also a black commons and a queer commons) that persists beyond the meager life chances that its participants negotiate. It is an account of a persistent brownness. In a later clip, Tsang uses transcripts from the UCLA archives to re-create an interview. The difference in these reperformances is that Livingstone's exchange during the interview is not cut out. The fan of *Paris Is Burning* hears the familiar citations from Livingstone's film but also hears something else: Livingstone's questions, which solicit these fantastic speeches. It feels revelatory to hear Livingstone's words, cut from her documentary and now conjured from the trash bin of history. Indeed, much of the criticism of Livingstone's film amounted to a critique of the director for not including her own white queer lesbian voice in the film. Livingstone has gone to the balls, won the confidence of her interview subjects, and is encouraging them to make the extravagant statements they make.

The point of inserting Livingstone back in the narrative is not to out her as nonobjective. The reenactments of the interviews show the kind of touch that I think is at the center of this mode of organization, which I describe as a commons. It is useful to see how Livingstone too lived and thrived in the commons of the ball culture, found a kind of touching that let her know her singularity as always plural. This clip also explains Tsang's rationale for inserting herself in all the *Wildness* project's various iterations. Tsang is at the center of the party, the documentary, and every other iteration of *Wildness*. Indeed, Tsang helped organize La Prensa, a free legal clinic for the women of the Silver Platter and the local community to help with their immigration and other legal issues. Spade was also involved with this effort. La Prensa was staffed with volunteer queer lawyers who wished to somehow be of assistance, and the Wildness party's promoters chiefly organized it. For Tsang, the women of the Silver Platter, and the performers in *A Life Perceived*, this desire to be with, and to be alongside in the face of the various enclosures that consume us, is all part of why the language of commonness takes shape. This move to practice our commons otherwise, to know the brownness of the world despite the impediments that manifest themselves as enclosure, is a necessary project of dis-enclosure. Our commonness is here and it is now, and we know it when we look at and feel the logics of enclosure and harm. But rather than buckling to the force of this encroaching threat, an attunement to the brownness of the world promises an unboundedness that is not knowable in advance. Instead, it functions, stridently and beautifully, as the queer dis-enclosure of a brown commons. This mode of dis-enclosure is the attunement that Sylvia Rivera demanded throughout her difficult life of struggle. It is also a return or resurrection of the voices of Venus, Octavia, Crystal, and all those who insisted on wanting more despite the ways in which their chances at achieving this full life were radically diminished, and in part constituted, through this diminishment. Young queer bodies, moving for another 16 mm camera, over twenty years later, reoccupy these lost voices. Tsang's artistic practice responds to these lines of radical thought and expression within the gay movement that persists in the ways in which the brownness of the world persists. This is to say that the capacity for striving in the face of potential and actualized harm is manifest as the salient call for "Power for *all* the people."

Vitalism's Afterburn

THE SENSE OF ANA MENDIETA

What is attempted when one looks for Ana Mendieta? What does her loss signify in the here and now? More importantly: What comes after loss? What is the afterlife of a violent and tragic end, a crash, resonating across decades and felt through that which remains not only after violent cessation, but also after an art practice that was attuned to the frenzy of experience marked by historical dispossession? In this chapter, I suggest that Mendieta's art practice was saturated with an intense vitalism, a concentrated interest in life itself. Work about life itself is often most poignant for its ability to represent death-in-life. This said, it is certainly important to strive for a perspective where one sees and feels the work detached from any singular life, no matter how tragic it might have been. But at the same time, it's difficult to do insofar as many today still feel a mysterious sense of connection to the work, to Mendieta, and to the various historical coordinates that allow us to locate her, or at least make that attempt. For some, Mendieta's work is experienced through a shared sense of feminist outrage and mourning; for others, the central point was her poetics of the primal and its emphasis on blood, fire, wood, and earth as medium; for others still, hers is a story of displacement and exile; for still others, it is all about the accounts of her small brown female body manifesting itself in a field of possibility dominated by often hostile white men. It's all of these potential nodes of attachment with the work and the artist that I index under the term "brownness."

In the introduction to a graphic novel on the life of Ana Mendieta, Lucy Lippard asserts that even though she was a white Cuban, Ana was in fact "Brown."[1] This is to say that even though she was born to a well-to-do family who were white in Cuba, her life in the United States had made her feel anything but white, and indeed all her sense of self was composed of feelings of alignment and commonality with others who found an important resource for self-description in the term "people of color." Lippard easily describes Mendieta as brown. In her case, this is a personal reflection about a deceased friend, and she need not theorize that sense of Mendieta as performing, radiating, enacting, and being brownness. This is the project that I take up in this writing. I wish to offer an account of life lived as brownness, attending to the mimetic practices that help one encounter brownness. Mendieta's work poignantly offers us access to a sense of brownness.

The slogan "Where is Ana Mendieta?" famously emerged during a 1992 protest outside the opening of the Guggenheim Museum in SoHo. The phrase was featured on one of the banners held by the approximately five hundred protesters outside of a group show that included the artist Carl Andre, who had been accused of murdering Mendieta, his wife. Those words were a cry of feminist outrage, a call born out of militancy. The question spoke to a moment where the politics of representational and actual lived modes of violence collided. But it is more than that. It's a question we ask for the purpose of making sense of Mendieta's work, life, and death. Such an undertaking often, as in the case of her death, seems like a futile attempt to make sense of the senseless, but indeed this impossibility of (making) sense may be one of brownness's most salient characteristics. It is imperative to constantly reassert that while Mendieta's work powerfully vectors with her biography, it most certainly cannot be reduced to it. This is to suggest that it seems difficult to know Mendieta as separate from her life's end, what many believe to be a violent and tragic death.

In the same way that one can't make sense of Mendieta without confronting her violent end, we cannot know her without considering her origins, the displacement that marked her early life, her removal from Cuba via the Peter Pan program that relocated (or perhaps dislocated) her to Iowa. In roughly the same manner that the violence that ended her life is prefigured in so much of her early work, the displacement that brought her to make art in the United States is constantly signaled in what remains. So much of the weird vitality of Mendieta's endeavors emerged from the strain of the kind of negation that is loss of homeland, ethnos, and other vagaries of selfhood. It is the straining of life in the face of various modes of loss that constitutes the work's strange intensity. This is to say that through violence, the straining and making precarious of life, a vitalism emerges and lingers after the official ontological closure of life itself.

The works in Mendieta's *Silueta* series seem like the afterburns of mimetically generated intensity. So much of her work looks like world markings or markings of world. They can be glimpsed like stagings and renderings of élan vital that manifested the ontological force of brownness as a mode of particularity in multiplicity. However, it's important to note that this self-portraiture was not a figurative representation, but rather a deeply symbolic indentation in the world around her. In this series, a general female form is carved or indented or molded or sometimes burned into the earth itself. Sometimes, the form is captured in mud or dirt or the walls of a cave. All these *Siluetas* resemble a rough outline of something that was once present and is now absent or entombed but nonetheless partially unconcealed and lingering, like a visual echo. If we take the artist at her word in various artist statements, and consider the *Siluetas* a mode of self-portraiture, what may the work tell us about the self and/in the world? These *Siluetas* are the evidence of expired life that nonetheless hints at return or Prometheus-like regeneration. Mendieta's work insists on a kind of mysterious understanding of life and death-in-life as something like mystical force. She was certainly drawn to the metaphorics of magic and spirituality. But one need not simply know the intensities performed by Mendieta as spiritualist escapism. It is clear that Mendieta partially invested in a kind of vitalism or élan vital that many would dismiss as irrational.

In her study of the influence of Henri Bergson on the poets of Négritude, Donna Jones identifies a strain of philosophical vitalism whose implications lead to racialist thinking. Jones's study makes an excellent case for being wary of some of the repercussions of what she identifies as a New Bergsonism. Jones's careful genealogical approach identifies certain risks in Bergson's vitalism, particularly the manner in which race stands for God in Bergsonism's evolutionary schema. Jones's work deciphers an internalist metaphor of race in Bergson. She describes this as a "noumenal racism."[2] Her analysis also points out the way in which Négritude "share[d] the attempt to recover a sedimented African tradition, a syntax of revolutionary traditionalism." This careful study outlines the problems of an uncritical return to Bergson that so many contemporary critics, especially those influenced by Gilles Deleuze, participate in. Jones's work shores up serious misgivings about the racial implication of élan vital in Bergson and contemporary practices of thought that she classifies as New Bergsonisms.

Deleuze famously attempted to stage an escape from metaphysics through the revivification of older philosophers who had fallen out of vogue in the mid-1960s. He first turned to Bergson in an essay on Hume, and later in a book that was provocatively titled *Bergsonism*.[3]

Indeed, Deleuze's Bergson is a central presence in almost all of the younger philosopher's work. Bergson allows Deleuze to think through the affective and its relation to movement and duration. The example of Bergsonian thought permits Deleuze to think about intuition as method and the implications of multiplicity and subjectivity. Perhaps most importantly for Deleuze, Bergson allows him a certain grasp on multiplicity. Deleuze delineates two modes of multiplicity: one is an extensive multiplicity associated with space, while the other is an intensive multiplicity associated with time. Multiplicity is also described by another dyad of concepts: the virtual and the actual. For Deleuze, these two notions are not mutually exclusive but in fact complementary. In the virtual multiplicity, we encounter a pressing possibility for change. We live along actual multiplicities (these are the components of the world we engage daily), but it is through virtual counterparts to these actual multiplicities that something becomes shareable. This is the argument for a redeployed critical engagement with Bergson and élan vital.

At the center of Jones's critique of Bergsonism, old and new, is the idea that Bergson was an irrational thinker whose philosophical systems vectored on mysticism. In this respect, Jones's concerns recall those of Judith Butler, whom Jones cites and echoes throughout the book. In Butler's criticism of Deleuze, Deleuzians, and "New Bergsonists," she describes what she perceives as "Deleuze posing as 'an ahistorical absolute' his 'arcadian vision of precultural libidinal chaos.'"[4] Butler, a specialist in Hegel, would most certainly not be predisposed to find much use in Deleuze or his Bergsonism. It is important to recall that Deleuze turned away from what biographer François Dosse described as the Hegelianism that dominated French thought in the 1960s, by turning to Hume and Bergson first.[5] This particular refusal of the dialectic posited another and particularly reworked notion of élan vital or vitalism in Deleuze.

Jones's nuanced analysis parses out what she sees as a potentially critical vitalism in Aimé Césaire's and Léopold Senghor's oeuvres. She observes that "the negritude poets offered African poets the Bergsonian promise of rebecoming who they really are."[6] Jones is quick to explain that this notion is of course historically contingent on the legacy of new-world colonialism, and that one of the main points of her text is to call attention to the paradox at the center of Négritude, "that colonial writers would 'forge weapons' out of the 'arsenal' of this vitalist form of European irrationalism."[7] This forceful repudiation of any thought that can be interpreted as a racialist élan vital or racial thinking is nonetheless invested in the strange trajectory of Négritude's potentially liberating redeployment of vitalism. Thus, nineteenth-century European ideas about a life force, even those tinged with a racialist irrationalism, can be reframed differently when considering the work of twentieth-century artists like Césaire and Senghor who were interested in larger projects of decolonization and a genuine poetics of dispossession. The example of Négritude's creolized vitalism serves as a potential precursor to a story about what, through the path of aesthetic protocols like Mendieta's, may be a useful account of the sense of life and world that is brownness.

The goal here is not to take a definitive stance on the philosophical debate sketched above, nor is it to agree or disagree with Jones's admirable study. The point is to work through similar questions around the concept of élan vital for the purposes of describing a general concept of brownness and, more specifically, to unpack a particular notion of the idea in relation to the poetics of dispossession practiced by Ana Mendieta. When considering the world of Afro-Cuban imagery that Mendieta called upon, one need not visualize it as real or imaginary, nor as being about belief or disbelief. Mendieta relied on the figural language of African, Afro-Cuban, and Taíno Afro-Cuban religiosity. Olga M. Viso mentioned the concerns that surrounded her use of sacred symbolism. Some believed her use of this image lexicon inadvertently "conjured forces that she did not fully comprehend."[8]

The question of the artist's intention or deliberate belief in relation to these images is somewhat beside the point insofar as the work instead suggests a sense of the world as the shareabilty of life that is attentive to the precarity and affectivity of brownness. The images are all imprints of life that call upon some potentially unifying notion of a real or imagined past world, a plane of simultaneous difference and singularity. It is an image repertoire that works to perform redeployments of a symbolic notion of vital force by colonized or dispossessed people whose shared sense in common or common sense constitutes a central aspect of the performance and enactment of brownness. For some, racialist thinking is among the worst traps facing the intellectual or artist of color. Yet it seems that if we displace the predictable good dog/bad dog argumentation around concepts like essentialism, we might see the mimetic operations and enactments or doings presented in certain performances of élan vital (or what I am calling the vital force of brownness) as something other than a conservative or even reactionary appeal to heritage or common memory. It may indeed be a matter of building a cosmology that responds cogently to precarious histories of singular and multiple dispossessions that may seem different at first glance, like the histories of violence against women and the imperial subjection of Caribbean people. These histories of violence coalesce in Mendieta's art practice, in her life and her iconicity. Mendieta's work traded in captures of life as strivings in the face of negation, which is to say that her visual lexicon is detectable as a visualization of, and marking on, a precarious and valuable sense of world. Her earth and body art works all attempt to burn, dig, or mold a mark in the world. When we encounter the traces of life that we know as Mendieta's *Siluetas*, we see the indentation left by some kind of force. This inquiry suggests that what we might be seeing is the after trail of a vital force that is brownness encountering the actual multiplicities of studio walls, caves, beaches, fields, and other mounds of earth and world. Mendieta's work stages encounters with the actualities of a corresponding virtuality, as a performing something else, as a being keyed or signaled, and this is exactly the possibility of change signaled in the work. However, that change need not be understood as "a precultural libidinal chaos" but instead a composed commentary of what social life is and could ostensibly be for dispossessed people.

It may be productive to move in closer and describe one particular encounter with the traces of élan vital left by Mendieta. This is not the first essay to suggest that Mendieta's work called upon the affective. In his stunning book *Cuban Palimpsests*, José Quiroga offers a beautiful account of returning home to Cuba and looking for the famous earth works in the caves of Jaruco National Park in Cuba. Quiroga's chapter is a chronicle of his own return to Cuba in the wake of Mendieta's over a decade earlier. That trip ended in the frustration of not finding Mendieta's cave etchings, which most probably did their own temporal disappearing acts. Mendieta returned to Cuba on seven trips after 1980. Quiroga describes the artist writing the work as an attempt to reconstruct her belonging to a feeling of Cubanity as wholeness. This sense of Cuba from the perspective of politics is impossible. The Cuban people have been fragmented not only in relation to the island and its diaspora, but also in relation to various monolithic understandings of politics. Quiroga argues that "[the] nature of the engagement Mendieta produced through her art was affective at all levels; we script ourselves in the art, and read our own lives through it. There is nothing to be gained by resisting this process of identification because it was one she demanded."[9]

Through Quiroga's narration of the spectators' interface with a certain brown élan vital via the trace of the intensity which is brownness on and of world left behind, one can start the work of tracing lines of influence and brown-becoming that emanate not so much from Mendieta as source but indeed through Mendieta. Along these energized lines we can decipher Richard Move's powerful identification with Mendieta in the reconstructions he stages in his documentary *Blood Work*. Alongside that, we can consider some of the work produced by Cuban performance artist Tania Bruguera, who channeled the affective force of Mendieta in her early bodywork. Nao Bustamante's work powerfully resonates on some kind of axis with Mendieta's, in that the female form is a silueta that is performed as iconic. While Bustamante's work might not immediately remind the viewer of Mendieta's blood work in Iowa, it nonetheless insists on the female body as monumental in very elemental and visceral ways. Similarly, in a piece like *Given Over to Want* (2008), we see a new kind of blood work that depicts the often degrading trajectories of violence that mark the brownness of being in the world. All of this work displays Quiroga's description of a demand to identify with Mendieta. There are certainly various identifications, disidentifications, and counteridentifications in Mendieta's work that can be understood as interfaces with the vital force of brownness. In revisiting Quiroga's formulation, I suggest that there is something else in and about the work that is not so much about a demand to identify, but instead about the sharing out of the sense of brownness in and of the world that Mendieta's images present.

Jean-Luc Nancy reminds one that the work of existence isn't just about operativity or utility. Indeed, it is about a certain sharing (out) of that thing that is without value precisely because it is invaluable. While Mendieta could not absolutely defy the system of valuation that is essentially the art world, her work did point us to another way of desiring, of feeling, or radiating a value that resisted accumulation and ownership. Think of siluetas in the sand erased by the tides or time. So many of these earth works were not meant to last. Or picture the flickering of gunpowder flame sculptures that are now available to us only through documentation or reenactment.

The argument here is not that Ana Mendieta's work resisted the commodifying logic of the art world. Instead, I want to suggest that so much of it is about a sharing of the unshareable. For Nancy, the unshareable is that thing that is shared out as the incalculable, the inoperative, the invalu-

13.1 Nao Bustamante, *Given Over to Want*, 2019. Photograph by Jorge Aceituno. COURTESY OF NAO BUSTAMANTE.

13.2 Nao Bustamante, *Given Over to Want*, 2019. Photograph by Lauris Aizupietis. COURTESY OF NAO BUSTAMANTE.

able; he explains that we know these things as art, friendship, love, thought, knowledge, or, most importantly for me, emotion.[10]

Ana Mendieta radiates a world of brown that we can now begin to describe as that thing that is not politics but "not not" politics, something that is beyond a demand for recognition. Affect is contagious. Good and bad affects touch the world around us and permeate each other's sense of the world, and one's world is just that: plural senses of the world that are singular in their plurality. Another philosopher's words might help further illustrate that thing that can be deciphered as the convergences and correspondences of the virtual and the actual that I am describing as brownness. Antonio Negri describes the diagram, an idea borrowed from Foucault and carefully reworked by Deleuze: "Naked life and clothed life, poverty and wealth, critical desire and the construction of the real—these are the elements that constitute the [Foucauldian] diagram of immersion in true reality. Only then can one participate in the composition of the swarm of singularities. Singularities wish to flow together into the common, but they also want to maintain their own freedom, their difference."[11]

Mendieta's work demands identification as Quiroga suggests, but there may be more to the complicated ontological choreography I am calling brownness. Brownness is more than the providence of identifications or even counteridentifications. It is certainly akin to what I described as disidentification, but even that description may hinge too much on linearity of direct alignments. Brownness is about something else. As a concept, even a method, it offers us a sense of the world. This sense of the world is the simultaneous approach and object that Mendieta could so elegantly and urgently present, a sense of the world as brown. It represents a "swarm of singularities." These brown feelings are not the sole province of people who have been called or who call themselves brown. It is, instead, and more importantly, the sharing out of a brown sense of the world, a flowing into the common that nonetheless maintains the urgencies and intensities we experience as freedom and difference.

Notes

Editors' Introduction
1. José Esteban Muñoz, *Disidentifications: Queers of Color and the Performance of Politics* (Minneapolis: University of Minnesota Press, 1999), 170.
2. Chapter 10, this volume.
3. José Esteban Muñoz, *Cruising Utopia: The Then and There of Queer Futurity* (New York: NYU Press, 2009), 16.
4. José Esteban Muñoz, *Cruising Utopia: The Then and There of Queer Futurity*, 10th anniversary ed. (New York: NYU Press, 2019), 203.
5. Muñoz, *Disidentifications*, 174.
6. Zora Neale Hurston, "How It Feels to Be Colored Me," *The World Tomorrow* 11 (May 1928): 215–16.
7. W. E. B. Du Bois, *The Souls of Black Folk* (New York: Gramercy, 1994), 3; Hurston, "How It Feels to Be Colored Me," 216.
8. We can thus read Hurston's essay, and Ligon's appropriation of it, as a means of what Amber Musser (drawing on Freud) describes as a practice of "working through the word's affective charge": Amber Jamilla Musser, *Sensational Flesh: Race, Power, and Masochism* (New York: NYU Press, 2014), 115. Hurston's essay is also marked by a difficulty that is underscored by what Huey Copeland describes as its status as "a text larded with stereotypes that seem to fly in the face of its insistence on the contextual character of racial identity": Huey Copeland, *Bound to Appear: Art, Slavery, and the Site of Blackness in Multicultural America* (Chicago: University of Chicago Press, 2013), 132.
9. Muñoz, *Disidentifications*, 176.
10. The year 1971 would mark the beginning of a long and painful period of family separation for the artist when González-Torres and his sister were sent abroad, unaccompanied by their parents, first to Spain before settling with an uncle in Puerto Rico.
11. Chapter 11, this volume.
12. Muñoz, *Disidentifications*, 4; Muñoz, *Cruising Utopia*, 67–69.
13. Chapter 7, this volume.

14. We have opened the manuscript with the fragment "The Brown Commons" for reasons elaborated on in the unnumbered note to chapter 1.

15. Joshua Javier Guzmán, "Brown," in *Keywords for Latina/o Studies*, ed. Deborah R. Vargas, Lawrence La Fountain-Stokes, and Nancy Raquel Mirabal (New York: NYU Press, 2017), 28.

16. Jill Lane, *Blackface Cuba: 1840–1895* (Philadelphia: University of Pennsylvania Press, 2005).

17. Muñoz, *Disidentifications*, 182.

18. José Quiroga, *Tropics of Desire: Interventions from Queer Latino America* (New York: NYU Press, 2000), 76.

19. Jafari S. Allen, *¡Venceremos? The Erotics of Black Self-Making in Cuba* (Durham, NC: Duke University Press, 2011).

20. Quiroga, *Tropics of Desire*, 90.

21. Muñoz, *Disidentifications*, 187.

22. The other essay on Nao Bustamante is José Esteban Muñoz, "Feeling Brown, Feeling Down: Latina Affect, the Performativity of Race, and the Depressive Position," *Signs* 31, no. 3 (2006): 675–88.

23. Chapter 1, this volume.

24. Muñoz, *Disidentifications*, 7.

25. Chapter 5, this volume.

26. Guzmán, "Brown," 28.

27. Jared Sexton, *Amalgamation Schemes: Antiblackness and the Critique of Multiracialism* (Minneapolis: University of Minnesota Press, 2008).

28. José Esteban Muñoz, "Ephemera as Evidence: Introductory Notes to Queer Acts," *Women and Performance* 8, no. 2 (1996): 5–6, emphasis added.

29. Sandra Ruiz, "Waiting in the Seat of Sensation: The Brown Existentialism of Ryan Rivera," *Women and Performance: A Journal of Feminist Theory* 25, no. 3 (2015): 342.

30. Ruiz, "Waiting in the Seat of Sensation," 336.

31. Alexandra T. Vazquez, *Listening in Detail: Performances of Cuban Music* (Durham, NC: Duke University Press, 2013); Albert Sergio Laguna, *Diversión: Play and Popular Culture in Cuban America* (New York: NYU Press, 2017); Aisha Beliso-De Jesús, *Electric Santería: Racial and Sexual Assemblages of Transnational Religion* (New York: Columbia University Press, 2015).

32. Quiroga, *Tropics of Desire*, 124.

33. Fredric Jameson, *An American Utopia: Dual Power and the Universal Army* (New York: Verso, 2016).

34. This is witnessed in classic films like both Tomás Gutiérriez's 1993 film *Fresa y Chocolate* and the more recent Irish/Cuban confection *Viva* (2016)—and our thinking here is guided by the work of Hiram Pérez, *A Taste for Brown Bodies: Gay Modernity and Cosmopolitan Desire* (New York: NYU Press, 2015). Insofar as the latter film was the product of an Irish director and screenwriter, it literalizes the manner in which male homosexuality functions in excess of national and revolutionary culture. The young drag queen protagonist of the

film, who at one point turns to selling sex in order to support his ne'er-do-well ex-prizefighter father, epitomizes this excess logic of the homosexual. Reviewing *Viva* in 2016, critic Glenn Kenny exemplifies this logic when he writes: "The old cars, the record stores stocked with old LPs, the corner drag club providing a den of cheerful and proscribed iniquity in plain sight—the atmosphere carries a weirdly intoxicating quality in spite of its privation. The lifting of the U.S. embargo on trade with Cuba will, no doubt, bring more 100-percent Cuban cinema into the view of U.S. moviegoers. But it shall also, no doubt, change Havana itself. The city seen in 'Viva' may be disappearing even as I write these words." Glenn Kenny, "Viva," Roger Ebert.com, April 29, 2016, https://www.rogerebert.com/reviews/viva-2016. Here, the trope of a vanishing Cuba is deployed symptomatically in this passage to render the drag queen or maricón the "living currency" of a transaction between communism and capitalism, between Cuba and the world, and to perform a particularly triumphal version of what Renato Rosaldo has termed "imperialist nostalgia," or regret for the passage of that which one is actively destroying. Renato Rosaldo, "Imperialist Nostalgia," *Representations*, no. 26 (1989): 107–22.

35. Juana María Rodríguez, *Sexual Futures, Queer Gestures, and Other Latina Longings* (New York: NYU Press, 2014), 18. This discourse of proximity is also resonant with the work of Roy Pérez, "The Glory That Was Wrong: El 'Chino Malo' Approximates Nuyorico," *Women and Performance: A Journal of Feminist Theory* 25, no. 3 (2015): 277–97.

36. Chapter 1, this volume.

37. Chapter 1, this volume.

38. Chapter 12, this volume.

39. Kandice Chuh, *The Difference Aesthetics Makes: On the Humanities "After Man"* (Durham, NC: Duke University Press, 2019), 11.

40. One of us worked as a research assistant to Muñoz during this period and both of us were involved in the development of that project.

41. We have also silently corrected gender pronouns (noted in the text) where appropriate, but have not attempted to systematize his usage of the terms "Latina," "Latino," and "Latina/o," nor have we revised the text to include the usage of "Latinx," which has come into broad circulation since his death.

42. Vazquez, *Listening in Detail*, 206.

1. The Brown Commons

Munoz gave a lecture with the title "The Brown Commons" several times, including on April 4, 2012, as the Miranda Joseph Endowed Lecture at the University of Arizona, and October 12, 2012, at the University of Texas, Austin. Largely consisting of a reading of Wu Tsang's film *Wildness*, a version of that lecture appears as chapter 12 of this volume. This chapter comes from his unpublished manuscript, where he was working out the analytic for the project as a whole. An excerpt was previously published in a special issue of *GLQ* (24, no. 4 [2018]: 395–97) on the queer commons.

1. *Editors' note:* Muñoz here refers to a 2010 law in the state of Arizona banning ethnic studies, a ban that was subsequently ruled unconstitutional by a federal court in 2017.

2. Fred Moten and Stefano Harney, "The University and the Undercommons: Seven Theses," *Social Text* 22, no. 2 (2004): 101–15.

3. Jean-Luc Nancy, *Being Singular Plural* (Stanford, CA: Stanford University Press, 2005).

4. Jane Bennett, *Vibrant Matter* (Durham, NC: Duke University Press, 2010).

5. Jacques Rancière, *Disagreement: Politics and Philosophy* (Minneapolis: University of Minnesota Press, 2008).

6. Bennett, *Vibrant Matter*, xix.

7. Antonio Viego, "The Life of the Undead: Biopower, Latino Anxiety and the Epidemiological Paradox," *Women and Performance: A Journal of Feminist Theory* 19, no. 2 (2009): 131–47.

8. Lauren Berlant, *Cruel Optimism* (Durham, NC: Duke University Press, 2011), on slow death.

9. Plato, *The Republic*, trans. Tom Griffith (Cambridge: Cambridge University Press, 2000), 161.

10. Aristotle, *The Politics and The Constitution of Athens*, ed. Stephen Everson (Cambridge: Cambridge University Press, 1996).

11. Michael Hardt and Antonio Negri, *Commonwealth* (Cambridge, MA: Harvard University Press, 2011), 154.

12. For a discussion of Dewey and Spinoza, see Bennett, *Vibrant Matter*, 109.

13. Leon Trotsky, "Celine and Poincaré: Novelist and Politician," in *Leon Trotsky on Literature and Art*, ed. Paul N. Siegel (New York: Pathfinder, 1972), 191.

14. José Esteban Muñoz, *Cruising Utopia: The Then and There of Queer Futurity* (New York: NYU Press, 2009).

15. Graham Harman, "The Well-Wrought Broken Hammer: Object-Oriented Literary Criticism," *New Literary History* 43, no. 2 (2012): 183–203.

16. Timothy Morton, "An Object-Oriented Defense of Poetry," *New Literary History* 43, no. 2 (2012): 208.

17. Graham Harman, "Aesthetics as First Philosophy: Levinas and the Nonhuman," *Naked Punch* 9 (summer/fall 2007), http://www.nakedpunch.com/articles/147.

18. Harman, "Aesthetics as First Philosophy."

19. Jane Bennett, "Systems and Things: A Response to Graham Harman and Timothy Morton," *New Literary History* 43, no. 2 (2012): 227.

20. Bennett, "Systems and Things."

21. Graham Harman, "On Interface: Nancy's Weights and Masses," in *Jean-Luc Nancy and Plural Thinking*, ed. Peter Gratton and Marie-Eve Morin (Albany: State University of New York Press, 2012), 98.

2. Feeling Brown

An earlier version of this chapter previously appeared in *Theatre Journal* 52, no. 1 (2000): 67–79.

1. See Norma Alarcón, "Conjugating Subjects in the Age of Multiculturalism," in *Mapping Multiculturalism*, ed. Avery F. Gordon and Christopher Newfield (Minneapolis: University of Minnesota Press, 1996), 127–48.

2. Williams warns us that it is important to "on the one hand acknowledge (and welcome) the specificity of these elements—specific dealings, specific rhythms—and yet to find their specific kinds of sociality, thus preventing the extraction from social experience which is conceivable only when social experience itself has been reduced." Thus the trick here is to identify specific "dealings" and "rhythms" that might not be recognizable or identifiable in relation to already available grids of classification, while, on the other hand, understanding these specific "feelings" as part of a larger social matrix and historically situated. See Raymond Williams, *Marxism and Literature* (New York: Oxford University Press, 1978), 133.

3. Alarcón, "Conjugating Subjects," 136.

4. May Joseph, *Nomadic Identities: The Performance of Citizenship* (Minneapolis: University of Minnesota Press, 1999), 14.

5. Foucault discusses truth games (*les jeux de vérité*) throughout his oeuvre. In one particularly useful interview, Foucault describes truth games and their relation to the self: "I have tried to find out how the human subject fits into certain games of truth, whether they were to take the form of a science or refer to scientific models, or truth games such as those one may encounter in institutions or practices of control." Michel Foucault, "The Ethics of the Concern of the Self as a Practice of Freedom," in *Ethics: Subjectivity and Truth*, ed. Paul Rabinow, trans. Robert Hurley and others (New York: New Press, 1997), 281.

6. For more on Latino exoticism, see Frances R. Aparicio and Susana Chávez-Silverman, eds., *Tropicalizations: Transcultural Representations of Latinidad* (Hanover, NH: University Press of New England, 1997).

7. See my book *Disidentifications: Queers of Color and the Performance of Politics* (Minneapolis: University of Minnesota Press, 1999) for more on the cultural politics of disidentifications.

8. Jean-Paul Sartre, *Sketch for a Theory of Emotions*, trans. Philip Mairet (London: Methuen, 1962), 93.

9. Sartre, *Sketch for a Theory of Emotions*.

10. Miriam Hansen, "Benjamin and Cinema: Not a One-Way Street," *Critical Inquiry* 25, no. 2 (1999): 325. Also see Jonathan Flatley, *Affective Mapping: Melancholia and the Politics of Modernism* (Cambridge, MA: Harvard University Press, 2008).

11. David Román, "Latino Performance and Identity," *Aztlan: A Journal of Chicano Studies* 22, no. 2 (1997): 151–68.

12. For other crucial interventions that measure the political force of Latino performance, see Alberto Sandoval-Sanchez, *José, Can You See? Latinos on and*

off Broadway (Madison: University of Wisconsin Press, 1999); Alicia Arrizón, *Latina Performance: Traversing the Stage* (Bloomington: Indiana University Press, 1999); and Jorge Huerta, *Chicano Theatre: Themes and Forms* (Ypsilanti, MI: Bilingual Press, 1982).

13. See María Irene Fornés, *Plays* (New York: PAJ, 2007).

14. Cherríe Moraga, "Refugees of a World on Fire: Foreword to the Second Edition," in *This Bridge Called My Back: Writings by Radical Women of Color*, ed. Cherríe Moraga and Gloria Anzaldúa (New York: Kitchen Table Women of Color Press, 1983).

15. Cherríe Moraga, *The Last Generation* (Boston: South End Press, 1993), 33.

16. See my coauthored introduction to my volume coedited with Celeste Fraser Delgado, *Everynight Life: Culture and Dance in Latin/o America* (Durham, NC: Duke University Press, 1997), 10 and passim.

17. Robert Hurwitt, "Celebrating 'Hangover,'" *San Francisco Examiner*, April 14, 1997.

18. Hurwitt, "Celebrating 'Hangover.'"

19. Stephen Orgel, *The Illusion of Power: Political Theater in the English Renaissance* (Berkeley: University of California Press, 1975).

20. Here I mean "house" to describe the actual theater and the conceptual and ideological house built by radical women of color.

21. While gay culture generally moves to an assimilationist center, focusing on debates like gays in the military or gay marriage, Bracho's work and the work of a generation of radical gay men of color insist on resisting the terms of this national debate and instead investing in radicalized and unapologetic forms and practices of gay male difference.

22. The War on Drugs was understood in certain activist circles as the "war on the poor."

23. I borrow the term "nondiegetic" from the language of cinema studies. Nondiegetic action is part of the actual film text but not part of the plot or narrative.

24. All quotes from *The Sweetest Hangover* are from the unpublished play. My thanks to Ricardo Bracho for granting me permission to quote from his work. Subsequent quotations are taken from this text. *Editors' note:* A revised version of this play has since been published: Ricardo Bracho, *The Sweetest Hangover* (Alexandria, VA: Alexander Street Press, 2005).

3. The Onus of Seeing Cuba

This chapter originally appeared in *South Atlantic Quarterly* 99, nos. 2–3 (2000): 455–59.

1. Nilo Cruz, *Two Sisters and a Piano and Other Plays* (New York: TCG, 2005).

2. *Editors' note:* Muñoz here refers to the euphemistically designated Special Period in a Time of Peace beginning in 1989.

3. María Irene Fornés, *Plays* (New York: PAJ, 2007).

4. *Editors' note:* Muñoz's references to Cortiñas's play are based on his atten-

dance of the play's 1998 San Francisco debut production: Jorge Ignacio Cortiñas, *Maleta Mulata*, Campo Santo at Intersection for the Arts, San Francisco, April 8–26, 1998. Directed by Paulo Nunes-Ueno.

4. Meandering South

A version of this chapter was first published in Sean Kissane, ed., *Isaac Julien* (Dublin: Irish Museum of Contemporary Art, 2005).

1. I first published on Julien's *Looking for Langston* in my book *Disidentifications*. See also my consideration of his installation for *True North* in a catalog essay coauthored with Michael Wang for the Schindler House in Los Angeles. José Esteban Muñoz and Michael Wang, "Reaching the Open: Isaac Julien's *True North*," in *Isaac Julien: True North*, ed. Lauri Firstenberg (Los Angeles: MAK Center for Art and Architecture, 2005).

2. For more on "the third space" of contemplation aligned with the conditions of postcoloniality, see Teshome H. Gabriel, *Third Cinema in the Third World: The Aesthetics of Liberation* (Ann Arbor, MI: UMI Research Press, 1982).

3. Gilles Deleuze, *Francis Bacon: The Logic of Sensation*, trans. Daniel Smith (London: Continuum, 2004), 82.

4. Deleuze, *Francis Bacon*, 83.

5. See Leo Bersani, *Homos* (Cambridge, MA: Harvard University Press, 1995).

6. Eve Kosofsky Sedgwick, *Between Men: English Literature and Male Homosocial Desire* (New York: Columbia University Press, 1985).

7. Jennifer Doyle, Jonathan Flatley, and José Esteban Muñoz, eds., *Pop Out: Queer Warhol* (Durham, NC: Duke University Press, 1996).

8. Deleuze, *Francis Bacon*, 73.

5. "Chico, What Does It Feel Like to Be a Problem?"

This chapter was previously published in Juan Flores and Renato Rosaldo, eds., *A Companion to Latina/o Studies* (Malden, MA: Wiley-Blackwell, 2011).

1. W. E. B. Du Bois, *The Souls of Black Folk* (New York: Bantam 1989), 1–2.

2. Teresa Brennan, *The Transmission of Affect* (Ithaca, NY: Cornell University Press, 2004).

3. Suzanne Obater, *Ethnic Labels, Latino Lives: Identity and the Politics of (Re)Presentation in the United States* (Minneapolis: University of Minnesota Press, 1995), 14.

4. See chapter 2, this volume.

5. Patricia Gherovici, *The Puerto Rican Syndrome* (New York: Other Press, 2003), 21.

6. For more on the concept of reparative critical work, see Eve Sedgwick, "Paranoid Reading and Reparative Reading, or, You're So Paranoid, You Probably Think This Essay Is about You," in *Touching Feeling: Affect, Pedagogy, Performativity* (Durham, NC: Duke University Press, 2003), 123–51.

7. Richard Rodríguez, *Brown: The Last Discovery of America* (New York: Viking, 2002).

8. Brennan, *The Transmission of Affect*, 5–6.

9. Vijay Prashad, *The Karma of Brown Folks* (Minneapolis: University of Minnesota Press, 2001).

10. W. R. Bion, *Experiences in Groups and Other Papers* (New York: Brunner-Routledge, 2004).

11. Melanie Klein, *The Selected Melanie Klein*, ed. Juliet Mitchell (New York: Free Press, 1986), is a useful introduction to Klein's project. Another good introduction is Meira Likierman, *Melanie Klein: Her Work in Context* (New York: Continuum, 2001).

12. Antonio Viego, *Dead Subjects: Towards a Politics of Loss in Latino Studies* (Durham, NC: Duke University Press, 2007).

13. Antonio Viego, "The Unconscious of Latino/a Studies," *Latino Studies* 1 (2003): 335.

14. Du Bois, *The Souls of Black Folk*, 182.

15. Ann Cvetkovich, *An Archive of Feelings: Trauma, Sexuality, and Lesbian Public Cultures* (Durham, NC: Duke University Press, 2003).

16. Chon Noriega, *Shot in America: Television, the State, and the Rise of Chicano Cinema* (Minneapolis: University of Minnesota Press, 2000), 70.

17. José Feliciano, "Star-Spangled Banner," accessed February 6, 2020, https://www.josefeliciano.com/video-boxes-control/natonal-anthem-1968.

18. Brennan, *The Transmission of Affect*, 11.

19. Frantz Fanon, *Black Skin, White Masks*, trans. Charles Lam Markmann (New York: Grove Press, 1967). Teresa Brennan also makes an argument about the olfactory transmission of affect in *The Transmission of Affect*.

20. See J. L. Austin, *How to Do Things with Words* (Cambridge, MA: Harvard University Press, 1962).

21. Shamoon Zamir, *Dark Voices: W. E. B. Du Bois and American Thought, 1888–1903* (Chicago: University of Chicago Press, 1995), 117.

22. Zamir, *Dark Voices*.

6. The Vulnerability Artist

A version of this essay was previously published in *Women and Performance: A Journal of Feminist Theory* 16, no. 2 (2006): 191–200.

1. Sianne Ngai, *Ugly Feelings* (Cambridge, MA: Harvard University Press, 2005).

2. Ngai, *Ugly Feelings*, 3.

3. Coco Fusco, "The Other History of Intercultural Performance," in *English Is Broken Here: Notes on Cultural Fusion in the Americas* (New York: New Press, 1995), 37–63.

4. Saidiya Hartman, *Scenes of Subjection: Terror, Slavery, and Self-Making in Nineteenth-Century America* (New York: Oxford University Press, 1997).

5. Franz Kafka, *The Complete Stories*, ed. Nahum N. Glatzer (New York: Schocken, 1995).

6. Gilles Deleuze, "Spinoza and the Three 'Ethics,'" in *Essays Critical and*

Clinical, trans. Daniel W. Smith and Michael A. Greco (Minneapolis: University of Minnesota Press, 1997), 138–51.

7. *Editors' note:* See Sigmund Freud, *Three Essays on the Theory of Sexuality*, trans. James Strachey (New York: Basic Books, 2007).

8. Deleuze, "Spinoza and the Three Ethics."

9. Friedrich Wilhelm Nietzsche, *On the Genealogy of Morals and Ecce Homo*, trans. Walter Arnold Kaufmann and R. J. Hollingdale (New York: Vintage, 1989).

7. Queer Theater, Queer Theory

A version of this chapter appeared in Alisa Solomon and Framji Minwalla, eds., *The Queerest Art: Essays on Lesbian and Gay Theater* (New York: New York University Press, 2002), 227–46.

1. A similar case is made by David Román, who looks at Alfaro's work as a contribution to Chicano studies. See his *Acts of Intervention: Performance, Gay Culture, and AIDS* (Bloomington: Indiana University Press, 1998), 177–201.

2. Luis Alfaro grew up in the Pico-Union district of Central Los Angeles, as the son of farmworkers. While working as a custodian at a theater where LAPD, the Los Angeles Poverty Department, worked, Alfaro met director Scott Kelman, who became his mentor. He later went on to study with playwrights María Irene Fornés and Tony Kushner. Alfaro has worked as a member of different artist collectives and as a solo artist.

3. Luis Alfaro, "Cuerpo Politizado," in *Uncontrollable Bodies: Testimonies of Identity and Culture*, ed. Rodney Sappington and Tyler Stallings (Seattle: Bay Press, 1994).

4. Elizabeth Grosz, *Space, Time, and Perversion: Essays on the Politics of Bodies* (New York: Routledge, 1995), 108.

5. Quoted in Doug Sadownick, "Two Different Worlds: Luis Alfaro Bridges the Gap between Gay Fantasies and Latino Reality," *The Advocate*, no. 568 (January 15, 1991), 6–63.

6. Jonathan Boyarin, *The Storm from Paradise: The Politics of Jewish Memory* (Minneapolis: University of Minnesota Press, 1992), xvi.

7. See Norma Alarcón, "Making *Familia* from Scratch: Split Subjectivities in the Work of Helena María Viramontes and Cherríe Moraga," in *Chicana Creativity and Criticism: New Frontiers in American Literature*, ed. Maria Herrera-Sobek and Helena María Viramontes (Albuquerque: University of New Mexico Press, 1996), 220–32.

8. Michael Warner, "Introduction," in *Fear of a Queer Planet: Queer Politics and Social Theory*, ed. Michael Warner (Minneapolis: University of Minnesota Press, 1993), x.

9. Warner, "Introduction," xvii.

10. Warner, "Introduction," xix.

11. Karl Marx quoted in Warner, "Introduction," vii.

12. Karl Marx, "Theses on Feuerbach," in *The Marx-Engels Reader*, ed. Robert Tucker (New York: Norton, 1972), 145.

13. Etienne Balibar, *The Philosophy of Marx*, trans. Chris Turner (London: Verso, 1995), 13.

8. Performing the Bestiary

This previously unpublished chapter was originally drafted for inclusion in the volume *Animal Acts: Performing Species Today*, edited by Una Chaudhuri and Holly Hughes (Ann Arbor: University of Michigan Press, 2014). The text of the Carmelita Tropicana play under discussion can be found there, along with a commentary by Larry La Fountain-Stokes.

1. *Editors' note:* Many key concepts in this paragraph derive from the work of Gilles Deleuze and Félix Guattari, especially "assemblage," the "body without organs," and "becoming-animal." Gilles Deleuze and Félix Guattari, *A Thousand Plateaus: Capitalism and Schizophrenia* (Minneapolis: University of Minnesota Press, 1987). On "queer assemblages," see Jasbir Puar, *Terrorist Assemblages: Homonationalism in Queer Times* (Durham, NC: Duke University Press, 2007).

2. Una Chaudhuri and Shonni Enelow, "Animalizing Performance, Becoming-Theatre: Inside Zooesis with the Animal Project at NYU," *Theatre Topics* 16, no. 1 (2006): 2.

3. Margo Jefferson, "Critic's Notebook: On the Home Front, the Personal Becomes Theatrical (and Political, Too)," *New York Times*, December 11, 2004.

4. Jacques Derrida, *The Beast and the Sovereign*, 2 vols. (Chicago: University of Chicago Press, 2011, 2017).

9. Performing Greater Cuba

A version of this chapter was previously published in *Women and Performance: A Journal of Feminist Theory* 11, no. 2 (2002): 251–66.

1. This ambivalence is not a passive ambivalence. It is more nearly a passionate investment in Cuba that sees the promise of the revolution, its potential, and its various failures and shortcomings. The ambivalence of the Cuban American Left is perhaps as passionate as the obsessive rejection continually performed by a Cuban American right wing.

2. Silvan Tomkins, *Shame and Its Sisters: A Silvan Tomkins Reader*, ed. Eve Kosofsky Sedgwick, Adam Frank, and Irving E Alexander (Durham, NC: Duke University Press, 1995), 142.

3. Gustavo Pérez Firmat, *Life on the Hyphen: The Cuban-American Way* (Austin: University of Texas Press, 1994).

4. The phrase "memoria de la postguerra" was originally used by Bruguera as the title of a journal/newspaper/artwork that was initially censored by the Cuban cultural authorities. Later, it was used to describe the publication and a series of performances.

5. Tania Bruguera, "Tania Bruguera in Conversation with Octavio Zaya," in *Cuba: Maps of Desire* (Vienna: Kunsthalle, 1999).

6. Tania Bruguera, letter to author, 1999.

7. Slavoj Žižek, *Enjoy Your Symptom! Jacques Lacan inside Hollywood and Out* (New York: Routledge, 1992), 38.

8. Jean Laplanche and J. B. Pontalis, *The Language of Psychoanalysis* (New York: Norton, 1974), 349.

9. Eve Kosofsky Sedgwick, ed., *Novel Gazing: Queer Readings in Fiction* (Durham, NC: Duke University Press, 1997), 1–40.

10. Ricardo Ortiz, "Café, Culpa, and Capital: Nostalgic Addictions of Cuban Exile," *Yale Journal of Criticism* 10, no. 1 (1997): 69.

11. Ortiz, "Café, Culpa, and Capital," 72.

12. Bruguera, "Tania Bruguera in Conversation," 29.

13. Nicolas Abraham and Maria Torok, *The Shell and the Kernel: Renewals of Psychoanalysis*, ed. Nicholas T. Rand (Chicago: University of Chicago Press, 1994), 125.

14. By psychology here, I mean quite a bit more than the Lacanian paradigms that dominate psychological approaches to cultural critique in the United States and Britain. I am in fact more interested in the still-underexplored work of psychoanalysts like Melanie Klein and Donald Winnicott.

15. Jean Laplanche, *Essays on Otherness* (New York: Routledge, 1999), 136.

16. Hortense Spillers, "All the Things You Could Be by Now If Sigmund Freud's Wife Was Your Mother: Race and Psychoanalysis," *Critical Inquiry* 22, no. 7 (1996): 710–34.

10. Wise Latinas

A version of this essay was published in *Criticism* 56, no. 2 (2014): 249–65.

1. Citation from Sonia Sotomayor, "A Latina Judge's Voice," Olmos Memorial Lecture, delivered at the Berkeley School of Law, University of California, 2001.

2. Kandice Chuh, *Imagine Otherwise: On Asian Americanist Critique* (Durham, NC: Duke University Press, 2003).

3. Rey Chow, *The Protestant Ethnic and the Spirit of Capitalism* (New York: Columbia University Press, 2002).

4. Richard T. Ford, *Racial Culture: A Critique* (Princeton, NJ: Princeton University Press, 2005).

5. Antonio Viego, *Dead Subjects: Towards a Politics of Loss in Latino Studies* (Durham, NC: Duke University Press, 2007).

6. Viego, *Dead Subjects*.

7. For an excellent analysis of Sotomayor's confirmation and the ways in which it did not stage a break with the status quo of U.S. law, see Josh Takano Chambers-Letson, "Embodying Justice: The Making of Justice Sonia Sotomayor," *Women and Performance: A Journal of Feminist Theory* 20, no. 2 (2010): 149–72.

8. Gerard Malanga, "Interview with Jack Smith," *Film Culture*, no. 45 (summer 1967): 12–16, quotation on 14.

9. *Mario Banana* can be seen on YouTube, posted by user Dueci on April 3, 2008: http://www.youtube.com/watch?v=1Ku9sGT2Ugg.

10. *Editors' note:* Muñoz drew the dialogue from a screening copy of *Screen Test #2*.

11. *Editors' note:* In the months before José passed, Joshua Chambers-Letson read the manuscript for "Wise Latinas" and raised the fact that the text uses both male and female pronouns with reference to Montez throughout. Muñoz was uncertain as to how he would resolve this, or whether he should. The movement between "he" and "she" underlined the gender fluidity of Montez's performance practice. The slippage also seemed to evince a familiarity José felt with Montez, as he often playfully referred to queer friends as "she" and "he" interchangeably. Though it may pose some confusion, we have left the pronouns as they were when he died, inviting the reader to read queerly as they meditate on the implications of Montez's genderplay in Muñoz's account.

12. Stephen L. Barber and David L. Clark, eds., *Regarding Sedgwick: Essays on Queer Culture and Critical Theory* (New York: Routledge, 2002).

13. Douglas Crimp, "Mario Montez, for Shame!," in *"Our Kind of Movie": The Films of Andy Warhol* (Cambridge, MA: MIT Press, 2012), 20–36.

14. Eve Kosofsky Sedgwick, *Touching Feeling: Affect, Pedagogy, Performativity*, Series Q (Durham, NC: Duke University Press, 2003).

15. Crimp, "Mario Montez, for Shame!," 34.

16. Eve Kosofsky Sedgwick, "Queer Performativity: Warhol's Shyness, Warhol's Whiteness," in *Pop Out: Queer Warhol*, ed. Jennifer Doyle, Jonathan Flatley, and José E. Muñoz, Series Q (Durham, NC: Duke University Press, 1997), 134–43.

17. Lauren Berlant, *Cruel Optimism* (Durham, NC: Duke University Press, 2011), 12.

18. Lawrence La Fountain-Stokes, "Gay Shame, Latina- and Latino-Style: A Critique of White Queer Performativity," in *Gay Latino Studies: A Critical Reader*, ed. Michael Hames-García and Ernesto Javier Martínez (Durham, NC: Duke University Press, 2011), 55–80.

19. Richard Schechner, *Between Theatre and Anthropology* (Philadelphia: University of Pennsylvania Press, 1985).

20. Fred Moten, *In the Break: The Aesthetics of the Black Radical Tradition* (Minneapolis: University of Minnesota Press, 2003).

21. Mauren Dowd, "White Man's Last Stand," *New York Times*, July 14, 2009.

22. Frank Rich, "They Got Some 'Splaining to Do," *New York Times*, July 18, 2009.

23. *Editors' note:* Bustamante eventually adopted the title *Soldadera* to describe this project. *Soldadera* premiered in a solo exhibition of Bustamante's work. Curated by Jennifer Doyle, *Soldadera* was first exhibited at the Vincent Price Art Museum from May 16 to August 1, 2015.

24. The point here is not to malign Farah or suggest anything about his actual character. I am instead interested in remarking on how these different contestants were rendered as types through the protocols of reality television editing and production.

25. Wendy Brown, *States of Injury: Power and Freedom in Late Modernity* (Princeton, NJ: Princeton University Press, 1995), 74. See my discussion below.

26. Brown, *States of Injury*, 74.

27. Jean-Luc Nancy, *Being Singular Plural*, trans. Robert D. Richardson and Anne E. O'Byrne (Stanford, CA: Stanford University Press, 2000).

11. Brown Worldings

This previously unpublished chapter appears in this volume for the first time.

1. *Editors' note:* See José Esteban Muñoz, "Toward a Methexic Queer Media," *GLQ* 19, no. 4 (2013): 564.

2. Vijay Prashad, *The Karma of Brown Folk* (Minneapolis: University of Minnesota Press, 2001).

3. Cited in Tony Ortega, "Vietnam! Ed Koch! Party Raid! Vietnam! Vietnam! Flag Burning! Horrorshow, Droogies!," *Village Voice*, November 27, 2009, https://www.villagevoice.com/2009/11/27/vietnam-ed-koch-party-raid-vietnam-vietnam-flag-burning-horrorshow-droogies/.

4. Cedric Robinson, *An Anthropology of Marxism* (Burlington, VT: Ashgate, 2001), 138.

5. See Karl Marx, "The Poverty of Philosophy," in *Collected Works of Karl Marx and Friedrich Engels, 1843–44*, vol. 3 (New York: Progress, 1976), 105–212.

6. See Immigrant Movement International, http://immigrant-movement.us.

7. Sam Dolnick, "An Artist's Performance: A Year as a Poor Immigrant," *New York Times*, May 8, 2011.

8. Tania Bruguera with Kathy Nobles, "Useful Art," *Frieze*, January 1, 2012, https://frieze.com/article/useful-art/.

9. Bruguera with Nobles, "Useful Art."

10. Claire Bishop, "Speech Disorder," *Artforum*, summer 2009, 121–22.

11. Jacques Rancière, *The Names of History: On the Poetics of Knowledge*, trans. Hassan Melehy (Minneapolis: University of Minnesota Press, 1994), 30.

12. María Irene Fornés, *Mud*, in *Plays* (New York: PAJ, 2007), 13–40.

12. The Sense of *Wildness*

This previously unpublished chapter was given as a lecture in various locations in 2013, including Northeastern University, Duke University, Eastern Michigan University, Brown University, and the University of North Carolina, Asheville.

1. Paul B. Preciado, *Testo Junkie: Sex, Drugs, and Biopolitics in the Pharmacopornographic Era* (New York: Feminist Press, 2013).

2. Preciado, *Testo Junkie*, 347.

3. Preciado, *Testo Junkie*, 347. *Editors' note:* Operaismo ("workerism" in English) is an Italian Marxist movement that emphasizes the autonomous power of social movements.

4. Cited in Muriel Combes, *Gilbert Simondon and the Philosophy of the Transindividual*, trans. Thomas LaMarre (Cambridge, MA: MIT Press, 2013), 65; Gilbert Simondon, *L'Individuation psychique et collective: A la lumiere des*

notions de forme, information, potential, et métastabilité (Paris: Aubier, 1992). *Editors' note:* Simondon, not being widely translated at the time of composition, would have been accessible to the author largely via Combes's secondary source.

5. Cited in Combes, *Gilbert Simondon*, 65.

6. Preciado, *Testo Junkie*, 398.

7. *Editors' note:* For more on Simondon's "real collective," see David Gilbert Scott, "The Collective as Condition of Signification," in *Gilbert Simondon's Psychic and Collective Individuation: A Critical Introduction and Guide* (Edinburgh: Edinburgh University Press, 2014), 150–76.

8. Barack Obama, "Inaugural Address by President Barack Obama," White House, Office of the Press Secretary, January 23, 2013, https://obamawhitehouse.archives.gov/the-press-office/2013/01/21/inaugural-address-president-barack-obama.

9. This footage can be accessed on YouTube. *Editors' note:* "L020A Sylvia Rivera, 'Y'all Better Quiet Down' Original Authorized Video, 1973 Gay Pride Rally NYC," YouTube, posted May 23, 2019, https://www.youtube.com/watch?v=Jb-JIOWUw10.

10. Frantz Fanon, *Black Skin, White Masks*, trans. Charles Lam Markmann (New York: Grove Press, 1967).

11. See Gloria Anzaldúa, *Borderlands/La Frontera: The New Mestiza* (1987; reprint, San Francisco: Aunt Lute, 2012).

12. Amber Hollibaugh and Cherríe Moraga, "What We're Rollin Around in Bed With: Sexual Silences in Feminism," in *Powers of Desire: The Politics of Sexuality*, ed. Ann Snitow, Christine Sansell, and Sharon Thompson (New York: Monthly Review, 1983), 224–29.

13. *Editors' note:* Here, Tsang includes additional dialogue from a separate film, 1967's *The Queen*.

13. Vitalism's Afterburn

A version of this essay was published in *Women and Performance: A Journal of Feminist Theory* 21, no. 2 (2011): 191–98.

1. Lucy R. Lippard, Introduction to *Who Is Ana Mendieta?*, by Christine Redfern and Caro Caron (New York: Feminist Press, 2011).

2. Donna V. Jones, *The Racial Discourses of Life Philosophy: Négritude, Vitalism, and Modernity* (New York: Columbia University Press, 2010), 117.

3. Gilles Deleuze, *Bergsonism*, trans. Hugh Tomlinson and Barbara Hammerjam (New York: Zone, 1988). See also Gilles Deleuze, *Empiricism and Subjectivity: An Essay on Hume's Theory of Human Nature*, trans. Constantin V. Boundas (New York: Columbia University Press, 1991).

4. Jones, *The Racial Discourses of Life Philosophy*, 174.

5. François Dosse, *Gilles Deleuze and Félix Guattari: Intersecting Lives* (New York: Columbia University Press, 2010), 130.

6. Jones, *The Racial Discourses of Life Philosophy*.

7. Jones, *The Racial Discourses of Life Philosophy*.

8. Olga Viso, *Ana Mendieta: Earth Body* (New York: Hatje Cantz, 2004), 66.

9. José Quiroga, *Cuban Palimpsests* (Minneapolis: University of Minnesota Press, 2004), 174.

10. Jean-Luc Nancy, *The Truth of Democracy*, trans. Pascale-Anne Brault and Michael Naas (New York: Fordham University Press, 2010), 17.

11. Antonio Negri, *Art and Multitude*, trans. Ed Emery (Cambridge: Polity, 2011), 121.

Bibliography

Abraham, Nicolas, and Maria Torok. *The Shell and the Kernel: Renewals of Psychoanalysis*, edited by Nicholas T. Rand. Chicago: University of Chicago Press, 1994.
Alarcón, Norma. "Conjugating Subjects in the Age of Multiculturalism." In *Mapping Multiculturalism*, edited by Avery F. Gordon and Christopher Newfield, 127–48. Minneapolis: University of Minnesota Press, 1996.
Alarcón, Norma. "Making *Familia* from Scratch: Split Subjectivities in the Work of Helena María Viramontes and Cherríe Moraga." In *Chicana Creativity and Criticism: New Frontiers in American Literature*, edited by Maria Herrera-Sobek and Helena María Viramontes, 220–32. Albuquerque: University of New Mexico Press, 1996.
Alfaro, Luis. "Cuerpo Politizado." In *Uncontrollable Bodies: Testimonies of Identity and Culture*, edited by Rodney Sappington and Tyler Stallings. Seattle: Bay Press, 1994.
Anzaldúa, Gloria. *Borderlands/La Frontera: The New Mestiza*. San Francisco: Aunt Lute, 2012. First published 1987.
Aparicio, Frances R., and Susana Chávez-Silverman, eds. *Tropicalizations: Transcultural Representations of Latinidad*. Hanover, NH: University Press of New England, 1997.
Aristotle. *The Politics and The Constitution of Athens*. Edited by Stephen Everson. Cambridge: Cambridge University Press, 1996.
Arrizón, Alicia. *Latina Performance: Traversing the Stage*. Bloomington: Indiana University Press, 1999.
Austin, J. L. *How to Do Things with Words*. Cambridge, MA: Harvard University Press, 1962.
Balibar, Etienne. *The Philosophy of Marx*. Translated by Chris Turner. London: Verso, 1995.
Barber, Stephen L., and David L. Clark, eds. *Regarding Sedgwick: Essays on Queer Culture and Critical Theory*. New York: Routledge, 2002.

Bennett, Jane. "Systems and Things: A Response to Graham Harman and Timothy Morton." *New Literary History* 43, no. 2 (2012): 225–33.
Bennett, Jane. *Vibrant Matter.* Durham, NC: Duke University Press, 2010.
Berlant, Lauren. *Cruel Optimism.* Durham, NC: Duke University Press, 2011.
Bersani, Leo. *Homos.* Cambridge, MA: Harvard University Press, 1995.
Bion, W. R. *Experiences in Groups and Other Papers.* New York: Brunner-Routledge, 2004.
Bishop, Claire. "Speech Disorder." *Artforum,* summer 2009, 121–22.
Boyarin, Jonathan. *The Storm from Paradise: The Politics of Jewish Memory.* Minneapolis, University of Minnesota Press, 1992.
Brennan, Teresa. *The Transmission of Affect.* Ithaca, NY: Cornell University Press, 2004.
Brown, Wendy. *States of Injury: Power and Freedom in Late Modernity.* Princeton, NJ: Princeton University Press, 1995.
Bruguera, Tania. "Tania Bruguera in Conversation with Octavio Zaya." In *Cuba: Maps of Desire.* Vienna: Kunsthalle, 1999.
Bruguera, Tania, with Kathy Nobles. "Useful Art." *Frieze,* no. 144 (January 1, 2012). https://frieze.com/article/useful-art/.
Chambers-Letson, Josh Takano. "Embodying Justice: The Making of Justice Sonia Sotomayor." *Women and Performance: A Journal of Feminist Theory* 20, no. 2 (2010): 149–72.
Chaudhuri, Una, and Shonni Enelow. "Animalizing Performance, Becoming-Theatre: Inside Zooesis with the Animal Project at NYU." *Theatre Topics* 16, no. 1 (2006): 1–17.
Chow, Rey. *The Protestant Ethnic and the Spirit of Capitalism.* New York: Columbia University Press, 2002.
Chuh, Kandice. *Imagine Otherwise: On Asian Americanist Critique.* Durham, NC: Duke University Press, 2003.
Combes, Muriel. 2013. *Gilbert Simondon and the Philosophy of the Transindividual.* Translated by Thomas LaMarre. Cambridge, MA: MIT Press, 2013.
Crimp, Douglas. "Mario Montez, for Shame!" In *"Our Kind of Movie": The Films of Andy Warhol,* 20–36. Cambridge, MA: MIT Press, 2012.
Cruz, Nilo. *Two Sisters and a Piano and Other Plays.* New York: TCG, 2005.
Cvetkovich, Ann. *An Archive of Feelings: Trauma, Sexuality, and Lesbian Public Cultures.* Durham, NC: Duke University Press, 2003.
Deleuze, Gilles. *Bergsonism.* Translated by Hugh Tomlinson and Barbara Hammerjam. New York: Zone, 1988.
Deleuze, Gilles. *Empiricism and Subjectivity: An Essay on Hume's Theory of Human Nature.* Translated by Constantin V. Boundas. New York: Columbia University Press, 1991.
Deleuze, Gilles. *Francis Bacon: The Logic of Sensation.* Translated by Daniel Smith. London: Continuum, 2004.
Deleuze, Gilles. "Spinoza and the Three Ethics." In *Essays Critical and Clinical,*

translated by Daniel W. Smith and Michael A. Greco, 138–51. Minneapolis: University of Minnesota Press, 1997.

Deleuze, Gilles, and Félix Guattari. *A Thousand Plateaus: Capitalism and Schizophrenia*. Minneapolis: University of Minnesota Press, 1987.

Delgado, Celeste Fraser, and José Esteban Muñoz, eds. *Everynight Life: Culture and Dance in Latin/o America*. Durham, NC: Duke University Press, 1997.

Derrida, Jacques. *The Beast and the Sovereign*. 2 vols. Chicago: University of Chicago Press, 2011, 2017.

Dolnick, Sam. "An Artist's Performance: A Year as a Poor Immigrant." *New York Times*, May 8, 2011.

Dosse, François. *Gilles Deleuze and Félix Guattari: Intersecting Lives*. New York: Columbia University Press, 2010.

Dowd, Maureen. "White Man's Last Stand." *New York Times*, July 14, 2009.

Doyle, Jennifer, Jonathan Flatley, and José Esteban Muñoz, eds. *Pop Out: Queer Warhol*. Durham, NC: Duke University Press, 1996.

Du Bois, W. E. B. *The Souls of Black Folk*. New York: Bantam, 1989.

Fanon, Frantz. *Black Skin, White Masks*. Translated by Charles Lam Markmann. New York: Grove, 1967.

Firmat, Gustavo Pérez. *Life on the Hyphen: The Cuban-American Way*. Austin: University of Texas Press, 1994.

Flatley, Jonathan. *Affective Mapping: Melancholia and the Politics of Modernism*. Cambridge, MA: Harvard University Press, 2008.

Ford, Richard T. *Racial Culture: A Critique*. Princeton, NJ: Princeton University Press, 2005.

Fornés, María Irene. *Plays*. New York: PAJ, 2007.

Foucault, Michel. "The Ethics of the Concern of the Self as a Practice of Freedom." In *Ethics: Subjectivity and Truth*, edited by Paul Rabinow, translated by Robert Hurley and others. New York: New Press, 1997.

Fusco, Coco. "The Other History of Intercultural Performance." In *English Is Broken Here: Notes on Cultural Fusion in the Americas*, 37–63. New York: New Press, 1995.

Gabriel, Teshome H. *Third Cinema in the Third World: The Aesthetics of Liberation*. Ann Arbor, MI: UMI Research Press, 1982.

Gherovici, Patricia. *The Puerto Rican Syndrome*. New York: Other Press, 2003.

Grosz, Elizabeth. *Space, Time and Perversion: Essays on the Politics of Bodies*. New York: Routledge, 1995.

Hansen, Miriam. "Benjamin and Cinema: Not a One-Way Street." *Critical Inquiry* 25, no. 2 (1999): 306–43.

Hardt, Michael, and Antonio Negri. *Commonwealth*. Cambridge, MA: Harvard University Press, 2011.

Harman, Graham. "Aesthetics as First Philosophy: Levinas and the Non-human." *Naked Punch* 9 (summer/fall 2007). http://www.nakedpunch.com/articles/147.

Harman, Graham. "On Interface: Nancy's Weights and Masses." In *Jean-Luc*

Nancy and Plural Thinking, edited by Peter Gratton and Marie-Eve Morin, 95–108. Albany: State University of New York Press, 2012.

Harman, Graham. "The Well-Wrought Broken Hammer: Object-Oriented Literary Criticism." *New Literary History* 43, no. 2 (2012): 183–203.

Hartman, Saidiya. *Scenes of Subjection: Terror, Slavery, and Self-Making in Nineteenth-Century America*. New York: Oxford University Press, 1997.

Hollibaugh, Amber, and Cherríe Moraga. "What We're Rollin' Around in Bed With: Sexual Silences in Feminism." In *Powers of Desire: The Politics of Sexuality*, edited by Ann Snitow, Christine Sansell, and Sharon Thompson, 224–29. New York: Monthly Review, 1983.

Huerta, Jorge. *Chicano Theatre: Themes and Forms*. Ypsilanti, MI: Bilingual Press, 1982.

Hurwitt, Robert. "Celebrating 'Hangover.'" *San Francisco Examiner*, April 14, 1997.

Jefferson, Margo. "Critic's Notebook: On the Home Front, the Personal Becomes Theatrical (and Political, Too)." *New York Times*, December 11, 2004.

Jones, Donna V. *The Racial Discourses of Life Philosophy: Négritude, Vitalism, and Modernity*. New York: Columbia University Press, 2010.

Joseph, May. *Nomadic Identities: The Performance of Citizenship*. Minneapolis: University of Minnesota Press, 1999.

Kafka, Franz. *The Complete Stories*. Edited by Nahum N. Glatzer. New York: Schocken.

Klein, Melanie. *The Selected Melanie Klein*. Edited by Juliet Mitchell. New York: Free Press, 1986.

La Fountain-Stokes, Lawrence. "Gay Shame, Latina- and Latino-Style: A Critique of White Queer Performativity." In *Gay Latino Studies: A Critical Reader*, edited by Michael Hames-García and Ernesto Javier Martínez, 55–80. Durham, NC: Duke University Press, 2011.

Laplanche, Jean. *Essays on Otherness*. New York: Routledge, 1999.

Laplanche, Jean, and J. B. Pontalis. *The Language of Psychoanalysis*. New York: Norton, 1974.

Likierman, Meira. *Melanie Klein: Her Work in Context*. New York: Continuum, 2001.

Lippard, Lucy R. Introduction to *Who Is Ana Mendieta?*, by Christine Redfern and Caro Caron. New York: Feminist Press, 2011.

Malanga, Gerard. "Interview with Jack Smith." *Film Culture*, no. 45 (summer 1967): 12–16.

Marx, Karl. "The Poverty of Philosophy." In *Collected Works of Karl Marx and Friedrich Engels, 1843–44*, vol. 3, 105–212. New York: Progress, 1976.

Marx, Karl. "Theses on Feuerbach." In *The Marx-Engels Reader*, edited by Robert Tucker, 143–44. New York: Norton, 1972.

Moraga, Cherríe. *The Last Generation*. Boston: South End, 1993.

Moraga, Cherríe. "Refugees of a World on Fire: Foreword to the Second Edition." In *This Bridge Called My Back: Writings by Radical Women of Color*, edited

by Cherríe Moraga and Gloria Anzaldúa. New York: Kitchen Table Women of Color Press, 1983.
Morton, Timothy. "An Object-Oriented Defense of Poetry." *New Literary History* 43, no. 2 (2012): 205–24.
Moten, Fred. *In the Break: The Aesthetics of the Black Radical Tradition.* Minneapolis: University of Minnesota Press, 2003.
Moten, Fred, and Stefano Harney. "The University and the Undercommons: Seven Theses." *Social Text* 22, no. 2 (2004): 101–15.
Muñoz, José Esteban. *Cruising Utopia: The Then and There of Queer Futurity.* New York: New York University Press, 2009.
Muñoz, José Esteban. *Disidentifications: Queers of Color and the Performance of Politics.* Minneapolis: University of Minnesota Press, 1999.
Muñoz, José Esteban. "Toward a Methexic Queer Media." *GLQ* 19, no. 4 (2013): 564.
Muñoz, José Esteban, and Michael Wang. "Reaching the Open: Isaac Julien's *True North*." In *Isaac Julien: True North*, edited by Lauri Firstenberg. Los Angeles: MAK Center for Art and Architecture, 2005.
Nancy, Jean-Luc. *Being Singular Plural.* Translated by Robert D. Richardson and Anne E. O'Byrne. Stanford, CA: Stanford University Press, 2005.
Nancy, Jean-Luc. *The Truth of Democracy.* Translated by Pascale-Anne Brault and Michael Naas. New York: Fordham University Press, 2010.
Negri, Antonio. *Art and Multitude.* Translated by Ed Emery. Cambridge: Polity, 2011.
Ngai, Sianne. *Ugly Feelings.* Cambridge, MA: Harvard University Press, 2005.
Nietzsche, Friedrich Wilhelm. *On the Genealogy of Morals and Ecce Homo.* Translated by Walter Arnold Kaufmann and R. J. Hollingdale. New York: Vintage, 1989.
Noriega, Chon. *Shot in America: Television, the State, and the Rise of Chicano Cinema.* Minneapolis: University of Minnesota Press, 2000.
Obama, Barack. "Inaugural Address by President Barack Obama." White House, Office of the Press Secretary, January 23, 2013. https://obamawhitehouse.archives.gov/the-press-office/2013/01/21/inaugural-address-president-barack-obama.
Oboler, Suzanne. *Ethnic Labels, Latino Lives: Identity and the Politics of (Re)Presentation in the United States.* Minneapolis: University of Minnesota Press, 1995.
Orgel, Stephen. *The Illusion of Power: Political Theater in the English Renaissance.* Berkeley: University of California Press, 1975.
Ortega, Tony. "Vietnam! Ed Koch! Party Raid! Vietnam! Vietnam! Flag Burning! Horrorshow, Droogies!" *Village Voice*, November 27, 2009. https://www.villagevoice.com/2009/11/27/vietnam-ed-koch-party-raid-vietnam-vietnam-flag-burning-horrorshow-droogies/.
Ortiz, Ricardo. "Café, Culpa, and Capital: Nostalgic Addictions of Cuban Exile." *Yale Journal of Criticism* 10, no. 1 (1997): 63–84.

Plato. *The Republic*. Translated by Tom Griffith. Cambridge: Cambridge University Press, 2000.
Prashad, Vijay. *The Karma of Brown Folk*. Minneapolis: University of Minnesota Press, 2001.
Preciado, Paul B. *Testo Junkie: Sex, Drugs, and Biopolitics in the Pharmacopornographic Era*. New York: Feminist Press, 2013.
Puar, Jasbir. *Terrorist Assemblages: Homonationalism in Queer Times*. Durham, NC: Duke University Press, 2007.
Quiroga, José. *Cuban Palimpsests*. Minneapolis: University of Minnesota Press, 2004.
Rancière, Jacques. *Disagreement: Politics and Philosophy*. Minneapolis: University of Minnesota Press, 2008.
Rancière, Jacques. *The Names of History: On the Poetics of Knowledge*. Translated by Hassan Melehy. Minneapolis: University of Minnesota Press, 1994.
Rich, Frank. "They Got Some 'Splaining to Do." *New York Times*, July 18, 2009.
Robinson, Cedric. *An Anthropology of Marxism*. Burlington, VT: Ashgate, 2001.
Rodríguez, Richard. *Brown: The Last Discovery of America*. New York: Viking, 2002.
Román, David. *Acts of Intervention: Performance, Gay Culture, and AIDS*. Bloomington: Indiana University Press, 1998.
Román, David. "Latino Performance and Identity." *Aztlan: A Journal of Chicano Studies* 22, no. 2 (1997): 151–68.
Sadownick, Doug. "Two Different Worlds: Luis Alfaro Bridges the Gap between Gay Fantasies and Latino Reality." *The Advocate*, no. 568 (January 15, 1991): 6–63.
Sandoval-Sanchez, Alberto. *José, Can You See? Latinos on and off Broadway*. Madison: University of Wisconsin Press, 1999.
Sartre, Jean-Paul. *Sketch for a Theory of Emotions*. Translated by Philip Mairet. London: Methuen, 1962.
Schechner, Richard. *Between Theatre and Anthropology*. Philadelphia: University of Pennsylvania Press, 1985.
Sedgwick, Eve Kosofsky. *Between Men: English Literature and Male Homosocial Desire*. New York: Columbia University Press, 1985.
Sedgwick, Eve Kosofsky, ed. *Novel Gazing: Queer Readings in Fiction*. Durham, NC: Duke University Press, 1997.
Sedgwick, Eve Kosofsky. "Queer Performativity: Warhol's Shyness, Warhol's Whiteness." In *Pop Out: Queer Warhol*, edited by Jennifer Doyle, Jonathan Flatley, and José E. Muñoz, Series Q, 134–43. Durham, NC: Duke University Press, 1997.
Sedgwick, Eve Kosofsky. *Touching Feeling: Affect, Pedagogy, Performativity*. Series Q. Durham, NC: Duke University Press, 2003.
Simondon, Gilbert. *L'Individuation psychique et collective: A la lumiere des notions de forme, information, potentiel, et l'invention philosophique*. Paris: Aubier, 1992.

Simondon, Gilbert. *Psychic and Collective Individuation: A Critical Introduction and Guide*. Edinburgh: Edinburgh University Press, 2014.

Sotomayor, Sonia. "A Latina Judge's Voice." Olmos Memorial Lecture, Berkeley School of Law, University of California, 2001. Reprint, *New York Times*, May 14, 2009, https://www.nytimes.com/2009/05/15/us/politics/15judge.text.html.

Spillers, Hortense. "All the Things You Could Be by Now If Sigmund Freud's Wife Was Your Mother: Race and Psychoanalysis." *Critical Inquiry* 22, no. 7 (1996): 710–34.

Tomkins, Silvan. *Shame and Its Sisters: A Silvan Tomkins Reader*. Edited by Eve Kosofsky Sedgwick, Adam Frank, and Irving E Alexander. Durham, NC: Duke University Press, 1995.

Trotsky, Leon. "Celine and Poincaré: Novelist and Politician." In *Leon Trotsky on Literature and Art*, edited by Paul N. Siegel. New York: Pathfinder, 1972.

Viego, Antonio. *Dead Subjects: Towards a Politics of Loss in Latino Studies*. Durham, NC: Duke University Press, 2007.

Viego, Antonio. "The Life of the Undead: Biopower, Latino Anxiety and the Epidemiological Paradox." *Women and Performance: A Journal of Feminist Theory* 19, no. 2 (2009): 131–47.

Viego, Antonio. "The Unconscious of Latino/a Studies." *Latino Studies* 1 (2003): 333–36.

Viso, Olga. *Ana Mendieta: Earth Body*. New York: Hatje Cantz, 2004.

Warner, Michael. Introduction to *Fear of a Queer Planet: Queer Politics and Social Theory*, edited by Michael Warner, vii–xxxi. Minneapolis: University of Minnesota Press, 1993.

Williams, Raymond. *Marxism and Literature*. New York: Oxford University Press, 1978.

Zamir, Shamoon. *Dark Voices: W. E. B. Du Bois and American Thought, 1888–1903*. Chicago: University of Chicago Press, 1995.

Žižek, Slavoj. *Enjoy Your Symptom! Jacques Lacan inside Hollywood and Out*. New York: Routledge, 1992.

Index

Note: Page numbers in italics refer to illustrations.

Abraham, Nicolas, 98–99
"Abuelita" (performance), 68. *See also* Alfaro, Luis
aesthetic rationalities, xxxii
affect: affective belonging, 17, 19; affective difference, 12, 49, 58; affective excess, 11, 15, 21, 47, 49, 58; affective normativity, 9, 19, 28, 40–41, 45–46, 48–49, 58, 63–65; affective particularity, x, 28, 35, 40, 46, 49, 51, 58, 79, 101–5; affective understanding of the world, 26–27; the body and, 51, 56; brown, 3, 35, 37, 39–41, 44, 101, 108, 116, 145; as contagious, 149; *cubanía* and, 88, 92, 99; definition of, 3, 40; ethnic, 10, 13, 65; guilt/shame and, 92–93, 106, 108; Latino/a affect and, 10–11, 15, 19–20, 62–63, 65–66, 101–3, 117; management of, 47–49; minoritarian, 13, 65; music and, 20–21, 43; negative, 52, 56–58; official, 9–10, 14, 22, 40–41; performance and, 9, 15, 58, 62–63, 96, 101–3, 105, 108, 111; queerness and, 27; reason and, 101–2; shared, 6, 99; transmission of, 37, 41, 43–46
affirmative action, 63
African American studies, 36–37
Afrocubanismo, xxi
Afro-diaspora, xxi
After Paris Burned, 128
AIDS, 63

Alarcón, Norma, xxiii, 9, 12
Albertson, Jack, 43
Alfaro, Luis: background of, 159n2; family and, xvii, 67–68, 72–73, 76; memory and, 59–60, 62–66, 72, 74, 77; queerness and, 59, 63, 65, 68, 72–77. *See also* "Abuelita" (performance); *Chicanismos* (video); "Moo-Moo Approaches/A Story about Mamas and Mexico, A" (performance); "On a Street Corner" (performance); "Orphan of Aztlan" (performance); *Politicized Body* (performances); "Virgin Mary" (performance)
Allen, Jafari, xxi
All in the Family (television), 44
Amalgamation Schemes: Antiblackness and the Critique of Multiracialism (Sexton), xxv
America, the Beautiful (performance), 54–57. *See also* Bustamante, Nao
Andre, Carl, 142
"Andy's Shyness, Andy's Whiteness" (Sedgwick), 107
animalization, 79, 82
Anzaldúa, Gloria, xxiii–xxiv
Arenas, Reinaldo, xix
Aristotle, 5
Arizona, 3
arte util, 125–26
Art Institute of Chicago, 88
Asianness, xxxi, 133, 138

assemblage, xx, 6–7, 78, 80, 83, 121, 132
assimilation, 19, 60, 67–68, 156n21
attunement: to brownness, xiv, xxxii, 5, 118–19, 123, 126–27, 132–33, 138, 140; to our transformation, 129–30; performance and, x, xxii–xxiii, 72, 118–19, 124, 126; to queerness, 131
Austin, J. L., 46, 97
avant-garde, 14, 103, 111, 119

Bacon, Francis, 30–34
Bailey, Moya, xx
Balibar, Etienne, 77
"Ballad of the Green Berets" (song), 119
ball circuit, 139
banana republic, 82
Bard College, xxxii
Batería (film), xix, xxvi–xxviii
Beast and the Sovereign (lecture), 84
Being and Nothingness (Sartre), 12
being-with, 124, 129–30, 132, 137
Belpré, Pura, 79–80
Benjamin, Walter, 13–14; angel of history, 66
Bennet, Jane, 4, 6–7
Bergson, Henri, 143
Bergsonism (Deleuze), 144
Berlant, Lauren, 5, 107–8, 116
Bersani, Leo, 32
bestiary, 80
Between Men (Sedgwick), 32–33
Bion, W. R., 41
biopower, 22
Bishop, Claire, 125
blackness: animalization of, 79, 82; blackened by the world and, 132; black excess and, xxi, xxix; black feminists and, xxiii, 15, 22–23; brownness and, xxx–xxxi, 37, 40–42, 133, 138; in Cuba, xxi, xxvii; as a problem, 36–37; queerness and, xxi; sexism directed at black women and, xx; slavery and, 43, 45; U.S. and, 17, 37. *See also* race
blacktino, xviii
Blankita, xx–xxi, xxix
Blood Work (documentary), 147

body, 35, 50–52, 56, 58, 61, 66, 78, 91, 129, 147
Bogotá. *See* Colombia
Boyarin, Jonathan, 66, 68
Bracho, Ricardo, 15–23, 156n21
Brava Theater, 15, 18
Brennan, Teresa, 37, 40, 45
Bridge, the, 119
British Empire, xxv
Brown (Rodríguez), 39–40
Brown, Wendy, 114–16
brown commons: being without, 127; definition of, xv, 2; difference and, xxxi, 4, 39 133, 136; in the face of shared wounding, 6, 121; methexis and, 130, 133; within the metropolis, 134; as a movement, xxxii, 2; persistent, 139; plurality of, 3–4, 132; populating and animating the world, xxxi; potential of, 138; queer ecologies and, 4, 131, 140; shared flourishing and, xvi, 2, 121; as together in difference, xxxi, 39. *See also* brownness; commons
brownness: affect and, 3, 35, 39–41, 108, 145; as an alternative to Latino/a, 120–21; Asianness and, xxxi, 133, 138; attunement to, xiv, xxxii, 5, 118–19, 123, 126–27, 132–33, 138, 140; blackness and, xxx–xxxi, 37, 40–42, 133, 138; brown power and, 3–4, 39, 120; brown world and, 118, 122–23, 126–27, 138, 140, 149; in Cuba, xviii; excess and, xxix, 15; feeling brown and, 16, 19, 38–43, 45, 58, 101–2, 111, 116–17, 149; *latinidad* and, xxii, xxiv, xxxi, 15, 39–40, 46, 122, 133; methexis and, 130; miscegenation and, xxiv–xxv; negation and, 40; otherwiseness of, 100, 103, 105, 111–13, 116; performance of, 46, 101, 103, 111, 118–20, 122, 126–27, 142, 145; persistence of, 4–5, 42, 85, 108, 127, 139; political potential of, xxiv; poverty and, 122–24, 126–27; production of knowledge and, 4, 101; queerness and, xxvi, xxix, 4, 108, 121–22, 131, 133–34, 140; sharing out

of, 147–49; theorization/definition of, x, xxi, xxv, xxvii, 3, 149; touch across, 121, 123, 127, 137–38; trans and, xxxi, 130, 133; in the U.S., xxiv, 37, 41, 43–44; vital force of, 146–47. *See also* brown commons; ethnicity; Latinas

Bruguera, Tania, *89*; controversy and, 88, 95, 124–25; the Cuban condition and, 95–99; guilt and, 88–92, 95, 97–98; useful art and, 125–26. See also *Burden of Guilt, The* (performance); *Burden of Guilt II* (performance); *Displacement* (performance); *Head Down* (performance); *Memory of the postwar* (performance)

Buena Vista Social Club (band), xxi

Burden of Guilt, The (performance), 88, 95. See also Bruguera, Tania

Burden of Guilt II (performance), 92–93. See also Bruguera, Tania

Bustamante, Nao, *1, 53, 55, 57, 115, 148*; body and, 54, 56, 58 147; as excessive, 47–50, 54–56, 58; as muse, xxiii; as otherwise, 114–17; and reparative performance, 50, 52; as a vulnerability artist, 50–52, 54, 56; on *Work of Art*, 113–14. See also *America, the Beautiful* (performance); *Given Over to Want* (performance); *Indigurrito* (performance); *Personal Protection* (performance); *Rosa Does Joan* (performance); *Sans Gravity* (performance); *Sparkler* (performance); *Work of Art* (TV show)

Butler, Judith, 144

Cabeza abajo. See *Head Down* (performance)
Cabrera, Lydia, xxi
California, 63–64
Cal State Los Angeles, xxxii
camp, 54, 104, 110
capitalism, 5, 38, 40, 102, 122, 133, 152–53n34
Carmelita Tropicana. *See* Troyano, Alina

Castillo de San Carlos de la Cabaña, xix–xx
castration anxiety, 52
Castro, Fidel, 86, 91–92, 97
Castro, Mariella, xix
Castro, Raul, xix
Césaire, Aimé, 144–45
Chauduri, Una, 80–81
Chicanismos (video), 60–61. *See also* Alfaro, Luis
Chicano/a, 3, 16, 44, 59, 65, 74, 87
Chicas 2000, 83
Chico and the Man (TV show), 43–44
Chow, Rey, 102
Chuh, Kandice, xxxi–xxxii, 102
chusma, xxi–xxii
chusmería, xxi
city, 5, 60–61
Clark, Petula, 60
Cobra Woman (movie), 104
Cold War, 81, 87
Colombia, 124–25
colonialism, xxvii, 90, 95, 144–45
colorism, 39
commons, 5–6, 120, 132, 136, 139–40, 149. See also brown commons
Conduct of Life (play), 14
Con Qué Culo se Sienta la Cucaracha? See *With What Ass Does the Cockroach Sit?* (performance)
coolie labor, xxv
Cortiñas, Jorge Ignacio, 28
Crimp, Douglas, 106–10
critical theory, 77
Cruel Optimism (Berlant), 107
Cruising Utopia (Muñoz), x–xi, xiii, xvi, xix, xxv, xxxii, 121–22
Cruz, Nilo, 24, 25, 26–28
Cuba: Afrocubanismo and, xxi, 91, 96–97, 145; beyond an ideological fog, 27–28; blackness and, xx, xxi, xxvii; brownness and, xviii; Cuban Americans and, xxii, 81–82, 86–87, 91–92; Cuban art/performance and, 24, 88–99, 142; Cuban Revolution and, 24, 26–28, 87, 90; diaspora and, xvi, xxvii, xxx, 81, 97; Elián González and, xvii, 81, 83–84, 86, 91;

INDEX 177

Cuba (*continued*)
fragmentation of, 146; Greater, 87–95, 99; guilt and, 87–95; police and, xxviii; queerness and, xviii–xx, xix, xxvii–xxviii, xxxi, 27, 94; U.S. and, xix, xxvii, xxix, 24, 81–82, 152–53n34. See also *cubanía*; queerness
Cuban blackface, *xx*
cubanía: affect and, 88, 92, 99; guilt and, 93–95; melancholia of, 28; as a structure of feeling, 24, 87, 94; as a way of being, xvii–xviii, 24, 26. See also Cuba
Cuban Palimpsests (Quiroga), 146
Cuerpo Politizado. See *Politicized Body* (performances)

Dead Subjects: Towards a Politics of Loss (Viego), 42, 102–3
Deleuze, Gilles, 30, 33–34, 50, 56, 143–44
De Niro, Robert, 29
Derrida, Jacques, 7, 84–85
Destierro. See *Displacement* (performance)
deterritorialization, 35, 78, 80
Dewey, John, xvi, 6, 121, 123
disidentification, xvi, 11, 65, 83, 147
Disidentifications (Muñoz), x–xi, xxi, xxiii
Displacement (performance), 96–97. See also Bruguera, Tania
dispossession, 79, 83, 141, 145–46
dissensus, 4
Dosse, Francois, 144
double gesture, 66, 68, 72
Down, Maureen, 111–12
"Downtown" (song), 60
drag, xx, 103–5, 119, 152–53n34
"Dreaming of Other Planets" (Moraga), 15–16
drugs, 15, 19, 124–26
Du Bois, W. E. B., xiv–xv, 36–40, 42–44, 46
Duke University, x

East Africa, xxv
élan vital, 143–47

El Monte (Cabrera), xxi
El Morro, xix–xx
El peso de la culpa. See *Burden of Guilt, The* (performance)
El Tiempo, 124
emotion, 12–13, 27, 40, 47–48, 50, 52, 102, 111, 149
"Ephemera as Evidence" (Muñoz), xxv
Espacio Aglutinador gallery, 95
ethnicity: affect and, 10, 13; disparaging, 111–12; ethnic family and, 72–73, 76; ethnic normativity and, 9; ethnic particularity and, 102; ethnic studies and, 4; *latinidad* as, xxx, 8; paranoia and, 92–93; as performative, 12; separatists models and, 17; as a structure of feeling, 22. See also blackness; brownness; Latino/a
Ethnic Labels, Latina/o Lives (Oboler), 37
exhibitionism, 47–50
Exposé, 20

family, xvii, 72–73, 76
Fanon, Frantz, xiv, 45, 132
Fear of a Queer Planet (Warner), 73, 77
feeling: and affect, 40, 62–63; archive of, 43; brown, 16, 19, 38–43, 45–46, 49–50, 58, 101–2, 111, 117, 149; "colored," xiv; like a problem, xiv–xv, 36–39, 45; like a solution, 41; otherwise, 112; queer, 58. See also structure of feeling; ugly feelings
Feeling Brown (original title), ix, xi. See also Muñoz, José Esteban
"Feeling Brown: Ethnicity and Affect in Ricardo Bracho's *The Sweetest Hangover (and Other STDs)*" (Muñoz), xi, xviii
Feliciano, José, 44–46
femininity, xx, 13
feminism, 15, 18–19, 22, 137, 141–42
Fisher, Gary, xiii
Florida, x
Ford, Richard T., 102–3
For How We Perceived a Life (Take 3) (performance), 138
Fornés, María Irene, 14, 27–28, 126–27

Foucault, Michel, xx
Freud, Sigmund, 52
Friedman, Andrew, 125–26
Frieze, 125
Frutos, Javier de, 29, 32, 34
Fusco, Coco, 50

Gay Is Good (rally), 131
Gay Latino Studies (La Fountain-Stokes), 107
gayness: affect and, 27; as antinormative, 15, 19, 152–53n34; in Cuba, xviii–xx, xix, xxviii, xxxi, 27; gay liberation movement, 131–32, 140; gay men of color, 15, 22, 63, 156n21; guilt and, 94; homophobia and, xvii, 19, 33, 51, 54, 63; solitary, 32. *See also* queerness
gender, 27, 68, 77, 110, 162n11
generalizations, 107–8, 115–16
Gherovici, Patricia, 38–40
Given Over to Want (performance), *1*, 147, *148*. *See also* Bustamante, Nao
globalization, 35
going South, 35
Gomez, Marga, xvi
González, Elián, xvii, 81, 83–84, 86, 91
González-Torres, Felix, xi, xiii–xvi
Graham, Lindsey, 111
Greater Cuba, 87–95, 99
Green Room, The (installation), 137
Grosz, Elizabeth, 61
group identification, xxiv, 17, 40–41, 63
Guggenheim Museum, 142
guilt, 87–95, 97, 99
Guzmán, Joshua Javier, xviii, xxiv

Hansen, Miriam, 14
Hardt, Michael, 5
harm, xvi, 4, 6, 108, 121–23, 126, 132–33, 140
Harman, Graham, 6–7
Harney, Stefano, 4
Hartman, Saidiya, 50
Havana, x, xx, 81
Havana Art Institute, 88
Head Down (performance), 95–96. *See also* Bruguera, Tania

Hegel, Georg, 46
Hemispheric Center for Performance and Politics, 124
heteronormativity, 59, 73
heterotopia, xx, xxii–xxiii
Hispanic, xxiii–xxiv, xxx, 8, 37–39
HIV/AIDS, xxv
Hollibaugh, Amber, 137
homophobia, xvii, 19, 33, 51, 54, 63, 94
homosexuality. *See* gayness; queerness
homosocial, 32
"How It Feels to Be Colored Me" (Hurston), xiv–xv
hunger artist, 50, 54, 56
Hurston, Zora Neale, xiv–xv
Hurwitt, Robert, 18
"Hybrid Alternos" (performance), xxii
hybridity, xxiv–xxv

identity in difference, xxiii–xxiv, 9, 39
identity politics, 9, 17
"I Got a Crush on You" (song), 20
illegitimate speech, 126–27
Immigrant Movement International, 125–26
indigenous people, 88–91
Indigurrito (performance), 52–54. *See also* Bustamante, Nao
Instituto Superior de Arte. *See* Havana Art Institute
INTAR Theatre, 80
intraracial empathy, 42
introjection, 98
Iowa, 142, 147

Jaruco National Park, 146
Jefferson, Margo, 83
Jets, 20
Jones, Donna, 143–45
Joseph, May, 10
Julien, Isaac, 29–35
Just, Tony, xxv–xxvii

Kafka, Franz, 50
Karma of Brown Folks, The (Prashad), 40–41

INDEX   179

Klein, Melanie, 41, 51, 98
Knoble, Kathy, 125

Lacan, Jacques, 98
La Fountain-Stokes, Lawrence, 107–9
LaMarre, Thomas, 129
Lane, Jill, xx
Laplanche, Jean, 92
La Prensa, 140
Latina: identity of, 14, 49, 58; injuries against, 115–16; as otherwise, 102–3, 116; wise, 100, 111–12, 116. *See also latinidad*; Latino/a
latinidad: affect and, 15, 19, 62–63, 101; brownness and, xxiii, xxiv, xxxi, 15, 39–40, 46, 122, 133; as a coalition, 87; as an ethnicity, xxx, 8; melancholia of, 28; particularities of, 38, 62–63; the psychic and, 42; as a way of being, 14, 22–23, 62–63. *See also* Latina; Latino/a
Latino/a: affect and, 10–11, 15, 19–20, 62–63, 65–66, 101–3, 117; brown as an alternative to, 120–21; displacing the term, xxiv, 14, 38, 120–21; as excessive, xxix, 15, 50, 58; gay shaming and, 109; incoherence of term, 8, 37–38, 87–88; mental and physical health and, 5, 38, 122–23; political utility of term, xxiii; prevented from accessing normativity, 9; as a problem, 37–39; resistance, 103; stereotypes of, 11, 50; studies, 37, 39, 42, 103, 120; theater and performance, 9–10, 14, 62–63, 65, 103; U.S. definition of, xxx, 8, 39; violence against, 62–63, 79, 81, 133. *See also* brownness; ethnicity; Latina; *latinidad*
Latinx: analysis of Cuban diaspora, xxx; childhood and, xvii; scope and reach of term, xviii; sexual world making and, xxix
Latinx studies, x
LBJ (performance), 119–22
lesbianness, 76, 94
LGBT, xxv
"Life of the Undead, The" (Viego), 4–5
Ligon, Glenn, xiv–xv

Lippard, Lucy, 142
Livingstone, Jennie, 138–39
Locke, John, 5
London's Institute of Contemporary Arts, 59–60
Lonesome Cowboys (film), 29, 33
Long Road to Mazatlán (film), 29–35
López, Ana, 87–88
Lorde, Audre, xxiii–xxiv
Los Angeles, 60–61, 65, 134–35

MacArthur Park, 134, 136
Maleta Mulata (play), 28
manera de ser. See way of being
Mariel boatlift, 81, 86
Mario Banana (movie), 104–5
"Mario Montez, for Shame!" (Crimp), 106
Marx, Karl, 77
Marxism and Literature (Williams), 9
Marx's 1844 manuscripts, xiii
masculinity, 29, 32–33, 35, 54, 68. *See also* misogyny
materialism, 6–7, 24, 87, 92
Memoria de la postguerra. See Memory of the postwar (performance)
memory, 59–60, 62–66, 72, 74, 77, 92
Memory of the postwar (performance), 88–93, 95. *See also* Bruguera, Tania
Mendieta, Ana, 141–43, 145–49
mestizaje, xxv, xxvi
methexis, 121, 130–32
Miami, 28, 80–82
migration, x, xxii, xxvii, 3, 67, 122
Milk of Amnesia (performance), 83
mimesis, 101–3, 110, 130, 142, 145–46
minoritarian subjects: affect and, 13, 65; animalization of, 79, 82; difference and, xxxi; erasure of histories and, xxvi; obstacles for, 22–23, 64; paranoia and, 93; particularity of, 40; performance and, 17, 114, 116; politics and, 66; as problematic, 11, 36–37; sorrow of, 45
miscegenation, xxiv–xxv
misogynoir, xx
misogyny, xx, 13, 63. *See also* masculinity

model minority, 41
Montez, María, 104–5, 116–17
Montez, Mario, 101, 103–12, 115–17, 162n11
"Moo-Moo Approaches/A Story about Mamas and Mexico, A" (performance), 66–68. *See also* Alfaro, Luis
Moraga, Cherríe, xxiii–xxiv, 15–16, 72, 137
Morton, Timothy, 6
Moten, Fred, 4, 110
Move, Richard, 147
Mud (play), 27
multiculturalism, xxiv–xxv, 9, 39–40, 76
multiplicity, 143–44
Mundos Alternos (exhibition), xxii
Muñoz, José Esteban: childhood of, x; Cuba and, xvii–xviii; influences on, xi–xiii, xxiii–xxiv; making of *Sense of Brown*, x–xi, xviii, xxxii; queerness and, xxv–xxvi. See also *Feeling Brown* (original title)
music, 20–21, 44, 46, 93–94, 110

Nancy, Jean-Luc, xii, 4, 7, 116–17, 132, 147
narco-economies, 125
national anthem, 45
negation, xxvi–xxvii, 40, 46, 99, 142–43, 146
Negri, Antonio, 5, 149
Négritude poets, 143–45
New Bergsonism, 143–44
New York, x, 103–4, 119
New York Post, 122
New York State Governor's Advisory Committee on Hispanic Affairs, 37–38
New York Times, 83, 111–12, 125–26
New York University, Department of Performance Studies, x
Ngai, Sianne, 49–50
nightlife, 17
Nixon, Richard, xxx
nkisi nkonde, 96–97
normativity: affect and, 9, 19, 28, 40–41, 45–46, 48–49; gender and, 110; heterosexuality and, 32, 59; in the majoritarian public sphere, 9, 13, 45, 49, 54; refusal to conform to, 15, 19, 46, 49–50; white, 11, 17, 54, 65, 73, 76
North American Free Trade Agreement, 34–35

Obama, Barack, 82, 100, 111
Oboler, Suzanne, 37
"On a Street Corner" (performance), 62–64. *See also* Alfaro, Luis
ontological condition, xxxii
ontology, xxiv, 6, 9, 14, 27, 101, 121, 143, 149
"Onus of Seeing Cuba: Nilo Cruz's *Cubanía*, The" (Munoz), xviii
Orgel, Stephen, 18
"Orphan of Aztlan" (performance), 73–76. *See also* Alfaro, Luis
Ortiz, Ricardo, 93
otherwiseness, 100, 102–3, 105, 110–14, 116
"*Our Kind of Movie*": *The Films of Andy Warhol* (Crimp), 106
Oz (television), 54

paranoia, 92–93
Paris Is Burning (film), 128, 138–39
Passions: How to Manage Despair, Fear, Rage and Guilt and Heighten Your Capacity for Joy, Love, Hope and Awe (Witkins), 47
Peforma biennale, 138
people of color, 9, 13, 17–19, 47–48, 63, 73, 79, 82–83, 93, 142
perestroika, 26–27
Pérez-Firmat, Gustavo, 88
Perez y Martina (Belpré), 79–80
performance: affect and, 9, 15, 48, 58, 62–63, 96, 101–3, 105, 108, 111; becoming animal in, 79–81, 83–84; of brownness, 46, 101, 111, 118–20, 122, 126, 142, 145; as challenge to stereotypes, 11, 14, 112; of citizenship, 10, 63; compulsory, 50, 111, 116; of Cuba, 88–99; ethnicity and, 12; guilt/shame and, 90, 95–98, 106;

INDEX 181

performance (*continued*)
of institutional critique, 124–25; Latino/a drama and, 9–10, 14, 62–63, 65, 103; memory and, 59–60, 63–66, 72, 74, 77; methexis and, 130; minoritarian, 17, 60, 114, 116; of normativity, 9, 11, 48, 63; of otherwiseness, 110–13, 116; performance attunes and, x, xxii–xxiii, 72, 118–19, 124, 126; performance studies and, x; performative mimesis, 110, 116; producing theory/knowledge through, 60, 77, 101; of queerness, 59–60, 63, 68, 77, 106, 118–20, 134; as reparative, 50, 52; use value of, xxxii. *See also individual artists*
Personal Protection (performance), 113–16. *See also* Bustamante, Nao
Peter Pan program, 142
pharmacopornographic regime, 128–30
Phenomenology (Hegel), 46
Plato, 5
plurality, 3–4, 117, 132–33, 149
"Point of No Return" (song), 20
Politicized Body (performances), 60–77. *See also* Alfaro, Luis
Politics, book 2 (Aristotle), 5
Pontalis, J. B., 92
pornopunk, 128
poverty, 27, 122–23, 139
"Poverty of Philosophy, The" (Marx), 123
Prashad, Vijay, 40–41, 121
Preciado, Paul B., xxxi, 128–30
Prinze, Freddie, 43–44
projection, 92
projective identification, 41
Proposition 187, 63–64
psychoanalysis, 41–42, 91–92, 98–99
public cruising, xxv–xxvi, xxvii, xxviii
public sex, xxvi, xxvii, 49, 112
Puerto Rican Syndrome, The (study), 38

"Qué culpa tengo yo" (song), 93–94. *See also* Rodríguez, Albita
queerness: assemblage and, xx, 78; blackness and, xxi; brownness and, xxvi, xxix, 4, 108, 121–22, 131, 133–34, 140; Cuba and, xviii–xx, xxviii, xxxi, 27, 94; erasures of queer existence and, xxv–xxvi, 49–50, 63, 76, 133; excess and, xxix, 49, 58; feminism and, 18, 68; interventions in meaning of, 30, 32, 34, 59, 73–74, 76, 107, 134, 156n21; mainstream LGBT culture and, xxv, 60, 72; methexis and, 131, 134; modalities of, 19, 30, 32, 34; performance of, 59–60, 63, 68, 77, 106, 118–20, 134; queer commons and, 131–32, 134; queer history and, xxvi, 54; queer incarceration and, xix, 131–32; queer theory and, 54, 60, 72, 76–77; queer ventriloquism, 27; restructuring relationality and, 33; shame and, 106–9; utopianism and, x, xxii–xxiii, xxix, 59–60. *See also* gayness
queer of color: family and, xvii, 67–68, 72–73, 76; feminism and, 15, 22; homophobia and, 19; identities-in-difference in relation to, xxiv; liminality of, 75; memory and, 63, 65; negotiating identity as, 65; shame and, 108–9
queer of color critique, xvii, 108
Quiroga, José, xxi, xxviii, 146–49

race: animalization and, 79, 82; blackness as, xxx; "colored" feeling, xiv–xv; psychic and, 99; racial hierarchy, xxv, 41; racialist thinking, 143–45; racial mixing, xxiv–xxvi; racial normativity, 9; racial profiling, 3, 122; racial separatist models, 17; racial slurs, xxi, 35, 82, 112; racism, xx, 13, 35, 40, 44–45, 51, 82; reverse racism, 100; and sex as intractable, 35; shame and, 107. *See also* blackness; brownness
Rancière, Jacques, 4
Reagan, Ronald, 19
Rechy, John, 32
Regarding Sedgwick (anthology), 106
relationality, 6–7, 33, 99, 108, 137

Reno, Janet, 81
reparative, 50–52, 58, 93
reparative reading, 93
reproductive futurity, xxvi
Republic, The, book 5 (Plato), 5
Republicans, 100, 111–12
Rich, Frank, 112
Rivera, René, 103–4
Rivera, Ryan, xxvi
Rivera, Sylvia, 131–34, 140
Rivers, Joan, 47
Robinson, Cedric, 123
Rockefeller Foundation, 124
Rodríguez, Albita, 93–95
Rodríguez, Juana María, xxix
Rodríguez, Richard, 39–40
Rodríguez-Soltero, José, 119–22
Rosa Does Joan (performance), 47–50, 113. See also Bustamante, Nao
Rosaldo, Renato, 152–53n34
Rousseau, Jean-Jacques, 5
Ruiz, Sandra, xxvi–xxvii

safe space, 135–36
Sainz, Damian, xix–xx, xxv, xxvii–xxviii
Sandler, Barry, 119
Sandoval, Chela, xxiii–xxiv
San Francisco, 15
San Francisco Examiner, 17–18
Sans Gravity (performance), 51–52. See also Bustamante, Nao
Santana, Matthew Leslie, xx
Santería, 96–97, 120
Sarah Lawrence College, x
Sarita (play), 14
Sartre, Jean-Paul, 12–13
SB 1070, 4
Screen Test #2 (movie), 103, 105–10, 115
Sedgwick, Eve Kosofsky, xiii, 32–33, 93, 106
Senghor, Léopold, 144–45
sense, ix–xiii
Sense of Brown, The, manuscript for, ix–xiii, xxiii, xxxii
Serrano, Andres, 113
Sevan, Adriana, 25

sexism, xx
Sexton, Jared, xxv
Sexual Futures, Queer Gestures, and Other Latina Longings (Rodríguez), xxix
sexual politics, xxvi
shame, theory of, 106–9
Siluetas (art), 143, 145–49
Silver Platter, 134–37, 140
Simondon, Gilbert, xxxi, 129–30
singularities, 5–6, 32, 115–17, 121, 132–33, 145, 149
Sixth Havana Biennial, 90–91
Sketch for a Theory of Emotions (Sartre), 12
slavery, 43, 45, 50
Smith, Jack, 103–4, 110
sorrow songs, 43, 45
Sotomayor, Sonia, 100, 102, 111, 115–17
Souls of Black Folk, The (Du Bois), 41–42, 46
sound, 20–21, 33–34
South Asia, xxv, 41, 121
Spade, Dean, 133–34, 140
Sparkler (performance), 56–58. See also Bustamante, Nao
speculative realism, 6
Spillers, Hortense, 99
Spinoza, Baruch, 6
STAR. See Street Transvestite Action Revolutionaries
Stonewall rebellion, 131
stop and frisk, 122
Street Transvestite Action Revolutionaries, 131–32, 134
structure of feeling: *cubanía* as, 24, 87, 94; ethnicity and, 22; as experience of a sense, xvi; guilt as, 88, 94; in Latino and queer communities, xvi; queer and brown experiences of childhood and, xvi–xvii; utility of the term, 9; utopia and, 17. See also feeling
Supreme Court, 100
Swan Theater, 18
Sweetest Hangover (and Other STDs), The (play), 15–23
Sylvia Rivera Law Project, 133

Tavel, Ronald, 105–7, 109, 112, 115
Taxi Driver (film), 29
teatro bufo. *See* Cuban blackface
technology, 13–14, 128–29
Testo Junkie (Preciado), xxxi, 128–30
Theatre of the Ridiculous, 105, 119
Theses on Feuerbach (Marx), 77
This Bridge Called My Back (anthology), 15, 18–19, 23
Tompkins, Silvan, 87
Torok, Maria, 98–99
touch, 7, 118–19, 121–23, 127, 138–39
Touching Feeling (Sedgwick), 106–7
Tourmaline, 133–34
transcultural avant-garde, 14
transgender, xxxi, 106–7, 128–31, 133–36. *See also* queerness
transindividuation, xxxi, 130
triptych format, 29, 34
Tropics of Desire (Quiroga), xxviii
Trotsky, Leon, 6
Troyano, Alina, xxi, 78–85
Troyano, Ela, xxi
Troyano sisters, xxii–xxiii
Trump, Donald J., xxii–xxiii
Tsang, Wu, xxxi, 130–31, 134–40
Two Sisters and a Piano (play), 25, 26–28

ugly feelings, 49–52, 58
undercommons of the academy, 4
United States of America: blackness in, 17, 37; brownness and, xxiv, 37, 41, 43–44, 122–23; citizenship and, 10, 21; Cuba and, xix, xxvii, xxix, 24, 27–28, 81–82, 152–53n34; Cuban Americans and, xxii, 81–82, 86–87, 91–92; cultural and political hegemony and, 11; defining Hispanic and Latino and, xxx, 8, 39; demographic transition in, xxx; Supreme Court and, 100
University of California, Los Angeles (UCLA), 138–39
University of California, Riverside, xxii
"Untitled" (Madrid 1971) (photograph), xiii–xvi

useful art, 125–26
utopia: critical utopianism and, 6; enacting utopianism and, 15–16, 39; queerness and, x, xxii–xxiii, xxix, 59–60; structures of feeling and, 17; technology and, 13–14; utopian socialism and, 123–24

Vargas, Deb, 120
Vazquez, Alexandra T., xxxii
Vega, Daphne Rubin, 25
Venceremos: The Erotics of Black Self-Making in Cuba (Allen), xxi
vibrant matter, 6
Viego, Antonio, 4–5, 42–43, 102–3
violence: family and, 73; historical, xxvi–xxvii; justification of, 83; against marginalized groups, 3, 33, 39, 62, 79, 122, 131, 134, 146; racialized, 45, 90; reimagining, 50; vitalism and, 143
"Virgin Mary" (performance), 64. *See also* Alfaro, Luis
Viso, Olga M., 145
vitalism, 141–44
vulnerability artist, 50–52, 54, 56

Warhol, Andy, 29, 33, 103–7, 109–10, 112
Warner, Michael, 73, 76–77
War on Drugs, 19
Washington Square Park, 131
way of being: *cubanía* as, xviii, 24, 26; deemed illicit, 19; ethnicity as, 22–23; feeling brown as, 39; Latino/a as, 14, 22–23; whiteness as, 65
Weber, Nancy, 122
West Indies, xxv
"What We're Rollin Around in Bed With: Sexual Silences in Feminism" (dialogue), 137
whiteness, 10–11, 18–19, 41–42, 52, 65, 72, 76, 111
white supremacy, xxiv–xxv, 63
Whitney Biennial (2012), 138
Wildness (film), xxxi, 134, 138
Williams, Raymond, xi, 9, 12
Williams, Tennessee, 26–27, 32

"wise Latina," 100
"Wise Latinas" (Muñoz), xii
With What Ass Does the Cockroach Sit? (performance), 78–80, 82–85
Witkins, Georgia, 47, 51
women: desire and, 27; femininity, xx, 13; feminism and, 15, 18–19, 22, 137, 141–42; meltdowns and, 111; misogynoir, xx; misogyny, 13; violence against, 33; woman of color feminists, xxiii, 15, 22–23
Work of Art (TV show), 113–14. *See also* Bustamante, Nao
wounded attachment, 114–16

Zamir, Shamoon, 46
Žižek, Slavoj, 91–92
zooësis, 80–81, 83–84

www.ingramcontent.com/pod-product-compliance
Lightning Source LLC
Chambersburg PA
CBHW070842160426
43192CB00012B/2278